Introduction to
assembler language programming for
the IBM system/360/370

Introduction to
assembler language
programming
for the
IBM system/ 360/370

H. C. Brearley, Jr.

Iowa State University

Macmillan Publishing Co., Inc.
New York
Collier Macmillan Publishers
London

Macmillan Publishing Co., Inc.
866 Third Avenue, New York, New York 10022

Collier-Macmillan Canada, Ltd.

Library of Congress Cataloging in Publication Data

Brearley, Harrington Cooper, Jr. (date)
    Introduction to assembler language programming for the IBM system/360/370.

    1. Assembler language (Computer program language)   2. IBM 360 (Computer)–Programming.   3. IBM 370 (Computer)–Programming.   I. Title.
QA76.73.A8B73   1974   001.6'424   73-8354
ISBN 0-02-313800-9

Printing: 1 2 3 4 5 6 7 8   Year: 4 5 6 7 8 9 0

Preface

This volume is an elementary introduction to machine and assembler language programming. One of its purposes is to describe the various representations of data inside a computer and the operations that can be performed on it. This will give the reader an understanding of what is happening inside a computer when it is executing a program he wrote in a higher level language. Another purpose is to teach the reader how to write assembler language programs. These are useful when the higher level languages otherwise being used make it difficult to do a particular computation or when the utmost in execution speed is needed.

These purposes could have been achieved using as the example computer either a real or hypothetical computer. In this book the example computer is the IBM System/360/370. One reason for picking the 360/370 is its wide availability—many thousands of them are now in use. Another reason is that the 360/370 contains a large variety of features, so it is a rather useful example computer.

This book is intended for a second course in computing, corresponding in part to Course B2 in the report of the ACM Curriculum Committee on Computer Science.[1] The reader of this book is presumed to know some higher level programming language, such as Fortran, Algol, or PL/1, so he knows, for example, about loops and subroutines. However, he is presumed to know little about the internal operation of a computer or the internal representation of data. That is the subject of this book. The level of detail of this book is approximately that of a computer reference manual. Machine instructions are described in terms of "before" and "after" register contents and memory contents, but the details of implementation of registers, counters, adders, and so on in hardware or in microprograms are not discussed. Assembler features are discussed at an elementary level. The syntax of various assembler language statements is given along with a description of the result, but how the assembler translates from one to the other is not discussed. Most features of the hardware and of the software are introduced as simple cases without so stating. More general cases are introduced subsequently as they are needed. For the most general case, the reader should consult the appropriate manual.

---

[1] Curriculum 68, Communications of ACM, March 1968, pp. 151-197.

In discussing the 360/370, or any computer system containing elaborate hardware and software, one faces a circularity problem. Each part of the material depends somewhat on the other parts. One is tempted to think that every chapter needs to be last and almost none can be first. We have found no uniquely best solution to this problem but think the sequence in this volume is one of the better orderings. For example, we discuss fixed point arithmetic first (Chapter 3) even though assembler language and the establishment of addressability are not covered until Chapter 4. This means that the programs in Chapter 3 have to be written using some apparently arbitrary rules. As another example, in Chapter 4 the BALR instruction is used for establishing addressability, but its most general usage, from which it takes its name, does not occur until Chapter 10 on subprograms. And there are other examples. These problems are not only pedagogic, some of them are inherent in the nature of a large computer system which is normally approachable only via an executive system that will not allow the user sole occupancy of the machine, and will not allow the user to use absolute addressing.

Possibly the most serious circularity problem relates to input-output. It is clearly undesirable for the assembler language programmer to have to wait until he understands input-output thoroughly before he can input or output his first data. So we provide in Chapter 6 a rather cookbook approach to input-output, using the Operating Systems macros GET and PUT. An alternative to this method is to use one of the simplified 360 assemblers that have been developed at various universities specifically for use by beginners. One of these, named ESP, is described in Appendix A. In either case the reader is able to begin running machine problems early in the course and to see his results in the assembler listing and memory dump. Except for Chapter 6 and Appendix A, this book is largely independent of the details of which 360/370 assembler or assembler-interpreter is used for running programs, so it can be used in conjunction with any of them.

Various versions of this material have been used at Iowa State University for several years in a one quarter (ten week) course for students familiar with algorithms and Fortran. This is not enough time for a student to become an expert assembler language programmer, but he can become thoroughly familiar with the problems of flow of control and representation of data and instructions in a computer. This provides a solid foundation for the future study of other computers, other assembler languages, compilers and assemblers, channel programs, loaders, and operating systems.

The material in this book is derived largely from the following IBM publications: System/360 Principles of Operation, Form GA22-6821; System/370 Principles of Operation, Form GA22-7000; and Assembler Language, Form GC28-6514. For additional details the reader should consult these manuals. I express my appreciation to IBM Corporation for permission to quote tables from forms GA22-6810, GX28-6509, GC28-6603, and GA22-7001, copyrighted in 1964, 1966, 1967, 1968, 1969, 1970, and 1972.

I want to thank the students, teaching assistants, and faculty members of the Computer Science department who used early versions of this material and contributed comments and interest. In addition I am grateful to the reviewers for their very helpful suggestions. And I would like to express appreciation to C. G. Maple, R. M. Stewart, and W. B. Boast for their encouragement.

H. C. B., Jr.

Ames, Iowa

Contents

1
Computer organization   1

2
Number systems   11

3
Fixed-point instructions   37

4
Assembler language
and the translation process   65

5
Relocation, loading, and execution   81

6
Mechanics of running a program   93

7
Branching, loops, and arrays   113

8
Character manipulation   131

9
Decimal conversions   155

10
Subprograms   169

Appendix A   The ESP assembler-interpreter   197

Appendix B   IBM system/360 reference data   207

Index   215

Introduction to
assembler language programming for
the IBM system/360/370

1

Computer organization

In this chapter we begin the study of computer organization and computer instructions. Some of the material presented here applies to all computers; some applies specifically to the IBM System/360/370, which we use as our example computer. However, this is not an exhaustive treatment of the 360/370; it is only an introduction. For the numerous details not discussed here, the reader should consult *IBM System/360 Principles of Operation,* Form GA22-6821; *IBM System/370 Principles of Operation,* Form GA22-7000; and other manuals.

The 360 and 370 computers are almost identical, but not quite. The 370 has all the 360 instructions plus a few more. All programs written for a 360 will run on a 370, but some 370 programs will not run on a 360. In this book everything said about the 360 computer also applies to the 370 computer, except where noted otherwise.

It is our hope that after studying the material presented here and running a number of practice problems the reader will understand machine and assembler language well enough to dig whatever else he needs out of the manuals for these or for other computers. He will also be prepared to study additional topics, such as macros, design of assemblers and loaders, channels and input-output programming, data set organization, and operating systems.

The organization of a typical computer is shown in Figure 1-1. Normally a computation begins by loading the program and possibly the input data into the memory through an input device, such as a card reader. Then the control unit begins to execute the program step by step as follows:

1. Examine the first instruction, see what to do.

2. Do it.

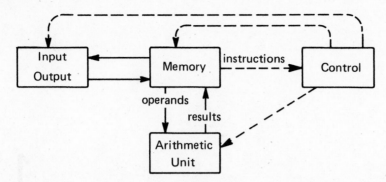

Figure 1-1. Computer block diagram. The solid lines indicate the flow of information being processed; the dashed lines indicate the flow of control.

3. Examine the next instruction, see what to do.

4. Do it.

.

.

.

and so on to the end of the program.

Most of the "doing" consists of carrying operands from the memory to the arithmetic unit, manipulating them in various ways to form intermediate or final results, and putting them back in the memory.

Consider the problem of forming the sum

$$Z = A + B + C$$

where *A, B,* and *C* represent three numbers (operands) that have already been loaded into the memory, and *Z* represents the desired result. The program causes each of the three operands to be carried (usually one at a time) to the arithmetic unit, where the sum is formed. The sum may be kept in the arithmetic unit or put back in the memory, depending on what is supposed to happen next. The final result is usually transmitted back to the memory and thence to an output device (such as a printer) to be transmitted to the human user.

MEMORY

The memory unit holds

1. Operands.

2. Intermediate and final results.

3. Instructions.

All three kinds of information are stored as sequences of 1's and 0's.

The location in memory of a particular string of bits is indicated by a numerical *address*. Instead of addressing each bit individually, the 360 memory is addressable in groups of eight bits called *bytes*. An example is shown in Figure 1-2, where both the bits and the bytes are numbered consecutively beginning with 0.

     1. Byte 0 is bits 0 through 7.

     2. Byte 1 is bits 8 through 15.

     3. Byte 2 is bits 16 through 23; and so on.

In the example shown in Figure 1-2, the *contents* of byte 5 is 11101000. Several other groupings of bits are provided for. A *full word* is a group of four consecutive bytes beginning at a byte address that is exactly divisible by 4. The integer +26 can be stored in full-word format as[1]

$$0000 \quad 0000 \quad 0000 \quad 0000 \quad 0000 \quad 0000 \quad 0001 \quad 1010$$

where we write the bits in groups of four only for convenience. The contents of this full word may also be written in hexadecimal as

$$00 \quad 00 \quad 00 \quad 1A$$

where two hex digits represent the contents of one byte. A *half-word* is a group of two consecutive bytes beginning at an address that is exactly divisible by 2. The integer +26 can be represented in half-word format as

$$0000 \quad 0000 \quad 0001 \quad 1010$$

or as

$$00 \quad 1A_H$$

bit position	01234567	111111 89012345	11112222 67890123	22222233 45678901	33333333 23456789	44444444 01234567	44 89
contents	10110010	11110000	00000101	00001001	00100100	11101000	11
byte	0	1	2	3	4	5	
	halfword		halfword		halfword		
	word				word		

Figure 1-2. Information boundaries in 360 memory.

---

[1]See Chapter 2.

In Figure 1-2 the contents of the half-word at byte address 2 is

$$0000 \quad 0101 \quad 0000 \quad 1001$$

For compactness, the memory addresses and contents are usually shown in hexadecimal, as in the example in Figure 1-3. Here four bytes are shown on each line, and the two hex digits representing the contents of each byte are grouped together. The addresses shown correspond to the leftmost byte in each line. Thus the contents at byte address 9 is C1. In addition to integers in full-word and half-word format, the memory may also contain data in other formats, which will be described subsequently. It also contains the instructions of the program in formats that will be described later. Instructions are 16, 32, and 48 bits long, and they always begin on a half-word boundary.

Various sizes of memory are available on 360/370 computers up to a maximum of $2^{27} = 134,217,728$ bits, or 2^{24} bytes. The range of byte addresses in the largest 360/370 memory is

$$0 \text{ through } 2^{24} - 1 = 16,777,215_{10} = \text{FFFFFF}_H$$

The computer has instructions that allow one or more bytes to be read or written. *Reading* does not destroy the contents of the byte(s) in memory; rather, it transmits a copy of the byte(s) to some other part of the computer. *Writing* does destroy the old contents of the byte(s) and replaces it with the new information.

The speed of writing or reading data in the memory varies from model to model within the 360/370 line, as shown in Table 1-1. For example, the time needed to read a 32-bit word in the Model 50 is 2 microseconds (μs). The time to read through a 262,144-byte region (the size of the whole memory for some Model 50's) is

$$262,144 \text{ bytes} \times \frac{1 \text{ word}}{4 \text{ bytes}} \times \frac{2 \times 10^{-6} \text{ second}}{1 \text{ word}} = .13 \text{ second}$$

Byte Addresses	Contents
000000	47 F0 F0 0C
000004	07 40 40 40
000008	D4 C1 C9 D5
00000C	90 EC D0 0C
000010	98 9C F0 88
000014	41 40 F0 40
000018	50 40 D0 08
00001C	50 D0 40 04
.	.
.	.
.	.
.	.

Figure 1-3. Example of memory addresses and contents in hexadecimal.

Table 1-1.   Some 360/370 Speeds

Model	CPU Basic Cycle (μs)	Memory Cycle (μs)	Memory Width (bytes)
360 Model 22	.750	1.5	1
25	.900	1.8	2
30	.750	1.5	1
40	.625	2.5	2
44	.250	1.0	4
50	.500	2.0	4
65	.200	.75[a]	8
67	.200	.75[a]	8
75	.195	.75[a]	8
195	.054	.756[a,b]	8
370 Model 135	.275 — 1.43	.770 read / .935 write	2 or 4
145	.202 — .315	.540 read / .607 write	8
155	.115	2.070[b]	16
165	.080	2.000[a,b]	8
195	.054	.756[a,b]	8

[a]Times given do not reflect the time reductions that are due to storage interleaving.

[b]Times given do not reflect the time reductions that are due to the high-speed buffer.

Source: Reproduced by permission from *360 System Summary,* Form GA22-6810, © 1964, 1967, 1968, 1969, and *370 System Summary,* Form GA22-7001, © 1970, 1972 by International Business Machines Corporation.

The data rate is

$$\frac{4 \text{ bytes}}{2 \times 10^{-6} \text{ second}} = 2,000,000 \text{ bytes per second}$$

Most computer peripheral devices operate at much slower data rates. About the only devices commonly used in computer systems that can handle data rates as fast as this are arithmetic units.

There are several physical mechanisms for storing 1's and 0's in a memory. A common one is by means of an array of very small magnetic toroids called *cores,* one for each bit. A 1 is stored by magnetizing the core in one direction, say clockwise; a 0 is stored by magnetizing it in the other direction, as shown in Figure 1-4. The magnetizing is done by passing a current through a winding around the core. After a core is driven to the 1 or the 0 state, it retains that state indefinitely unless disturbed.

A core memory is a *random access* device; that is, the time needed to fetch a word from a particular address does not depend on what address was accessed previously. For example, in the Model 50, words can be stored or fetched in any order at a rate of one word every 2 μs.

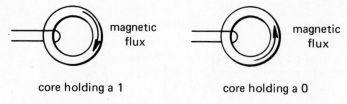

core holding a 1   core holding a 0

Figure 1-4. Magnetic cores.

In addition to the main core memory, a computer frequently has additional memories, such as magnetic drums, magnetic disks, and magnetic tapes. In these devices the data are physically distributed along a movable magnetic surface, and the access time depends in part on the distance along the surface from the last byte accessed to the desired byte. These moving magnetic memories usually provide large-volume storage at a lower cost per bit than main memory, but at the price of slower speed and a speed that is a function of the present and previous address.

ARITHMETIC UNIT

The arithmetic unit is the part of the computer that performs arithmetic and logical operations. The 360 arithmetic unit contains 16 general-purpose registers, numbered 0 to 15_{10} or 0 to F_H, as shown in Figure 1-5. Each register is 32 bits long. A general register is quite similar to a full-word location in memory in that

1. Data can be held in it, indefinitely if necessary.

2. Data can be copied from it to another part of the computer.

3. New data can be stored in it, obliterating the old data.

Arithmetic Unit

General Registers

0

1

2

.
.
.

15

Figure 1-5. 360 Arithmetic Unit.

In addition, the general registers have other properties. They are connected to adders, subtracters, and so on (not shown in Figure 1-5), which allow arithmetic and other operations to be performed.

Consider the problem of adding the two numbers in location 000F00 and 000F04 and storing the sum at location 000F08. We can do this with a sequence of three instructions using general register 0 to accumulate the sum.

Instruction	Meaning
58000F00	Load (that is, copy) the contents of 000F00 into general register 0.
5A000F04	Add the contents of 000F04 to the contents of general register 0, leaving the sum in general register 0.
50000F08	Store the contents of general register 0 (the sum) in 000F08.

These instructions will be discussed in detail later.

Many early computers had only two general registers. One was frequently called the accumulator and was used for most purposes, including addition and subtraction. The other was frequently called the multiplier-quotient register and was used mostly during multiplication and division. One even-odd pair of general registers in the 360 is similar to the accumulator multiplier-quotient register pair of older machines. The use of 16 general registers instead of two does allow more flexibility, since more intermediate results can be kept readily available in the arithmetic unit, instead of having to store them away in the memory and then retrieve them from time to time.

A more important reason for providing multiple registers is related to the base-displacement addressing scheme and to indexing, which are described later.

CONTROL UNIT

The control unit controls the actions of the whole computer. It does this by executing a program. The program consists of a sequence of *instructions* that are *executed* one at a time.

In the 360, each instruction is stored in memory as a string of 16, 32, or 48 bits, but for the moment we consider only 32-bit, that is, 4-byte, instructions. The instructions are stored in the memory in the order in which they are to be executed. For example, we might store the previous program segment in locations 0100, 0104, and 0108, since these instructions are four bytes long. Then the memory would look as shown in Figure 1-6. The program is in one part of the memory, the data and results are in another part, and other parts are unused.

To keep track of what instruction is being executed at each moment, the control unit contains an *instruction counter*. It points first to 0100, then to 0104, then to 0108, and so on. To execute the preceding program segment, the instruction counter must be set to 0100. Then the computer proceeds as follows[2]:

1. Fetch the instruction at location 000100.

---

[2] The notation C(*xx*) means the contents of *xx*.

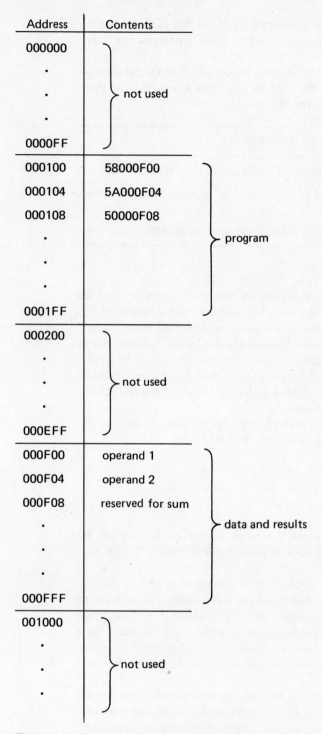

Address	Contents
000000	
•	
•	} not used
•	
0000FF	
000100	58000F00
000104	5A000F04
000108	50000F08
•	
•	} program
•	
0001FF	
000200	
•	
•	} not used
•	
000EFF	
000F00	operand 1
000F04	operand 2
000F08	reserved for sum
•	
•	} data and results
•	
000FFF	
001000	
•	
•	} not used
•	

Figure 1-6. Example of a memory assignment.

2. Execute it; that is, load C(000F00) into R0.

3. Fetch the instruction at location 000104.

4. Execute it; that is, add C(000F04) to C(R0); leave sum in R0.

5. Fetch the instruction at location 000108.

6. Execute it; that is, store C(R0) into location 000F08.

7. Fetch the instruction at location 00010C; and so on.

Note that the *fetch* and *execute* steps alternate. Prior to each instruction fetch, the instruction counter must be incremented by the proper amount (four bytes in this case) to point to the next instruction.

Normally, the instructions are taken in sequence, but it is also possible to set the instruction counter to a completely new value to jump to another part of the memory. Thus the program need not be in one contiguous part of the memory, but may be in several noncontiguous sections. In theory, the human programmer can assign portions of the memory to program or data in an almost completely arbitrary manner. In practice, this freedom is often restricted. For example, the executive system that supervises the use of the computer by various programs may allocate to one program a region of 6000 bytes and restrict that program to operate only in that region.

INPUT-OUTPUT

Computers in general use a variety of input media. A common one is punched paper cards. The card code used on the 360 computer is shown in Figure 1-7. Each card has 80 *columns* into which the code for a character (a letter, digit, or other symbol) can be punched. Each column is divided into 12 rows, which are named, starting from the top,

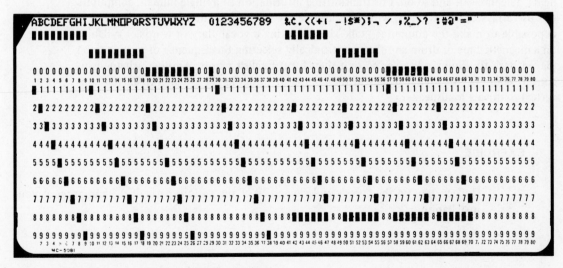

Figure 1-7. Card code used by IBM System/360.

the 12 row, 11 row, 0 row, . . ., 9 row. The punched card code for A is 12-1, for B is 12-2, for J is 11-1, for $ is 11-3-8, and so on.

The card in Figure 1-7 was prepared on a typewriter-like device called a *keypunch*. When a key on the keyboard is pressed, the machine punches the appropriate holes in the card and prints the character at the top. After a deck of cards has been punched, it is fed into the computer via a *card reader*. This is an electromechanical device that pulls the cards off the stack one at a time, examines the holes, and lets the cards that have been read fall through into another stack. As a consequence of this, a deck of cards cannot be read twice without manually moving the cards from the output stack back to the input stack. The holes are read by brushes carrying a small electric voltage, or by light beams and photoelectric cells. The printed characters on the cards are ignored, as are all extraneous pencil or ink marks. However, tears and bends in the card may cause card jams in the reader, and tears may be falsely interpreted as holes. Card readers are available with speeds up to about 1000 cards per minute.

The output device we shall be most concerned with is the printer. Various speeds and paper sizes are available. One model prints on fan-folded continuous-form paper 14 inches wide. Each page is 11 inches high. Each line can contain up to 132 characters, and each page can contain up to 66 lines. The speed is 1100 lines per minute.

In addition to the card reader and printer, a wide variety of other input and output devices is available on various computers. Another common input medium is punched paper tape; it is similar to a stream of punched cards fastened end to end, except that the paper tape usually has 5, 6, 7, or 8 rows of holes instead of 12 rows as in a punched card. Some computers accept inputs directly from keyboards, such as Teletype or electric typewriters. Some computers have document readers that accept sheets of paper with writing on them. Usually the writing or marks on the paper are constrained to a rather rigid format.

Other common output devices are card punches and Teletype machines. The latter frequently combine an output device (a printer) and an input device (a keyboard) in one unit. However, the number of possible computer output devices is very large, since practically any device that can be controlled electrically can be controlled by a computer and thought of as an output device. The list of possibilities includes guidance of vehicles of all types, control of processes (oil refineries, paper mills), control of networks (traffic lights, telephones), and so on. For transmitting information to a single human, computers can use arrays of lamps, bells, whistles, cathode ray tubes, and other kinds of displays. It is possible to make the computer "talk" by recording a vocabulary of words or syllables on a magnetic tape or drum and then electronically selecting the sequence of sounds to be played back to a human listener so that they form English words. Another scheme is to convert some of the digital signals in the computer to audio (in a digital-to-analog converter) to drive a loudspeaker.

EXERCISE

1. Collect data on the speeds and capacities of the various parts of the computer at your installation.

2

Number systems

Computers can handle alphabetic data, punctuation marks, special symbols, and numbers. In this chapter we consider some of the various systems that can be used to represent numbers, first for hand calculation, and then for machine calculation. The reader who is already familiar with this material may skip this chapter without loss of continuity.

For hand calculations, we usually write numbers in decimal form as follows:

$$3 \quad 2 \quad 1 \quad . \quad 7 \quad 4$$

hundreds   units   tenths   hundredths

tens   decimal point

Each *digit position* or column has associated with it a *weight*: 100, 10, 1, $\frac{1}{10}$, $\frac{1}{100}$, and so on. Each digit position contains a *digit*: 0, 1, 2, 3, 4, 5, 6, 7, 8, 9. The meaning of this number is

$$N = 3 \times 100 + 2 \times 10 + 1 \times 1 + 7 \times \frac{1}{10} + 4 \times \frac{1}{100}$$

This decimal representation of a number is one example of a *positional number representation* using a positive integer base. The general form is

$$N = \ldots x_3 \ \ x_2 \ \ x_1 \ \ x_0 \ \ . \ \ x_{-1} \ \ x_{-2} \ \ x_{-3} \ldots$$
$$\text{weights} \quad b^3 \ \ b^2 \ \ b^1 \ \ b^0 \quad b^{-1} \ \ b^{-2} \ \ b^{-3}$$

where b is the base of the number system and the digits x_i can have values $0, 1, 2, \ldots,$ $b - 1$. The meaning of this representation is

$$N = \ldots x_3 b^3 + x_2 b^2 + x_1 b^1 + x_0 b^0 + x_{-1} b^{-1} + x_{-2} b^{-2} \ldots$$
$$= \sum_i x_i b^i$$

For example, 123.4 interpreted as a base 7 number means

$$1 \times 7^2 + 2 \times 7^1 + 3 \times 7^0 + 4 \times 7^{-1}$$

$$= 1 \times 49 + 2 \times 7 + 3 \times 1 + 4 \times \frac{1}{7}$$

$$= 66\frac{4}{7} = 66.571\ldots_{10}$$

We usually indicate the base of the number system by a subscript, thus: 123.4_7.

If the base is larger than 10, there is a notation difficulty in representing the digit values from 10 up to $b - 1$. This is usually solved by using letters. In the base 16 or *hexadecimal* system, the digit values from 0 through 15 are usually represented by the 16 symbols

$$0, 1, 2, 3, 4, 5, 6, 7, 8, 9, A, B, C, D, E, F$$

For example, $E3.B_{16}$ means

$$E \times 16 + 3 + B \times \frac{1}{16} = 224 + 3 + \frac{11}{16} = 227\frac{11}{16}$$

We denote the hexadecimal number system by the subscript 16 or H.

In the base 2 or *binary* number system, the only binary digit values, or *bit* values, are 0 and 1. For example, 1010.11_2 means

$$1 \times 2^3 + 0 \times 2^2 + 1 \times 2^1 + 0 \times 2^0 + 1 \times 2^{-1} + 1 \times 2^{-2}$$

$$= 8 + 0 + 2 + 0 + \frac{1}{2} + \frac{1}{4} = 10\frac{3}{4}$$

Several schemes for representing the integers 0 through 20_{10} are shown in Table 2-1.

Most digital computers store data internally in binary form. The digit values 0 and 1 are represented by two states of a circuit. For example, a current may be present or absent, a voltage may be high or low, a magnetization may be north or south, and so on.

Table 2-1.   Four Number Systems.

Decimal	Binary	Octal	Hexadecimal
0	00000	0	0
1	00001	1	1
2	00010	2	2
3	00011	3	3
4	00100	4	4
5	00101	5	5
6	00110	6	6
7	00111	7	7
8	01000	10	8
9	01001	11	9
10	01010	12	A
11	01011	13	B
12	01100	14	C
13	01101	15	D
14	01110	16	E
15	01111	17	F
16	10000	20	10
17	10001	21	11
18	10010	22	12
19	10011	23	13
20	10100	24	14

Numbers containing, for example, 32 bits are stored in a circuit containing an array of 32 one-bit storage elements. The data contained in such an array might be

$$10110011101010111100011100100000$$

A computer can handle this without difficulty, but humans find it difficult to read or write long strings without error. For humans, a somewhat more manageable form can be obtained by arranging the bits in groups of four and then replacing each group by its hexadecimal equivalent, thus:

$$1011 \quad 0011 \quad 1010 \quad 1011 \quad 1100 \quad 0111 \quad 0010 \quad 0000._2$$
$$B \qquad 3 \qquad A \qquad B \qquad C \qquad 7 \qquad 2 \qquad 0._H$$

This grouping scheme can be used to convert a binary number to any base that is a power of 2. For example, the same binary number can be represented in base 8 or *octal* by grouping bits in groups of three, thus:

$$10 \quad 110 \quad 011 \quad 101 \quad 010 \quad 111 \quad 100 \quad 011 \quad 100 \quad 100 \quad 000._2$$
$$2 \quad 6 \quad 3 \quad 5 \quad 2 \quad 7 \quad 4 \quad 3 \quad 4 \quad 4 \quad 0._8$$

When grouping bits, always begin at the binary point and work out in both directions.

CONVERSION BETWEEN BASES: INTEGERS

The procedures for converting from one base to another are different for integers and fractions. We examine integers first.

Let the given number be expressed in positional notation in base b_1, thus:

$$[y_2 \quad y_1 \quad y_0.]_{b_1}$$

We wish to find the digits in the equivalent representation in base b_2:

$$[x_3 \quad x_2 \quad x_1 \quad x_0.]_{b_2}$$

In general the number of digits in the two representations are not equal. We write

$$[y_2 \quad y_1 \quad y_0.]_{b_1} = x_3 \; b_2^3 + x_2 \; b_2^2 + x_1 \; b_2^1 + x_0 \; b_2^0$$

Dividing both sides by b_2, we obtain

$$\frac{[y_2 \quad y_1 \quad y_0.]_{b_1}}{b_2} = \underbrace{x_3 \; b_2^2 + x_2 \; b_2^1 + x_1 \; b_2^0}_{\text{integer}} + \underbrace{\frac{x_0}{b_2}}_{\text{fraction}}.$$

We compare this to integer division:

$$\frac{\text{dividend}}{\text{divisor}} = \text{quotient} + \frac{\text{remainder}}{\text{divisor}}$$

and identify x_0 as the remainder obtained after dividing $[y_2 \quad y_1 \quad y_0.]_{b_1}$ by b_2. The division has to be performed in a single number system, so we must express b_2 in the b_1 number system and carry out the division in the b_1 system. This process produces a value of x_0, the least significant digit of the converted number. To obtain x_1, apply the same process to the quotient first obtained, and, by repeating this process, obtain, $x_2, x_3, \ldots$.

Example: Convert $347._{10}$ to base 8.

$$\frac{347._{10}}{8_{10}} = 43\frac{3}{8}, \quad x_0 = 3$$

$$\frac{43.}{8} = 5\frac{3}{8}, \quad x_1 = 3$$

$$\frac{5.}{8} = 0\frac{5}{8}, \quad x_2 = 5$$

$$x_3 = 0$$

Thus

$$347._{10} = 533._8$$

A more compact conversion notation is as follows:

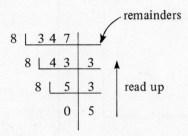

Example: Convert 347._{10} to binary.

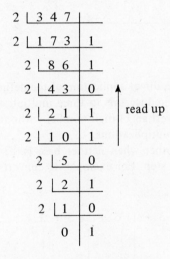

Thus $347._{10} = 101\ 011\ 011._2 = 533._8$, as before.

When the first base is not 10, the preceding scheme is still valid, but it is awkward to use because it requires doing division in a nondecimal number system. Another scheme is to expand the given number using the definition of positional number notation. For example, convert $2327._8$ to decimal:

$$2327._8 = 2 \times 8^3 + 3 \times 8^2 + 2 \times 8^1 + 7$$
$$= ((2 \times 8 + 3)\, 8 + 2)\, 8 + 7$$

$$
\begin{array}{r}
2 \\
\underline{\times 8} \\
16 \\
\underline{+3} \\
19 \\
\underline{\times 8} \\
152 \\
\underline{+2} \\
154 \\
\underline{\times 8} \\
1232 \\
\underline{+7} \\
1239
\end{array}
$$

Thus $2347._8 = 1239._{10}$. In this example, direct application of the definition requires six multiplications, but by nesting terms we reduce this to three multiplications. For larger numbers, the savings are greater. To convert an 11-digit number without nesting takes 55 multiplications; with nesting it takes 10 multiplications.

    Conversion from one base to another when neither base is 10 can be done by converting to decimal as an intermediate step. For example, to convert $4123._5$ to base 9 we write

$$4123._5 = ((4 \times 5 + 1)\, 5 + 2)\, 5 + 3$$

$$
\begin{array}{r}
4 \\
\underline{\times 5} \\
20 \\
\underline{+1} \\
21 \\
\underline{\times 5} \\
105 \\
\underline{+2} \\
107 \\
\underline{\times 5} \\
535 \\
\underline{+3} \\
538
\end{array}
$$

$$
\begin{array}{c|cc}
9 & 5\ \ 3 & 8 \\ \hline
9 & 5\ \ 9 & 7 \\ \hline
9 & 6 & 5 \\ \hline
 & 0 & 6
\end{array}
\quad \uparrow \text{ read up}
$$

Hence $4123._5 = 538._{10} = 657._9$. All the arithmetic in this example is in decimal.

CONVERSION BETWEEN BASES: FRACTIONS

Let the given number be expressed in positional notation in base b_1, thus:

$$[.y_{-1} \quad y_{-2} \quad y_{-3} \quad \ldots]_{b_1}$$

We wish to find the equivalent representation in base b_2, namely

$$[.x_{-1} \quad x_{-2} \quad x_{-3} \quad \ldots]_{b_2}$$

We write

$$[.y_{-1} \quad y_{-2} \quad y_{-3} \quad \ldots]_{b_1} = \frac{x_{-1}}{b_2^1} + \frac{x_{-2}}{b_2^2} + \frac{x_{-3}}{b_2^3} + \ldots$$

Multiplying by b_2, we obtain

$$[.y_{-1} \quad y_{-2} \quad y_{-3} \quad \ldots]_{b_1} \times b_2 = \underbrace{x_{-1}}_{\substack{\text{integer} \\ \text{part}}} + \underbrace{\frac{x_{-2}}{b_2^1} + \frac{x_{-3}}{b_2^2} + \ldots}_{\substack{\text{fraction} \\ \text{part}}}$$

The integer part of the product is the first converted digit, x_{-1}. By repeating this process on the fraction part, we obtain x_{-2}, x_{-3}, and so on. For example, to convert $.912_{10}$ to octal, we write

$$.912$$
$$\underline{\times 8}$$
$$\not{7}.296 \quad \therefore x_{-1} = 7$$
$$\underline{\times 8}$$
$$\not{2}.368 \quad \therefore x_{-2} = 2$$
$$\underline{\times 8}$$
$$\not{2}.944 \quad \therefore x_{-3} = 2$$
$$\underline{\times 8}$$
$$\not{7}.552 \quad \therefore x_{-4} = 7$$
$$\underline{\times 8}$$
$$\not{4}.416 \quad \therefore x_{-5} = 4 \quad \text{etc.}$$

Hence $.912_{10} = .72274\ldots_8$. At each step we multiply the fraction by 8, but not the integer. We indicate this by crossing out the integer obtained at each step.

In this conversion scheme, the multiplication must be done in the b_1 number system. For example, to convert $.E8_H$ to decimal, we multiply by $b_2 = 10_{10} = A_H$ using hexadecimal arithmetic. (A hexadecimal multiplication table is useful here.)

$$.E8$$
$$\underline{\times A}$$
$$\not{9}.10$$
$$\underline{\times A}$$
$$\not{0}.A0$$
$$\underline{\times A}$$
$$\not{6}.40$$
$$\underline{\times A}$$
$$\not{2}.80$$
$$\underline{\times A}$$
$$\not{5}.00$$

Hence $.E8_H = .90625_{10}$.

Fractions with repeated digits are indicated by drawing a bar or vinculum over the group of digits to be repeated. For example,

$$.2_3 = \frac{2}{3} = .666\ldots_{10} = .\overline{6}_{10}$$

Conversion of fractions containing a vinculum can be done using a finite (and small) number of digits by taking care to restore the repetitive pattern at each step. For example, convert $.\bar{6}_{10}$ to base 8. We begin using four digits:

$$.6666$$
$$\underline{\times 8}$$
$$\cancel{5}.3328 \quad \therefore \ x_{-1} = 5$$

We restore the repetitive pattern and continue:

$$.3333$$
$$\underline{\times 8}$$
$$\cancel{2}.6664 \quad \therefore \ x_{-2} = 2$$

We restore the repetitive pattern and obtain .6666, which is the number we started with. The converted number will have repeated digits, thus:

$$.\bar{6}_{10} = .525252\ldots_8 = .\overline{52}_8$$

BINARY ARITHMETIC

The addition and multiplication tables for one-digit binary arithmetic are as follows:

Sum	0	1
0	0	1
1	1	10

Product	0	1
0	0	0
1	0	1

Multicolumn calculations can be performed by using these tables and by propagating carries and borrows as in decimal arithmetic, except that the carries and borrows represent weight 2 instead of weight 10. In the following examples, carries and borrows are indicated by arrows.

```
    1 0 1 1 1 0  (augend)        1 0 0 1 1 1  (minuend)
  + 1 0 1 0 1 0  (addend)      -   1 1 0 1 0  (subtrahend)
  -------------                -------------
    1 0 1 1 0 0 0  (sum)         0 0 1 1 0 1  (difference)
```

```
            1  0  1  0  1   (multiplicand)
         ×  1  1  0  1  0   (multiplier)
            0  0  0  0  0
         1  0  1  0  1
      0  0  0  0  0
   1  0  1  0  1
1  0  1  0  1
1  0  0  0  1  0  0  0  1  0   (product)
```

```
                     1  1  0  0 .  (quotient)
(divisor) 1 0 1 1 ) 1 0 0 0 0 1 1 1 . (dividend)
                  1  0  1  1
                     1  0  1  1
                     1  0  1  1
                        0  1  1   (remainder)
```

HEXADECIMAL ARITHMETIC

The hexadecimal (base 16) digits are

$$0, 1, 2, 3, 4, 5, 6, 7, 8, 9, A, B, C, D, E, F$$

One-digit hexadecimal addition and subtraction can be done mentally after a little practice, or one can use the hexadecimal addition table shown as Table 2-2.

Multicolumn hexadecimal arithmetic can be done as in decimal by (1) using this table and (2) noting that a carry or borrow represents 16 units. Another approach is to mentally convert each column to decimal, perform the operation, and then convert the result back to hexadecimal. For example,

```
    1 A D . 7 2           2 3 4 . F 9
  +     D . 0 F         - 1 F C . 7 A
    1 B A . 8 1            3 8 . 7 F
```

Multiplication can be done by repeated addition, or by constructing a hexadecimal multiplication table (Exercise 5).

Table 2-2. *Hexadecimal Addition Table.*

	0	1	2	3	4	5	6	7	8	9	A	B	C	D	E	F
0	0	1	2	3	4	5	6	7	8	9	A	B	C	D	E	F
1		2	3	4	5	6	7	8	9	A	B	C	D	E	F	10
2			4	5	6	7	8	9	A	B	C	D	E	F	10	11
3				6	7	8	9	A	B	C	D	E	F	10	11	12
4					8	9	A	B	C	D	E	F	10	11	12	13
5						A	B	C	D	E	F	10	11	12	13	14
6							C	D	E	F	10	11	12	13	14	15
7								E	F	10	11	12	13	14	15	16
8									10	11	12	13	14	15	16	17
9										12	13	14	15	16	17	18
A											14	15	16	17	18	19
B												16	17	18	19	1A
C													18	19	1A	1B
D														1A	1B	1C
E															1C	1D
F																1E

OTHER NUMBER SYSTEMS

So far we have considered only nonredundant positional number systems with positive integer bases. Positional number systems also exist for positive and negative, integer and fraction bases. However, these are less important than positive integer bases; in fact, most computers use some version of a base 2 or base 10 system.

As examples of positional number representations with a noninteger base, we show that 1.5 can be expressed in bases $\frac{3}{4}$ and $\frac{4}{3}$ using digit values 0 and 1. For base $\frac{3}{4}$ we write

$$1.5 = \sum_i x_i \left(\frac{3}{4}\right)^i \qquad \text{where } x_i = 0 \text{ or } 1$$

and solve for the digits x_i. For base $\frac{4}{3}$ we write

$$1.5 = \sum_i y_i \left(\frac{4}{3}\right)^i \qquad \text{where } y_i = 0 \text{ or } 1$$

and solve for the y_i. Since the bases are reciprocals, we see that

$$x_j = y_{-j}$$

so the two problems reduce to one. We choose to solve the base $\frac{4}{3}$ problem first. We write

$$1.5 = \ldots y_2\left(\frac{4}{3}\right)^2 + y_1\left(\frac{4}{3}\right)^1 + y_0 + y_{-1}\left(\frac{4}{3}\right)^{-1} + y_{-2}\left(\frac{4}{3}\right)^{-2} + \ldots$$

Since $\left(\frac{4}{3}\right)^2 = \frac{16}{9} \geqslant 1.5$, we conclude that $y_i = 0$ for all $i \geqslant 2$. We also note that y_1 or y_0 can be 1, but not both. The representation of a number in this number system is not unique. We choose $y_1 = 1, y_0 = 0$. The expansion becomes

$$1.5 = 1\left(\frac{4}{3}\right) + 0 + y_{-1}\left(\frac{4}{3}\right)^{-1} + y_{-2}\left(\frac{4}{3}\right)^{-2} + \ldots$$

or

$$\frac{3}{2} - \frac{4}{3} = \frac{1}{6} = y_{-1}\left(\frac{4}{3}\right)^{-1} + \ldots$$

This can be handled as a fraction conversion problem, multiplying by the base and examining the integer part at each step.

$$\frac{4}{3} \times \frac{1}{6} = \frac{4}{18} = y_{-1} + y_{-2}\left(\frac{4}{3}\right)^{-1} + \ldots, \quad y_{-1} = 0$$

$$\frac{4}{3} \times \frac{4}{18} = \frac{16}{54} = y_{-2} + \ldots, \quad y_{-2} = 0$$

$$\frac{4}{3} \times \frac{16}{54} = \frac{64}{162} = y_{-3} + \ldots, \quad y_{-3} = 0$$

$$\frac{4}{3} \times \frac{64}{162} = \frac{256}{486} = y_{-4} + \ldots, \quad y_{-4} = 0$$

$$\frac{4}{3} \times \frac{256}{486} = \frac{1024}{1458} = y_{-5} + \ldots, \quad y_{-5} = 0$$

$$\frac{4}{3} \times \frac{1024}{1458} = \frac{4096}{4374} = y_{-6} + \ldots, \quad y_{-6} = 0$$

$$\frac{4}{3} \times \frac{4096}{4374} = \frac{16,384}{13,122} = y_{-7} + \ldots, \quad y_{-7} = 1$$

$$\frac{4}{3} \times \left(\frac{16,384}{13,122} - 1\right) = \frac{13,048}{39,366} = y_{-8} + \ldots, \quad y_{-8} = 0 \quad \text{etc.}$$

As a check, we add the weights of the nonzero digits.

$$y_1: \quad \frac{4}{3} \quad = \quad\quad\quad 1.3333$$

$$y_{-7}: \quad \left(\frac{4}{3}\right)^{-7} = \frac{.2187}{16,384} = \frac{.1335}{1.4668}$$

The correct sum is 1.5, so the error is $1.5 - 1.4668 = .0332$. This error could be made smaller by taking more terms.

The weights of the digit positions and the digit values are summarized next.

weight:
$$\left(\frac{4}{3}\right)^{1} \quad \left(\frac{4}{3}\right)^{0} \quad \left(\frac{4}{3}\right)^{-1} \quad \left(\frac{4}{3}\right)^{-2} \quad \left(\frac{4}{3}\right)^{-3} \quad \left(\frac{4}{3}\right)^{-4} \quad \left(\frac{4}{3}\right)^{-5} \quad \left(\frac{4}{3}\right)^{-6} \quad \left(\frac{4}{3}\right)^{-7} \quad \left(\frac{4}{3}\right)^{-8}$$

digit
value: 1   0   0   0   0   0   0   0   1   0

y digits
$\left(\text{base } \frac{4}{3}\right)$: $y_1 \quad y_0 \quad y_{-1} \quad y_{-2} \quad y_{-3} \quad y_{-4} \quad y_{-5} \quad y_{-6} \quad y_{-7} \quad y_{-8}$

x digits
$\left(\text{base } \frac{3}{4}\right)$: $x_{-1} \quad x_0 \quad x_1 \quad x_2 \quad x_3 \quad x_4 \quad x_5 \quad x_6 \quad x_7 \quad x_8$

Thus the positional representation of 1.5 in base $\frac{4}{3}$ is

$$\ldots y_2 \quad y_1 \quad y_0 \quad . \quad y_{-1} \quad y_{-2} \quad y_{-3} \ldots = [10.00000010\ldots]_{4/3}$$

and the representation in base $\frac{3}{4}$ is

$$\ldots x_2 \quad x_1 \quad x_0 \quad . \quad x_{-1} \quad x_{-2} \quad x_{-3} \ldots = [\ldots 010000000.1]_{3/4}$$

$$\underbrace{\text{fraction}} \quad \underbrace{\text{integer}}$$

The digits representing the fraction part are on the left of the radix point when the base is less than 1.

The number system just described does not yield a unique representation for 1.5. We could have begun the expansion with $y_1 = 1$, $y_0 = 0$ or with $y_1 = 0$, $y_0 = 1$. This redundancy does not occur only in noninteger bases. For example, we can make a redundant base 2 system by allowing digit values 0, 1, and -1 (which we write as $\bar{1}$). Some representations in this system are

Base 10	Redundant Binary
0	0
1	$1, 1\bar{1}, 1\bar{1}\bar{1}, \ldots$
2	$10, 1\bar{1}0, 1\bar{1}\bar{1}0, \ldots$
3	$11, 10\bar{1}, 1\bar{1}0\bar{1}, \ldots$
4	$100, 1\bar{1}00, 1\bar{1}\bar{1}00, \ldots$
5	$101, 11\bar{1}, 10\bar{1}\bar{1}, 1\bar{1}01, \ldots$
6	$110, 10\bar{1}0, 1\bar{1}\bar{1}0, \ldots$
7	$111, 100\bar{1}, 10\bar{1}1, \ldots$

One application of this number system is in speeding up multiplication. For example, in the multiplication

$$101011001011 \times 011111111111$$

$$\text{(multiplicand)} \qquad \text{(multiplier)}$$

the multiplier contains eleven 1's, so we must add the multiplicand to the partial product eleven times. But by rewriting the multiplier as

$$011111111111 = 10000000000\bar{1}$$

we obtain a version requiring only two additions, one of which is negative, a saving of nine additions. For multipliers containing only short strings of consecutive 1's, the savings are less. A similar example in base 10 is

$$567 \times 999 = 567(1000 - 1) = 567,000 - 567 = 566,433$$

The number systems we have been considering were all positional number systems with a unique weight associated with each digit position. There are also number systems in which the digit positions do not have a unique weight. Examples are (1) the Roman number system and (2) the "excess 3" code, which is used in some computers to represent the decimal digits 0 to 9 in a four-bit pattern.

Arabic	Roman	Excess 3
0		0011
1	I	0100
2	II	0101
3	III	0110
4	IV or IIII	0111
5	V	1000
6	VI	1001
7	VII	1010
8	VIII	1011
9	IX or VIIII	1100

EXERCISES

1. Complete the following table. Carry each fraction conversion to at least four digits.

Decimal	Binary	Octal	Hexadecimal
13.25	1101.01	15.2	D.4
14.			
	1101101.01		
			4F.9
		$13.\overline{25}$	
	11000.00001		
$3.\overline{7}$			

2. Convert 39. base 14 to base 11.

3. Convert .231 base 8 to base 10 by doing multiplication in octal. Carry conversion to four places.

4. Convert 143 base 5 to base 10_{10} ($= 20_5$)
   a. By division in base 5.
   b. By multiplication in base 10.

5. Construct a hexadecimal multiplication table.

6. Convert .44 base 16 to decimal (eight places) using hexadecimal arithmetic.

7. Perform the indicated binary arithmetic:

$$1010111.01 \ + \ 111.001$$

$$1110011. \ - \ 101111.$$

$$111.001 \ \times \ 1010.1$$

$$1100010. \ \div \ 1101.1$$

8. Perform the indicated hexadecimal arithmetic

$$234.56 \ + \ FFF0.0E7$$

$$93.311A \ - \ 73.312$$

$$BA. \ \times \ DA.$$

9. Construct a multiplication table for a base 6 positional number system that uses digit values 0, 1, 2, 3, 4, and 5.

10. Consider a base 36 number system that uses digit values 0, 1, 2, 3, . . ., 8, 9, A, B, C, . . ., X, Y, Z. Convert $CAT._{36}$ to base 10.

11. In the derivation of the conversion procedure for fractions on page 17, the sum of a series was denoted "fraction part." Prove that this sum is indeed less than 1.

12. Show that the expansion of 1.5 in base $\frac{3}{4}$ is not unique by finding the first few nonzero digits of three different expansions. How many expansions are there?

13. Use the digit values 0 and 1 to express 2 in base $\frac{3}{2}$.

14. Find the first two nonzero digits of the positional representation of $\frac{3}{4}$ in base $+\sqrt{2}$, allowing digit values 0 and 1. Evaluate this approximate representation numerically and compare it to .75.

15. Consider a positional number system with base $+4$ with digit values -1, 0, 1, and 2. Use this system to write out representations of the integers 0 through 20. Is this a redundant number system? Why?

16. Consider a positional number system with base $+3$ and digit values -1, 0, 1, 2, 3. Write out the digits of two different representations of each of the numbers 1 through 10 using this system.

17. Using a higher level language (Fortran, Algol, PL/I, etc.) write a program to read a positive integer from columns 1 to 4 of a card and print on one line the decimal and base seven representations of that integer. Then repeat for the next card. For example, if the data deck is

    b b b 0
    b b 1 2
    b 1 2 3

    where b indicates blank, then the printed output should be

              0   0
           1 2   1 5
        1 2 3   2 3 4

    You may print leading zeros if you wish.

18. Using a higher level language, write a program to read a positive integer from columns 1 and 2 of a card and print on one line the decimal and Roman representations of that number. Then repeat for the next card. For example if the input deck is

    2 9
       3
    8 7

    then the printed output should be

    2 9   X X V I I I
       3   I I I
    8 7   L X X X V I I

    To simplify the problem use the "old style" for 4, that is use I I I I instead of I V.

POSITIVE AND NEGATIVE INTEGER REPRESENTATIONS

Integers may be represented in a computer by appropriate bit patterns in a register. Consider an $(n + 1)$-bit register with bit positions numbered as follows:

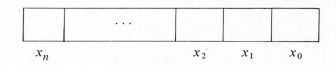

We indicate the contents of the register by the array of bits $[x_n, x_{n-1}, \ldots, x_3, x_2, x_1,$

x_0]. What code do we use to represent integers; that is, what bit pattern represents 7, 13, -3, and so on?

For the positive integers, the obvious code is the binary integer representation:

[0000]   represents   0

[0001]   represents   +1

...

[1111]   represents +15

This binary system can be extended to allow representation of negative integers in three important ways:

1. Sign-magnitude representation.

2. Two's complement representation.

3. One's complement representation.

Four-bit examples of the three systems are shown in Table 2-3. Some details are discussed next.

Table 2-3.   *Three Base 2 Number Systems.*

Decimal Representation	Sign-Magnitude Representation	Two's Complement Representation	One's Complement Representation
+7	0111	0111	0111
+6	0110	0110	0110
+5	0101	0101	0101
+4	0100	0100	0100
+3	0011	0011	0011
+2	0010	0010	0010
+1	0001	0001	0001
0	0000	0000	0000
−0	1000	a	1111
−1	1001	1111	1110
−2	1010	1110	1101
−3	1011	1101	1100
−4	1100	1100	1011
−5	1101	1011	1010
−6	1110	1010	1001
−7	1111	1001	1000
−8	a	1000	a

[a]Not representable in this system.

SIGN-MAGNITUDE REPRESENTATION

Sign-magnitude representation is the system humans ordinarily use, except that the first bit is written 0 or 1 instead of + or -, respectively. Thus, in a six-bit sign-magnitude system, the representation of +9 is 001001 and the representation of -9 is 101001.

The rules are as follows. Let $[y_n, \ldots, y_2, y_1, y_0]$ be the binary vector representing the integer X in the sign-magnitude system. We denote this as

$$R_{SM}(X) = [y_n, \ldots, y_2, y_1, y_0] \quad \text{where } y_i = 0 \text{ or } 1$$

We define the rule for obtaining this binary vector from the number X thus:

$$R_{SM}(X) = \begin{cases} X & \text{for } X \geqslant 0 \\ 2^n + |X| & \text{for } X < 0 \end{cases} \tag{S1}$$

where the positive integer on the right is expressed as an $(n + 1)$-bit unsigned binary integer $[y_n, \ldots, y_2, y_1, y_0]$. The inverse problem is, given the y digits, to find the corresponding X:

$$X = (1 - 2 \cdot y_n) \sum_{i=0}^{n-1} y_i 2^i \tag{S2}$$

For example, the representation of -5 in a four-bit system is, from (S1),

$$R_{SM}(-5) = 2^3 + 5$$
$$= 1000 + 0101 = 1101$$

The inverse transformation is, from (S2),

$$X = (1 - 2 \cdot 1) \sum_{i=0}^{2} y_i 2^i$$
$$= -(1 \cdot 2^2 + 0 \cdot 2^1 + 1 \cdot 2^0)$$
$$= -(4 + 1) = -5$$

Sign-magnitude representation works well for humans. It also has been used in a number of computers. However, it has the disadvantage that when adding signed numbers, the signs and the relative magnitudes must be inspected to see which magnitude to subtract from which. Consider the addition $A + B = S$. There are three cases.

Case	Required Action
Operand signs match	Form $|A| + |B|$, append common sign
Signs differ: $|A| > |B|$	Form $|A| - |B|$, append sign of A
Signs differ: $|B| > |A|$	Form $|B| - |A|$, append sign of B

For humans, the inspection of signs and relative magnitudes of A and B is trivially easy; for computers it may require a subtraction. Another disadvantage of the sign-magnitude system is that when counting up or down the computer has to sense when the count crosses 0 and change from subtractions to additions, or vice versa. The two's complement and one's complement systems avoid these difficulties, but they have difficulties of their own. Computers have been built using each of these three systems, and some computers use more than one. For example, the IBM System/360 represents fixed-point numbers in two's complement form, and represents the fraction part of floating-point numbers in sign-magnitude form.

TWO'S COMPLEMENT REPRESENTATION

The two's complement (or, more properly, the two-to-the-n-plus-one complement) of X is $2^{n+1} - X$. In a four-bit system, the two's complement of 0011 is $2^4 - 0011$. But $2^4 = 10000$ cannot be represented in a four-bit system, so we write

$$
\begin{array}{r}
0\ \ 0\ \ 0\ \ 0 \\
-\ 0\ \ 0\ \ 1\ \ 1 \\
\hline
1\ \ 1\ \ 0\ \ 1
\end{array}
$$

where there was a borrow from the (nonexistent) bit position just to the left of the most significant bit. The two's complement of X is used as the representation of $-X$ in the two's complement number system.

More formally, we have the following. Let X be any integer. We represent X in the two's complement number system by the bit string

$$R_{TC}(X) = [z_n, \ldots, z_2, z_1, z_0] \qquad \text{where } z_i = 0 \text{ or } 1$$

We define the rule for obtaining $R_{TC}(X)$ as follows:

$$R_{TC}(X) = \begin{cases} X & \text{for } X \geqslant 0 \\ 2^{n+1} - |X| & \text{for } X < 0 \end{cases} \tag{T1}$$

where the positive integer on the right is expressed as an $(n + 1)$-bit unsigned binary integer $[z_n, \ldots, z_2, z_1, z_0]$. The inverse problem is, given the z_i digits, to find the corresponding X:

$$X = -2^n z_n + \sum_{i=0}^{n-1} z_i 2^i \tag{T2}$$

For example, the representation of -5 in a four-bit system ($n = 3$) is, by (T1),

$$R_{TC}(-5) = 2^4 - 5 = (1)0000 - 0101 = 1011$$

Evaluating 1011 using (T2), we have

$$X = -2^3 + 0 \cdot 2^2 + 1 \cdot 2^1 + 1 \cdot 2^0$$

$$= -8 + 2 + 1 = -5$$

An important property of the two's complement number system is that addition can be performed in it directly without prior inspection of the signs or magnitudes of the operands. We show this as follows. Consider the addition $S = A + B$. We show that we can obtain the correct representation of the sum by simply adding the representations of the operands as positive integers, modulo 2^{n+1}.

Prove: $R_{TC}(S) = R_{TC}(A) + R_{TC}(B)$, modulo 2^{n+1}.

Case 1. $A \geqslant 0$, $B \geqslant 0$, $S = |A| + |B|$

$$R_{TC}(A) = |A|$$

$$R_{TC}(B) = |B|$$

$$R_{TC}(A) + R_{TC}(B) = |A| + |B| = |S| = R_{TC}(+|S|)$$

Example:

$$A = +2 = 0010$$

$$B = +3 = \underline{0011}$$

$$0101 = +5$$

Case 2. $A < 0$, $B < 0$, $S < 0$, $|S| = |A| + |B|$

$$R_{TC}(A) = 2^{n+1} - |A|$$

$$R_{TC}(B) = 2^{n+1} - |B|$$

$$R_{TC}(A) + R_{TC}(B) = 2^{n+1} - |A| + 2^{n+1} - |B|$$

But since $2^{n+1} = 100. . .00$ has $n + 1$ zeros, only zeros appear in the register. Hence we can add or subtract 2^{n+1} at will. Then

$$R_{TC}(A) + R_{TC}(B) = 2^{n+1} - |A| - |B|$$

$$= 2^{n+1} - (|A| + |B|)$$

$$= R_{TC}[-(|A| + |B|)]$$

$$= R_{TC}(-|S|)$$

$$= R_{TC}(S)$$

Example:

$$A = -2 = 1110$$

$$B = -3 = \underline{1101}$$

$$1011 = -5$$

carry
lost

Note that even though a carry was lost at the left end, the result is correct.

Case 3A. $A < 0,\quad B \geqslant 0,\quad |A| > |B|$

$$S < 0,\quad |S| = |A| - |B|$$

$$S = -(|A| - |B|)$$

$$R_{TC}(A) = 2^{n+1} - |A|$$

$$R_{TC}(B) = |B|$$

$$\begin{aligned}
R_{TC}(A) + R_{TC}(B) &= 2^{n+1} - |A| + |B| \\
&= 2^{n+1} - (|A| - |B|) \\
&= R_{TC}[-(|A| - |B|)] \\
&= R_{TC}(S)
\end{aligned}$$

Example:

$$A = -5 = 1011$$
$$B = +2 = \underline{0010}$$
$$1101 = -3$$

Case 3B. $A < 0,\quad B \geqslant 0,\quad |A| < |B|$

$$S > 0,\quad S = +(|B| - |A|)$$

$$R_{TC}(A) = 2^{n+1} - |A|$$

$$R_{TC}(B) = |B|$$

$$\begin{aligned}
R_{TC}(A) + R_{TC}(B) &= 2^{n+1} - |A| + |B| = |B| - |A| \\
&= R_{TC}[+(|B| - |A|)] = R_{TC}(S)
\end{aligned}$$

Example:

$$A = -2 = 1110$$
$$B = +4 = \underline{0100}$$
$$0010 = +2$$

carry
lost

Case 4. $A \geqslant 0, B < 0$. Same as case 3 by interchanging A and B.

This concludes the proof that addition in the two's complement system can be done by adding the two's complement representations of the operands to obtain the two's complement representation of the sum. We leave two's complement subtraction until a later section.

The two's complement representation is an example of a *radix complement* representation. Another example is the *ten's complement*. The ten's complement (or, more accurately, the ten-to-the-three complement) of 738 is $10^3 - 738$, or

$$\begin{array}{r} 000 \\ -\ 738 \\ \hline 262 \end{array}$$

This subtraction requires a borrow from the (nonexistent) digit just to the left, and this borrow must propagate the whole length of the number. We can subtract without borrowing by writing

$$1000 - 738 = 999 - 738 + 1$$

or

$$
\begin{array}{r}
999 \\
- 738 \\
\hline
261 + 1 = 262
\end{array}
$$

The result of subtracting from a string of 9's is called the *nine's complement* or *radix-minus-one complement* or *diminished radix complement*. The analogous quantity in binary is called the *one's complement*.

ONE'S COMPLEMENT REPRESENTATION

The one's complement of X is $2^{n+1} - 1 - X$. For example, the one's complement of 6 in a four-bit system is

$$
\begin{aligned}
2^4 - 1 - 6 &= (1)0000 - 0001 - 0110 \\
&= \quad 1111 - 0110 \\
&= \quad 1001
\end{aligned}
$$

Thus the one's complement of X is the bitwise complement[1] of X. The one's complement of X is used as the representation of $-X$ in the one's complement number system.

Let X be any integer. We represent X by the bit string

$$R_{OC}(X) = [w_n, w_{n-1}, \ldots, w_2, w_1, w_0] \quad \text{where } w_i = 0 \text{ or } 1$$

We define the rule for obtaining $R_{OC}(X)$ as follows:

$$R_{OC}(X) = \begin{cases} X & \text{for } X \geqslant 0 \\ 2^{n+1} - 1 - |X| & \text{for } X < 0 \end{cases} \tag{O1}$$

where the positive integer on the right is expressed as an $(n + 1)$-bit unsigned binary

---

[1] The complement of 1 is 0; the complement of 0 is 1.

integer $[w_n, \ldots, w_2, w_1, w_0]$. The inverse problem is, given the w_i digits, to find the corresponding X:

$$X = w_n(-2^n + 1) + \sum_{i=0}^{n-1} w_i 2^i \qquad \text{(O2)}$$

For example, the representation of -5 in a four-bit system ($n = 3$) is

$$R_{OC}(-5) = 2^4 - 1 - 5$$
$$= 16 - 1 - 5$$

or

$$\begin{array}{r} 1111 \\ -\ 0101 \\ \hline 1010 \end{array}$$

The inverse calculation is

$$X = 1(-2^3 + 1) + 0 \cdot 2^2 + 1 \cdot 2^1 + 0 \cdot 2^0$$
$$= -7 + 2 = -5$$

From (T1) and (O1) we have, for negative numbers,

$$R_{TC}(-|X|) = R_{OC}(-|X|) + 1 \qquad \text{(O3)}$$

Since the one's complement is easily obtained as the bitwise complement, this is a convenient way to calculate the two's complement of a number.

Addition in the one's complement system can be done by adding the representations of the operands as if they were positive integers, plus adding an *end-around carry* if one occurs. This can be shown algebraically as before, but we show only examples:

$$
\begin{array}{ll}
\begin{array}{rl}
+4 & 0100 \\
+3 & \underline{0011} \\
+7 & 0111 \\
& \searrow 0 \\
& \underline{} \\
& 0111 = +7
\end{array}
\qquad
\begin{array}{rl}
+4 & 0100 \\
-3 & \underline{1100} \\
+1 & 0000 \\
& \searrow 1 \\
& \underline{} \\
& 0001 = +1
\end{array}
\end{array}
$$

$$
\begin{array}{ll}
\begin{array}{rl}
-4 & 1011 \\
+3 & 0011 \\
\hline
-1 & 1110 \\
& \searrow 0 \\
\hline
& 1110 = -1
\end{array}
&
\begin{array}{rl}
-4 & 1011 \\
-3 & 1100 \\
\hline
-7 & 0111 \\
& \searrow 1 \\
\hline
& 1000 = -7
\end{array}
\end{array}
$$

Subtraction in the one's complement system can be done by adding the one's complement of the subtrahend to the minuend. In hand calculation the bitwise complement is written down by inspection; in machine calculation simple circuits provide the complement of each bit. For example,

$$
\begin{array}{lll}
\begin{array}{r}
+4 \\
(-)+3 \\
\hline
+1
\end{array}
&
\begin{array}{r}
0100 \\
(-)0011 \\
\hline
\end{array}
&
\begin{array}{r}
0100 \\
(+)1100 \\
\hline
0000 \\
\searrow 1 \\
\hline
0001 = +1
\end{array}
&
\begin{array}{r}
+4 \\
(-)-3 \\
\hline
+7
\end{array}
&
\begin{array}{r}
0100 \\
(-)1100 \\
\hline
\end{array}
&
\begin{array}{r}
0100 \\
(+)0011 \\
\hline
0111 \\
\searrow 0 \\
\hline
0111 = +7
\end{array}
\end{array}
$$

$$
\begin{array}{lll}
\begin{array}{r}
-4 \\
(-)+3 \\
\hline
-7
\end{array}
&
\begin{array}{r}
1011 \\
(-)0011 \\
\hline
\end{array}
&
\begin{array}{r}
1011 \\
(+)1100 \\
\hline
0111 \\
\searrow 1 \\
\hline
1000 = -7
\end{array}
&
\begin{array}{r}
-4 \\
(-)-3 \\
\hline
-1
\end{array}
&
\begin{array}{r}
1011 \\
(-)1100 \\
\hline
\end{array}
&
\begin{array}{r}
1011 \\
(+)0011 \\
\hline
1110 \\
\searrow 0 \\
\hline
1110 = -1
\end{array}
\end{array}
$$

TWO'S COMPLEMENT SUBTRACTION

To perform the subtraction $Z = X - Y$, we write $Z = X + (-Y)$. Representing the numbers in the two's complement number system, we have, from (O3),

$$
\begin{aligned}
R_{TC}(Z) &= R_{TC}(X) + R_{TC}(-Y) \\
&= R_{TC}(X) + R_{OC}(-Y) + 1
\end{aligned}
$$

Thus, we can subtract in the two's complement system by adding the bitwise complement of the subtrahend plus 1 to the minuend. For example,

$$
\begin{array}{lll}
\begin{array}{r}
+5 \\
(-)+2 \\
\hline
+3
\end{array}
&
\begin{array}{r}
0101 \\
(-)0010 \\
\hline
\end{array}
&
\begin{array}{r}
0101 \\
1101 \\
1 \\
\hline
0011 = +3
\end{array}
\end{array}
$$

Note that the carry out of the left bit position is discarded instead of being added end around as in the one's complement system.[2]

$$\begin{array}{rcc}
-4 & 1100 & 1100 \\
\underline{(-)-3} & \underline{(-)1101} & 0010 \\
-1 & & \underline{1} \\
& & 1111 = -1
\end{array}$$

EXERCISES

1. Express the following numbers in sign-magnitude binary, two's complement, and one's complement representations: -3, +4, -127. What is the minimum register length that will hold each of these numbers?

2. What is the meaning of the following bit arrays if they are interpreted as sign-magnitude, two's complement, and one's complement numbers:

$$\begin{array}{cccccc}
1 & 1 & 1 & 1 & 1 & 1 \\
0 & 0 & 0 & 0 & 0 & 0 \\
1 & 0 & 1 & 0 & 1 & 0 \\
0 & 1 & 0 & 1 & 0 & 1
\end{array}$$

3. Show how the following additions and subtractions would be performed in a computer that represents all operands and results in eight-bit sign-magnitude form.

$$+14 + (+29)$$
$$+14 - (+29)$$
$$-29 + (-14)$$
$$+29 + (-14)$$
$$-14 - (+29)$$

4. Repeat Exercise 3 using two's complement representations.

5. Repeat Exercise 3 using one's complement representations.

6. Find the most positive and the most negative numbers that can be represented in each of the following number systems.
   6 bit sign-magnitude
   6 bit two's complement
   6 bit one's complement
   Repeat for lengths of 10 bits.

---

[2] A carry out of the left bit position does not necessarily mean that the result is too big to fit; that is, it does not indicate overflow. For a discussion of overflow in two's complement arithmetic, see Chapter 3.

7. When the end-around carry that may occur in one's complement addition is added in, can it produce another end-around carry, and then another and another and so on? Why? Give examples of the worst cases.

3

Fixed-point instructions

Integers may be stored in IBM System/360 in full-word (32-bit) fixed-point format,

S	integer

0 1   31

or in half-word (16-bit) fixed-point format,

S	integer

0 1   15

In this chapter we consider only the full-word format. Negative numbers are represented in two's complement form; for example,

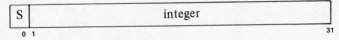

$$0000\ 0000\ 0000\ 0000\ 0000\ 0000\ 0001\ 0111 = +23$$

$$1111\ 1111\ 1111\ 1111\ 1111\ 1111\ 1110\ 1001 = -23$$

(The grouping into four-bit groups is only for convenience.) The instructions that describe operations on full-word fixed-point numbers come in several formats. We discuss the simplest first.

RR FORMAT

RR format instructions describe *register-to-register* operations. An RR format instruction is 16 bits long and can be stored anywhere in memory, beginning on a half-word boundary (an even-numbered byte). The RR format is

op code	R_1	R_2

Register address 1 · Register address 2

(bits: 0 · 7 8 · 11 12 · 15)

The 16 bits are divided into three *fields*, as shown. The leftmost field, bits 0 to 7, represents the instruction code, or operation code, or *op code*. For example, 0001 1000 in this field means "load." The next two fields represent the addresses of operands. However, these are not main memory addresses, which would need to be 24 bits long. These addresses are four bits long. They indicate which of the 16 general registers contains the operands. The meaning of the load instruction is

> copy the second operand (the contents of the general register whose address is in the R_2 field) into the first operand location (the general register whose address is in the R_1 field). The contents of register R_2 are not disturbed.

Thus, if we find the bit pattern 0001 1000 1101 1000 in the memory lying on a half-word boundary, and if we interpret it as an instruction,[1] we can identify the fields as follows[2]:

$$0001 \quad 1000 \qquad 1101 \qquad 1000$$
$$\text{op code} = \text{load} \qquad R_1 = 13 \qquad R_2 = 8$$

Thus the meaning of this bit pattern is

> copy the contents of R8 into R13, do not disturb R8

which we indicate symbolically as

$$C(R13) \leftarrow C(R8)$$

where C(*xxx*) means the contents of *xxx* and the arrow means transfer (copy) the contents as indicated.

In subsequent sections, we shall sometimes show the contents of pertinent registers before and after execution of an instruction as follows:

---

[1] The contents of the memory are not marked to distinguish between instructions and numbers; the distinction is made at the time these contents are used. For example, the bit pattern discussed could also be interpreted (purposely or by mistake) as a number in half-word fixed-point format, namely $+6360._{10}$.

[2] Note the use of subscripts. R_1, R_2, and so on, are symbols denoting arbitrary registers. On the other hand, R2 denotes general register 2.

Before: C(R8) = 0000 0000 0000 0000 0000 0000 1111 1111

C(R13) = 0000 0000 0000 0000 0000 0000 1010 0000

C(other general registers) = not shown

Execute: 0001   1000   1101   1000

After: C(R8) = 0000 0000 0000 0000 0000 0000 1111 1111

C(R13) = 0000 0000 0000 0000 0000 0000 1111 1111

C(other general registers) = same as before

REPRESENTATION OF INSTRUCTIONS

The load instruction was shown previously as

$$0001 \quad 1000 \quad 1101 \quad 1000$$

This is the form in which the instruction exists as it sits in the memory waiting to be executed. However, this form is awkward to write, particularly for 32- and 48-bit instructions. It is somewhat more convenient to write the instruction in hexadecimal form as 18D8. A still more convenient form is to replace the operation code (of which there are more than 100) with a more easily remembered mnemonic abbreviation. In this case the standard abbreviation is LR, which means "load, register to register." It is also slightly more convenient to describe the register addresses with decimal rather than hexadecimal numbers. Then the instruction becomes   LR   13,8. This form is known as *assembler language*. The three representations of an instruction are

Representation of Instruction	Example
Binary	0001 1000 1101 1000
Hexadecimal	1 8 D 8
Assembler language	LR 13,8

Human programmers frequently write computer programs in assembler language. The translation from assembler language to binary is done by the computer itself under the control of a program called an *assembler*.[3] The assembler also produces a printed listing showing (1) the original assembler language instruction and (2) its hexadecimal equivalent. The listing does not show the binary form. After the program is translated from assembler language to binary, it is ready to be loaded into the memory and executed.

_____

[3]Most assemblers have many features in addition to the two mentioned here: (1) use of mnemonic op code abbreviations and (2) use of decimal rather than binary operands. A few of the other features of the 360 assembler will be discussed in later sections. For further information, see *IBM System/360 Operating System Assembler Language*, Form C28-6514.

Add instruction

Machine format:

1A	R_1	R_2
0 7	8 11	12 15

Assembler format: AR R_1, R_2

Meaning: $C(R_1) \leftarrow C(R_1) + C(R_2)$

There are two operands. When the addition occurs, the contents of R_2 remain unchanged but the contents of R_1 are obliterated and replaced by the sum. The addition is 32 bits wide, and follows the rules for two's complement addition. The following example shows the contents of the registers in hexadecimal for compactness, and it omits the locations that are not involved.

    Example:

Before: $C(R3) = 00\ 00\ 00\ 0D = +13$

               $C(R5) = FF\ FF\ FF\ F1 = -15$

Execute: $1A35_H = AR \qquad 3,5$

After: $C(R3) = FF\ FF\ FF\ FE = -2$

               $C(R5) = FF\ FF\ FF\ F1 = -15$

Subtract instruction

Machine format:

1B	R_1	R_2
0 7	8 11	12 15

Assembler format: SR R_1, R_2

Meaning: $C(R_1) \leftarrow C(R_1) - C(R_2)$

For hand calculation the subtraction may be done directly, or it may be done by adding the two's complement of the second operand (the one's complement of the second operand plus 1 in the last place) to the first operand.

    Example: Calculate $-10 - (-3) = -7$.

In binary we have

$$\text{minuend} = 111\ldots \quad 1110110 = -10$$
$$\text{subtrahend} = 111\ldots \quad 1111101 = -3$$

Take the two's complement of the subtrahend and add it to the minuend:

$$111\ldots \quad 1110110 = -10$$
$$000\ldots \quad 0000011 = -(-3)$$
$$\overline{111\ldots \quad 1111001 = -7}$$

Doing this calculation in registers 3 and 6 would give the following results:

Before:	C(R6) =	FF	FF	FF	F6	= -10
	C(R3) =	FF	FF	FF	FD	= -3
Execute:	1B63$_H$ =	SR		6,3		
After:	C(R6) =	FF	FF	FF	F9	= -7
	C(R3) =	FF	FF	FF	FD	= -3

OVERFLOW

The range of integers representable in 32-bit full-word fixed-point format is from

$$1000\ 0000\ 0000\ 0000\ 0000\ 0000\ 0000\ 0000_2 = 80000000_H$$
$$= -2^{31}$$
$$= -2,147,483,648$$

to

$$0111\ 1111\ 1111\ 1111\ 1111\ 1111\ 1111\ 1111_2 = 7FFFFFFF_H$$
$$= 2^{31} - 1$$
$$= +2,147,483,647$$

An attempt to produce a result outside this range by addition or otherwise will produce *overflow* and an incorrect result.

Consider a four-bit two's complement arithmetic unit with bits numbered from the left 0, 1, 2, 3, which is otherwise like the 360. The range of integers representable in this machine is

+7	0111
+6	0110
+5	0101
+4	0100
+3	0011
+2	0010
+1	0001
0	0000
-1	1111
-2	1110

$$-3 \quad 1101$$
$$-4 \quad 1100$$
$$-5 \quad 1011$$
$$-6 \quad 1010$$
$$-7 \quad 1001$$
$$-8 \quad 1000$$

Note that the range is not symmetric about 0; that is, -8 can be represented, but +8 cannot be represented. We can also visualize this range as shown in Figure 3-1. Note that +7 is "next to" -8. Starting at a point in the range and adding a positive number can be visualized as a counterclockwise motion. But an attempt to move counterclockwise beyond +7 will give an answer that is incorrect and negative; for example,

$$0111 = +7$$
$$(+)\ 0001 = +1$$
$$\overline{1000} = -8 \quad \text{incorrect}$$

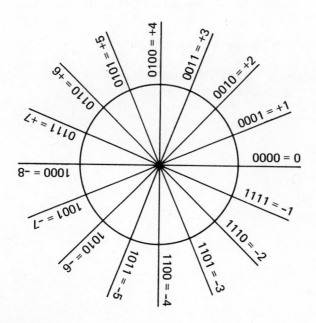

Figure 3-1. Graphical representation of a four-bit two's complement number system.

Overflow during the addition of two positive numbers may be detected as follows. Let the sum be

first operand	a_0	a_1	a_2	a_3
second operand	b_0	b_1	b_2	b_3
sum	c_0	c_1	c_2	c_3

For positive operands, $a_0 = 0$ and $b_0 = 0$. If the sum is to be correct, it must be positive; that is, c_0 must be 0. If c_0 is 1, indicating a negative sum, we know that overflow occurred. An alternative criterion is to note that a carry from bit position 1 to bit position 0 during the addition also indicates overflow.

When adding a negative (or subtracting a positive) number, an attempt to move clockwise beyond −8 will give an answer that is incorrect and positive. For example,

$$
\begin{array}{rl}
1011 = & -5 \\
(+)\ 1101 = & -3 \\
\hline
1000 = & -8 \quad \text{correct} \\
\end{array}
\qquad
\begin{array}{rl}
1011 = & -5 \\
(+)\ 1100 = & -4 \\
\hline
0111 = & +7 \quad \text{wrong} \\
\end{array}
$$

no overflow   overflow

Overflow during the addition of two negative operands may be detected as follows. For this case, $a_0 = 1$ and $b_0 = 1$. If the sum is to be correct, c_0 must be 1, or alternatively a carry *must* occur from bit position 1 to bit position 0. If not, overflow has occurred. (A carry out of bit position 0 always occurs when adding two negative numbers; it should be ignored.)

When adding one negative and one positive operand, overflow cannot occur. (Why?)

To avoid overflow there are several possible strategies:

1. Arrange that all operands, intermediate results, and final results have magnitudes smaller than $2^{31} \cong 2 \times 10^9$ by multiplying and dividing by suitable scaling factors. Scaling a simple program to handle one particular set of numbers is fairly straightforward. Scaling a complicated program to handle a wide range of input data is usually more difficult.

2. Use floating-point numbers and the corresponding instructions. This allows numbers up to 10^{75} to be represented, although sometimes at the price of the loss of some of the less significant digits.

3. Test after addition to see if overflow occurred. See Chapter 7 on branching.

EXERCISES

1. Show the hexadecimal results of adding and subtracting the following numbers. In each case the instructions being executed (separately) are   AR   3,4   and   SR   3,4. State whether overflow occurs.

a. C(R3) = 80 00 00 00
   C(R4) = 90 00 00 00

b. C(R3) = 80 00 00 00
   C(R4) = 00 00 00 01

c. C(R3) = 7F FF FF FF
   C(R4) = 00 00 00 01

d. C(R3) = 01 23 45 67
   C(R4) = 89 AB CD EF

2. Develop criteria for the detection of overflow in one's complement addition analogous to the criteria given for two's complement addition.

MULTIPLY INSTRUCTION

The product of two full-word (32-bit) numbers may be up to 64 bits long, which requires two full words of storage.[4] In the 360, the fixed-point multiply instruction stores double-length products in an even-odd register pair, R_1 and $R_1 + 1$. The most significant 32 bits of the product are stored in R_1; the least significant 32 bits are stored in $R_1 + 1$. The register-to-register multiply instruction is

Machine format:

1C	R_1	R_2

0   7 8   11 12   15

Assembler format: MR R_1,R_2

Meaning: $C(R_1, R_1 + 1) \leftarrow C(R_1 + 1) \times C(R_2)$

$C(R_1)$ is ignored.

$C(R_1 + 1)$ is the multiplicand, $C(R_2)$ is the multiplier, and $C(R_1, R_1 + 1)$ is the double-length product.[5] R_1 must be even. If R_1 is odd, it is an error and an interruption will occur.[6] Note that although R_1 is shown as an operand the initial contents of R_1 do not participate in the multiplication unless R_1 happens to contain the multiplier.

---

[4] Recall that in decimal multiplication the product of two n-digit numbers may be up to $2n$ digits long; for example,

```
        9 9 9
      × 9 9 9
      8 9 9 1
    8 9 9 1
  8 9 9 1
  9 9 8 0 0 1
```

[5] $R_1 + 1$ refers to the next consecutively numbered register after R_1. Thus if R_1 = R6, then $R_1 + 1$ = R7.

[6] The 360 hardware checks for certain kinds of errors. When one occurs, an *interruption* usually takes place. Then the computer stops executing the user's program and begins executing a program that usually (1) diagnoses the error, (2) prints a message, and (3) terminates execution of the user's program. In some cases termination of the user's program can be prevented; but it is dangerous to attempt to resume execution after an error without careful consideration of the possible consequences of using incorrect numbers in subsequent calculations.

Example:

```
Before:     C(R4)  = 01  23  AB  CD
            C(R5)  = 12  00  00  12
            C(R11) = 04  00  00  01
Execute:    1C4B_H = MR      4,11
After:      C(R4)  = 00  48  00  00
            C(R5)  = 5A  00  00  12
            C(R11) = 04  00  00  01
```

For positive operands, the multiplication may be checked by hand using hexadecimal arithmetic for compactness, thus:

```
            1 2 0 0 0 0 1 2  =  multiplicand  =  C(R5)
        *   0 4 0 0 0 0 0 1  =  multiplier    =  C(R11)
          ─────────────────
            1 2 0 0 0 0 1 2
    4 8 0 0 0 0 4 8
  ─────────────────────────
  0 0 4 8 0 0 0 0 5 A 0 0 0 0 1 2  =  product
  ‿‿‿‿‿‿‿‿‿‿‿‿‿‿   ‿‿‿‿‿‿‿‿‿‿‿‿‿‿
       C(R4)              C(R5)
```

Note that the old contents of R4 were destroyed without taking part in the multiplication.

Products shorter than 32 bits will fit entirely into the odd register of the even-odd pair; for example,

```
Before:     C(R6) = XX  XX  XX  XX
            C(R7) = 00  00  A4  01
            C(R4) = 00  00  00  33
Execute:    MR      6,4
After:      C(R6) = 00  00  00  00
            C(R7) = 00  20  AC  33
            C(R4) = 00  00  00  33
```

The contents of R6 are shown as X's to indicate that R6 could have contained any number.

If the product is negative and has less than 32 significant bits, the even register will be filled with 1's; for example,

Before: C(R2) = XX XX XX XX

               C(R3) = 00 00 00 0A = +10

               C(R9) = FF FF FF FC = -4

Execute: MR   2,9

After: C(R2) = FF FF FF FF

               C(R3) = FF FF FF D8 = -40

               C(R9) = FF FF FF FC

To check this by hand, one can multiply the magnitudes of the operands to obtain the magnitude of the product, and then complement to obtain the product.

Normally, the initial contents of the even register specified by R_1 are ignored. But not if this register happens to contain the second operand, thus:

Before: C(R8) = 43 00 00 21

               C(R9) = 00 00 00 80

Execute: MR   8,8

After: C(R8) = 00 00 00 21

               C(R9) = 80 00 10 80

In the 360, fixed-point multiplication can be performed in eight different places, namely in register pairs 0-1, 2-3, 4-5, 6-7, 8-9, 10-11, 12-13, and 14-15, although normally registers 0, 1, 13, 14, and 15 are not used for arithmetic.[7] In some earlier computers there was only one place where multiplication could be performed: the left part (corresponding to a 360 even register) was sometimes called the accumulator, and the right part (corresponding to a 360 odd register) was sometimes called the multiplier-quotient register.

The apparently arbitrary rules for the use of the even-odd register pair (R_1, $R_1 + 1$) may appear more reasonable in connection with the algorithm for multiplying positive integers given next. This algorithm is only an example of an algorithm for multiplying positive integers.

1. Begin with the multiplier in R_2 and the multiplicand in the odd register $R_1 + 1$. Clear the even register R_1 to 0. (If R_1 contains the multiplier, save it elsewhere.)

2. Examine the least significant bit of the odd register. If it is 1, then add the multiplier to the even register. If it is 0, do not add.

3. Shift the contents of the double-length even-odd register one bit position to the right, feeding in a 0 on the left, and discarding a bit from the right.

---

[7]By convention registers 0, 1, 13, 14, and 15 are reserved for use with linkages to subprograms. See Chapter 10.

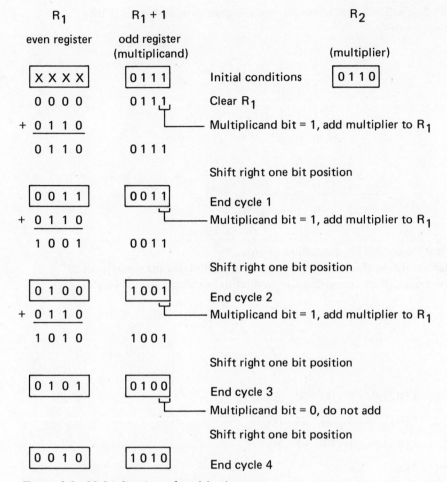

Figure 3-2. Multiplication of positive integers.

4. Repeat steps 2 and 3 once for each bit position of the multiplicand, that is, a total of
   32 times in a 32-bit system. At the end, the double-length product lies in the even-odd
   register pair.

For example, the multiplication of +6 by +7 in a four-bit positive integer system would
occur as shown in Figure 3-2. At the conclusion of four repetitions of steps 2 and 3, the
double-length product, $00101010_2 = 42_{10}$, lies in the even-odd register pair. The odd
register contains 1010. Note that in this case the left-hand bit of the odd register does *not*
represent the sign of the product.

The algorithm described applies only to positive operands. Algorithms for multiplying positive or negative numbers directly in the two's complement number system are
more involved and will not be discussed here.[8] The important property of the two's
complement number system—that addition can be performed in it just as if the operands
were positive—does *not* carry over to multiplication. For example, if one attempts to

[8]T. C. Bartee, I. L. Lebow, and I. S. Reed, *Theory and Design of Digital Machines* (New York:
McGraw-Hill, 1962), p. 199, and C. V. L. Smith, *Electronic Digital Computers* (New York: McGraw-
Hill, 1959).

multiply the numbers -2_{10} and -3_{10} in a four-bit two's complement system as if they were positive integers, one obtains

```
            1  1  1  0
            1  1  0  1
            1  1  1  0
         0  0  0  0
      1  1  1  0
   1  1  1  0
   ─────────────────
1  0  1  1  0  1  1  0
```

which emphatically is *not* the correct representation of $+6_{10}$.

For hand calculation, the product may be obtained by multiplying the magnitudes of the operands in decimal and then converting the product to hexadecimal and complementing if necessary.

EXERCISES

1. Before: C(R2) = 00 00 00 A0

   C(R3) = 08 00 04 00

   C(R4) = FF FF FF 80

   Execute: MR   2,4

   After: C(R2) = ?   C(R3) = ?   C(R4) = ?

2. The multiplications indicated are to be carried out using the instruction MR 10,12. What must be the hexadecimal "before" and "after" contents of registers 10, 11, and 12 if these multiplications are to take place? The factors shown are in decimal.

	Multiplicand	*Multiplier*
a.	12	2
b.	-3	-13
c.	2	-6
d.	2^{20}	11
e.	32,768	-4

3. Let P be the most positive and N the most negative numbers representable in full-word fixed-point format. Evaluate the following products:

$$P * P$$
$$P * N$$
$$N * N$$

What general conclusions can you draw about overflow during fixed-point multiplication?

4. Write out the steps in the multiplication of +3 and +4 as it would occur in a four-bit computer that handles positive integers only and uses the multiplication algorithm described on page 46.

DIVIDE INSTRUCTION

The divide instruction divides a 64-bit dividend in an even-odd pair of registers by a 32-bit divisor to produce a quotient in the odd-numbered register and a remainder in the even-numbered register.

Machine format:

1D		R_1	R_2
0	7 8	11 12	15

Assembler format: DR R_1,R_2

Meaning: $\dfrac{C(R_1,R_1 + 1)}{C(R_2)} \rightarrow \begin{cases} \text{quotient in } R_1 + 1 \\ \text{remainder in } R_1 \end{cases}$

$C(R_1, R_1 + 1)$ is the double-length dividend. $C(R_2)$ is the divisor. The quotient goes into $R_1 + 1$; the remainder goes into R_1. The sign of the quotient is determined by the rules of algebra. The sign of the remainder is the sign of the dividend, except when the remainder is zero. R_1 must be even; if it is odd, an interruption will occur.

Example:

$$\frac{39_{10}}{-4_{10}} = -9_{10}, \quad \text{remainder 3}$$

Using registers 6 and 7 for the dividend and register 3 for the divisor, we have

Before: $C(R6) = 00\ 00\ 00\ 00$
$C(R7) = 00\ 00\ 00\ 27$ $\Big\} = +39$ dividend

$C(R3) = FF\ FF\ FF\ FC = -4$ divisor

Execute: $1D63_H = DR\quad 6,3$

After: $C(R6) = 00\ 00\ 00\ 03 = +3$ remainder

$C(R7) = FF\ FF\ FF\ F7 = -9$ quotient

$C(R3) = FF\ FF\ FF\ FC = -4$ divisor, unchanged

If the relative magnitudes of the dividend and the divisor are such that the quotient cannot be expressed in a 32-bit fixed-point word, then successful division is not possible.

For example, if the dividend is

$$00200000 \quad 00000000_H$$

and the divisor is 00000001_H, both of which are perfectly legal, then the quotient should be $200000 \quad 00000000_H$; but this is too big to fit. In the 360 if one attempts a division which will give a quotient that is too big, then (1) the division will not occur, (2) the dividend and the divisor will remain unchanged, and (3) a *fixed-point divide interruption* will occur. This will also occur if one attempts to divide by zero.

The exact criterion for successful division is

$$-2^{31} \leqslant \text{quotient} \leqslant +2^{31} - 1$$

This criterion is inconvenient to use because it depends on the result of the division. A more convenient approximate criterion based on the dividend and the divisor before the division can be developed as follows. Visualize the dividend both as two 32-bit words and as one 64-bit word with the bits numbered thus:

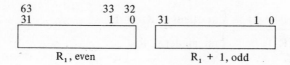

The division requires

$$\frac{C(R_1, R_1 + 1)}{C(R_2)} = Q + \frac{REM}{C(R_2)}$$

where Q is the quotient, REM is the remainder, and $REM/C(R_2) < 1$.

Approximating $C(R_1, R_1 + 1)$ by $C(R_1) * 2^{32}$, we have

$$\frac{C(R_1) * 2^{32}}{C(R_2)} \approx Q + \frac{REM}{C(R_2)}$$

Neglecting $REM/C(R_2) < 1$ and noting that Q must fit into a 32-bit word, we obtain

$$-2^{31} \leqslant \frac{C(R_1) * 2^{32}}{C(R_2)} \leqslant +2^{31} - 1$$

$$-\frac{1}{2} \leqslant \frac{C(R_1)}{C(R_2)} \leqslant +\frac{1}{2} - \frac{1}{2^{32}}$$

or approximately

$$\left| \frac{C(R_1)}{C(R_2)} \right| < \frac{1}{2}$$

If this (approximate) criterion is satisfied, successful division will occur.

Example (normal division): Consider the division

$$\frac{3 * 2^{32}}{8} = \frac{3}{8} * 2^{32} = .011_2 * 2^{32} = 011\underbrace{000...000}_{29 \text{ zeros}} {}_2$$

This quotient will fit correctly into a 32-bit register, so normal division will occur, thus:

$$
\begin{array}{lll}
\text{Before:} & C(R2) = 00 \;\; 00 \;\; 00 \;\; 03 & \left.\right\} \text{dividend} \\
& C(R3) = 00 \;\; 00 \;\; 00 \;\; 00 & \\
& C(R4) = 00 \;\; 00 \;\; 00 \;\; 08 & \text{divisor} \\
\text{Execute:} & \text{DR} \quad 2,4 & \\
\text{After:} & C(R2) = 00 \;\; 00 \;\; 00 \;\; 00 & \\
& C(R3) = 60 \;\; 00 \;\; 00 \;\; 00 & \\
& C(R4) = 00 \;\; 00 \;\; 00 \;\; 08 & \text{normal division}
\end{array}
$$

Example (fixed-point divide interruption): Consider the division

$$\frac{4 * 2^{32}}{8} = \frac{4}{8} * 2^{32} = .1_2 * 2^{32} = +1\underbrace{000...000}_{31 \text{ zeros}} {}_2$$

Even though the quotient contains only 32 digits, it cannot be represented correctly in a 32-bit two's complement scheme. Hence division will *not* occur. The before and after results will be as follows:

$$
\begin{array}{lll}
\text{Before:} & C(R2) = 00 \;\; 00 \;\; 00 \;\; 04 & \\
& C(R3) = 00 \;\; 00 \;\; 00 \;\; 00 & \\
& C(R4) = 00 \;\; 00 \;\; 00 \;\; 08 & \\
\text{Execute:} & \text{DR} \quad 2,4 & \\
\text{After:} & C(R2) = 00 \;\; 00 \;\; 00 \;\; 04 & \\
& C(R3) = 00 \;\; 00 \;\; 00 \;\; 00 & \text{fixed-point divide interruption} \\
& C(R4) = 00 \;\; 00 \;\; 00 \;\; 08 & \text{occurs, division does not take place}
\end{array}
$$

When dividing a single-length dividend by a (single-length) divisor, the significant digits of the dividend lie entirely in the odd register, and the even register contains only

00 00 00 00 or FF FF FF FF, depending on the sign; so the requirement for successful division is always satisfied, provided the divisor is not zero.[9]

Example:

$$\frac{-6 * 16^7}{8} = -.11_2 * 16^7 = -C_H * 16^6$$

Before:	$C(R8)$ =	FF FF FF FF
	$C(R9)$ =	A0 00 00 00
	$C(R2)$ =	00 00 00 08
Execute:	DR	8,2
After:	$C(R8)$ =	00 00 00 00
	$C(R9)$ =	F4 00 00 00
	$C(R2)$ =	00 00 00 08

The apparently arbitrary rules for the use of the even-odd register pair $(R_1, R_1 + 1)$ may appear more reasonable in connection with the algorithm given next for dividing positive integers.

1. Begin with the double-length dividend in the even-odd register pair R_1, $R_1 + 1$ and the divisor in R_2.

2. Shift the contents of the even-odd register pair left one bit position. Temporarily save the bit shifted off at the left until the subtraction in step 3 is carried out.

3. Subtract the divisor from the even register, treating both numbers as positive integers.

4. If the difference is positive or zero, the subtraction was successful and the corresponding quotient bit is 1. Set the right bit of the odd register to 1. If the difference is negative, the subtraction was unsuccessful and the corresponding quotient bit is 0. Restore the even register by adding the divisor back in, and set the right bit of the odd register to 0.

5. Repeat steps 2, 3, and 4 once for each bit position of the quotient, that is, a total of 32 times in a 32-bit system. At the end the quotient lies in the odd register and the remainder lies in the even register.

For example, the division of 17 by 3 in a four-bit positive integer system would occur as shown in Figure 3-3. After the execution of four cycles of steps 2, 3, and 4, the quotient, $0101 = 5$, lies in the odd register, and the remainder, $0010 = 2$, lies in the even register. This algorithm applies only to positive operands, it does not apply to a division problem involving negative operands expressed in two's complement form.

---

[9]In the special case $\frac{-2^{31}}{-1} = +2^{31}$, the dividend and the divisor are both legal single-length numbers; but the quotient is too big to fit correctly into a single register, so division will not occur.

R₁	R₁ + 1		R₂
even register	odd register		
dividend			divisor

R_1 $R_1 + 1$ R_2

even register   odd register

dividend   divisor

0 0 0 1	0 0 0 1	Initial conditions	0 0 1 1
0 0 1 0	0 0 1 -	Shift left one bit position	
- 0 0 1 1		Subtract divisor from even register	
1 1 1 1		Result negative, restore by adding divisor, set quotient bit = 0	
+ 0 0 1 1			
0 0 1 0	0 0 1 0	End cycle 1	
0 1 0 0	0 1 0 -	Shift left one bit position	
- 0 0 1 1		Subtract divisor from even register	
0 0 0 1		Result positive, set quotient bit = 1	
0 0 0 1	0 1 0 1	End cycle 2	
0 0 1 0	1 0 1 -	Shift left one bit position	
- 0 0 1 1		Subtract divisor from even register	
1 1 1 1		Result negative, restore by adding divisor, set quotient bit = 0	
+ 0 0 1 1			
0 0 1 0	1 0 1 0	End cycle 3	
0 1 0 1	0 1 0 -	Shift left one bit position	
- 0 0 1 1		Subtract divisor from even register	
0 0 1 0		Result positive, set quotient bit = 1	
0 0 1 0	0 1 0 1	End cycle 4	

Figure 3-3. Division of positive integers.

SEQUENCES OF INSTRUCTIONS

The four instructions just described can be combined into sequences of instructions to evaluate simple expressions such as $[+19 + (-29) + 4] * 6$.

Before: C(R6) = FF FF FF E3 = −29

C(R7) = 00 00 00 13 = +19

C(R8) = 00 00 00 04 = +4

C(R11) = 00 00 00 06 = +6

	Instruction		*Results*
Execute:	1A76 = AR	7,6	+19 + (−29) = −10 in R7
	1A78 = AR	7,8	−10 + 4 = −6 in R7
	1C6B = MR	6,11	(−6) ∗ (+6) = −36 in R6, R7
After:	C(R6) = FF FF FF FF		$\left.\begin{array}{l} \\ \\ \end{array}\right\} = -36$
	C(R7) = FF FF FF DC		
	C(R8) = 00 00 00 04		
	C(R11) = 00 00 00 06		

When doing calculations involving multiplications and divisions, one must move the operands to the right place before doing the operation. For multiply, the multiplicand must be in an odd register; if it is in an even register, it can be moved to an odd register with the LR instruction. For divide, a 32-bit dividend needs to be extended to 64 bits prior to the division. This can be done by multiplying by +1, as shown next, or by using a shift instruction.

In the following example we evaluate the expression

$$\frac{\dfrac{a + b}{c} + d}{e} + f$$

where *a, b, c, d, e,* and *f* represent 32-bit fixed-point numbers in registers 2, 3, 4, 5, 6, and 7, respectively. We also need the constant +1, which we assume to be in register 8. Each line of the table shows the contents of the registers after the execution of the corresponding instruction. We assume that each of the intermediate results will fit in 32 bits, and we ignore the remainders.

		C(R2)	C(R3)	C(R4)	C(R5)	C(R6)	C(R7)	C(R8)
Initially		a	b	c	d	e	f	+1
AR	3,2	a	$a + b$	c	d	e	f	+1
MR	2,8	←—— $a + b$ ——→		c	d	e	f	+1
DR	2,4	rem_1	$\dfrac{a + b}{c}$	c	d	e	f	+1
AR	3,5	rem_1	$\dfrac{a + b}{c} + d$	c	d	e	f	+1
MR	2,8	← $\dfrac{a + b}{c} + d$ →		c	d	e	f	+1
DR	2,6	rem_2	$\dfrac{\dfrac{a + b}{c} + d}{e}$	c	d	e	f	+1
AR	3,7	rem_2	$\dfrac{\dfrac{a + b}{c} + d}{e} + f$	c	d	e	f	+1

EXERCISES

1. The divisions indicated are to be attempted using the instruction   DR   2,4. Show the corresponding "before" and "after" contents of registers 2, 3, and 4 in hexadecimal. The operands shown are in decimal.

	Dividend	Divisor
a.	256	5
b.	-29	4
c.	-2^{36}	2^{10}
d.	$3 * 2^{32}$	-8
e.	$4 * 2^{32}$	-8
f.	$5 * 2^{32}$	-8

2. Assume that $a, b, c, x,$ and $+1$ are in registers 2, 3, 4, 5, and 7, respectively. Write sequences of RR instructions to evaluate the following expressions and store the result in register 6. Use the fewest possible steps. You may destroy operands when you no longer need them. Ignore remainders. Assume all intermediate results will fit in 32 bits, and that divide interruptions do not occur.

a. $\dfrac{a + c}{b + x}$

b. $\dfrac{a}{b} + \dfrac{c}{x}$

c. $\dfrac{ac}{b} + x$

RX FORMAT INSTRUCTIONS

So far we have considered only fixed-point RR format instructions of the form

op code	R$_1$	R$_2$
0 7	8 11	12 15

These instructions allow movement of data within the 16 general registers. To extend the range of action to the main memory, which can contain up to 2^{24} bytes, we need a new instruction format. One scheme would be to replace one or both of the four-bit register addresses in the RR format by a 24-bit main memory address. Such a scheme has been used in a number of computers, but it has the disadvantage that it makes the instruction rather long. Also, it does nothing to aid in the job of "relocating" a program, that is, moving it from one part of the memory to another without hurting its ability to run.[10]

----

[10]For a discussion of relocation, see Chapter 5.

RX format instructions allow data to be transferred to and from a 2^{24}-byte main memory. The mnemonic RX stands for *Register and Indexed Storage.* The RX format is

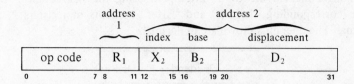

The first operand is in the register indicated by the R_1 field. The second operand is in the main memory at an *effective address* composed of

1. An *index*, a 24-bit positive integer in the register indicated by X_2.

2. A *base address*, a 24-bit positive integer in the register indicated by B_2.

3. A *displacement*, a 12-bit positive integer in the D_2 field of the instruction.

The rule for obtaining the effective address (EA) is

$$\text{effective address} = C(X_2) + C(B_2) + D_2$$

The addition is 24 bits wide, using the low-order 24 bits of $C(X_2)$ and $C(B_2)$ and ignoring overflow. The 12-bit displacement is extended to 24 bits by appending zeros on the left before adding. There is a special case: if X_2 or B_2 is 0, it means that 0 is to be added in forming the effective address, not the contents of register 0.

The range of displacements is 000_H to FFF_H or 0_{10} to 4095_{10}. Hence the displacement allows relative addressing up to 4095 bytes beyond the base address. Negative displacements are not allowed, so the effective address cannot refer to a lower-numbered byte than the base address. The index provides a convenient way of stepping through the elements of an array, as will be described later. For the present, we shall assume that X_2 is always 0.

Load

Machine format:

58	R_1	X_2	B_2	D_2
0 7	8 11	12 15	16 19	20 31

Assembler format: L $R_1,D_2(X_2,B_2)$

Meaning: An effective address is formed:

$$EA = C(X_2) + C(B_2) + D_2$$

Then

$$C(R_1) \leftarrow C(EA)$$

That is, copy the contents of the full word at the effective address in the main memory into general register R_1. The contents of the word in the main memory is not changed.

Example:

5	8	7	0	C	0	1	0

$$= 5870C010_H = \quad L \quad 7,16(0,12)$$

The meaning is

$$C(R7) \leftarrow C[C(R12) + 010_H]$$

If $C(R12) = 013000_H$ at the time this instruction is executed, then the effective address is $013000_H + 010_H = 013010_H$, and the meaning is "copy the contents of 013010_H into general register 7, do not disturb 013010."

Store

Machine format:

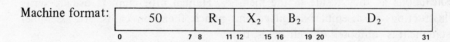

50	R_1	X_2	B_2	D_2
0	7 8	11 12	15 16	19 20 31

Assembler format: ST $R_1,D_2(X_2,B_2)$

Meaning: Copy the contents of general register R_1 into the main memory at an effective address as described previously. The contents of R_1 is not changed.

Example:

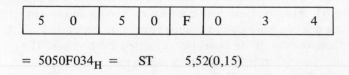

5	0	5	0	F	0	3	4

$$= 5050F034_H = \quad ST \quad 5,52(0,15)$$

This means "copy the contents of register 5 into the main memory at 52_{10} bytes beyond the address in register 15."

RX FIXED-POINT ADD, SUBTRACT, MULTIPLY, AND DIVIDE

The full-word fixed-point add, subtract, multiply and divide instructions described earlier were in RR format. There are also corresponding RX format instructions, where the second operand is at an effective address in the main memory, constructed as described previously, instead of in a register. All the previously stated rules still apply.

| Operation | RR Format | | RX Format | |
	Mnemonic	Op Code	Mnemonic	Op Code
Add	AR	1A	A	5A
Subtract	SR	1B	S	5B
Multiply	MR	1C	M	5C
Divide	DR	1D	D	5D

For example,   A   10,24(6,12)   means

$$C(R10) \leftarrow C(R10) + C[C(R6) + C(R12) + 24]$$

The effective address must refer to a full-word location (a byte address exactly divisible by 4); otherwise, a specification interruption will occur.

ASSEMBLER LANGUAGE FORMAT

The machine format for RX instructions was given on page 56, that is, the format of RX instructions as they reside in the memory. Human programmers usually write machine instructions in assembler language and punch them on cards. An assembler language statement is composed of four fields, thus:

name	operation	operands	comments

The *name* field begins in column 1 of the card. If column 1 is blank, the name field is assumed to be blank. (More about names later.)

The *operation* field contains a mnemonic abbreviation for the machine language instruction, for example, L or ST. The operation field contains no blanks, and is separated from the name field by one or more blanks. An operation entry must be present.

The *operand* field contains zero or more operands, separated by commas. The operand field contains no blanks. It is separated from the operation and comments fields by one or more blanks. The operand field may be blank.

The *comments* field is separated from the operand field by one or more blanks. It may contain anything the programmer wants to write, including blanks. The comments must not extend beyond column 71. A whole statement may be used entirely for comments by punching an asterisk in column 1.

The assembler language format described here allows the entries on the card to occur at various positions (except for the name entry, which if present must begin in column 1). However, for ease in reading the program it is convenient to put the name, operation, operand, and comments fields in fixed positions, for example, in columns 1, 10, 16, and 30, respectively.

The four fields described together constitute the statement field, which lies in columns 1 to 71 inclusive. If more space is needed for a statement, it may be continued on the next card by punching a nonblank character in column 72, and then continuing at column 16 of the next card. All columns to the left of column 16 must be blank. If a second continuation card is needed, punch a nonblank character in column 72 of each card to be continued. Only two continuation cards may be used for a statement, except for macro instructions.

The remaining space, columns 73 to 80, is called the identification-sequence field. It may be left blank or punched with identifying abbreviations or sequence numbers. The assembler reads and lists the contents of this field, but normally does not make any other use of it. When cards in a deck are to be numbered serially, it is convenient to number by fives or tens, for example, 0010, 0020, 0030, 0040, . . ., to allow for possible insertion of additional numbers without renumbering the whole deck.

The operand field for an RX instruction can be written in assembler language in several forms. One form, the *explicit* form, is

$$R_1, D_2(X_2, B_2)$$

where R_1, D_2, X_2, and B_2 represent decimal integers that describe the corresponding quantities, and the commas and parentheses occur as shown. An example is

        ST   10,20(0,12)

An RX operand field contains two fields, separated by a comma. The first field describes the first register operand, in the example, register 10. The second field gives the address in main memory of the second operand. The explicit form of the second field is $D_2(X_2, B_2)$. Note that the quantities in the second field are *not* in the same left-to-right order as in the machine format. In the example,

        ST   10,20(0,12)

the effective address of the second operand is

$$EA = C(R12) + 20$$

where nothing is added for the index since $X_2 = 0$. The meaning of the whole instruction is "copy the contents of register 10 into the main memory at address EA."

EXAMPLES USING RR AND RX INSTRUCTIONS

The following examples illustrate the use of RR and RX format instructions in simple programs subject to the following assumptions.

1. Assume that the program and data will be loaded into the memory beginning at location R by some means, not stated here.[11] Also assume that R15 will contain the address of the beginning of the program, namely R, and R15 will be used as a base register.

---

[11] For more on relocation, see Chapter 5.

2. Assume that execution begins at the address in R15, namely R + 000.

3. Terminate execution of the program with an unconditional branch to the address in R14 using the instruction 07FE = BCR 15,14. (For further discussion of branching, see Chapter 7.)

Example 1: Calculate

$$\frac{a}{x} + b * x + c \to f$$

where $a = 66$
$b = 13$
$c = -7$
$x = 4$

and store the result in the memory.

The steps in the solution are as follows. First we decide somewhat arbitrarily to put the variables a, b, c, and x at 200, 204, 208, and 20C bytes beyond the beginning of the program. We could have chosen any (not necessarily contiguous) full-word locations in the range R + 000 to R + FFF$_H$ that will not overlap the program. We also need places to put the answer f and the constant +1, so we pick R + 210 and R + 214, respectively. Next we decide on the register usage and the sequence of arithmetic operations to be performed, as indicated in the table. (This step might be done only mentally.)

Operation	Register Usage
$\dfrac{a * 1}{x}$	$\dfrac{C(R2,R3)}{x} \to C(R3)$
$b * x$	$C(R5) * b \to C(R4,R5)$
$\dfrac{a}{x} + (b * x)$	$C(R3) + C(R5) \to C(R5)$
$\dfrac{a}{x} + b * x + c$	$C(R5) + c \to C(R5)$
f	$C(R5) \to f$

Before the division, we expand the dividend to 64 bits by multiplying by +1. After the division, we ignore the remainder. We assume that the product $b * x$ will fit in a full word.

The complete program is shown next. On the left are the hexadecimal addresses relative to the beginning of the program and the hexadecimal instructions, or *object code*. On the right are the assembler language instructions and comments. Note that the operands are expressed as hexadecimal numbers in the object code and as decimal numbers in the assembler language version.

Locations Relative to Beginning of Program	Hexadecimal Object Code	Assembler Language			
		Name	Operation	Operand	Comments
000	5830F200		L	3,512(0,15)	a
004	5C20F214		M	2,532(0,15)	Expand to double length
008	5D20F20C		D	2,524(0,15)	a/x
00C	5850F20C		L	5,524(0,15)	x
010	5C40F204		M	4,516(0,15)	$x * b$
014	1A53		AR	5,3	$x * b + \dfrac{a}{x}$
016	5A50F208		A	5,520(0,15)	$x * b + \dfrac{a}{x} + c = f$
01A	5050F210		ST	5,528(0,15)	
01E	07FE		BCR	15,14	
.	.				
.	.				
.	.				
200	00000042				$a = +66$
204	0000000D				$b = +13$
208	FFFFFFF9				$c = -7$
20C	00000004				$x = +4$
210					f
214	00000001				$+1$

The instructions must lie in contiguous locations in memory. The AR instruction at address 014 is two bytes long; hence it occupies bytes 014 and 015. Thus the next instruction must begin at byte 016. All 360 instructions must begin on a byte address that is divisible by 2, but note that RX instructions, although they are four bytes long, do not necessarily begin on a byte address that is divisible by 4.

In this example the table represents the object code which is to be loaded into memory. The contents of the word at f (relative address 210_H) is shown as blank since nothing is to be put there at the time the program is loaded into memory. [Actually this word in memory will contain four bytes left over from previous computations, but they are unrelated to the problem at hand and are sometimes called garbage.] Later on, when this program is executed, the answer will be stored at f by the store instruction.

Example 2: Calculate

$$ax^2 + bx + c \rightarrow y$$

where $a = 10$
$\quad\ \ b = 3$
$\quad\ \ c = -9$
$\quad\ \ x = 13$

To save a multiplication we rewrite the expression as $(ax + b)x + c$. The program is shown next.

Locations Relative to Beginning of Program	Hexadecimal Object Code	Assembler Language			
		Name	Operation	Operand	Comments
000	5830F100		L	3,256(0,15)	*a*
004	5C20F10C		M	2,268(0,15)	*ax*
008	5A30F104		A	3,260(0,15)	*ax* + *b*
00C	5C20F10C		M	2,268(0,15)	(*ax* + *b*)*x*
010	5A30F108		A	3,264(0,15)	(*ax* + *b*)*x* + *c*
014	5030F110		ST	3,272(0,15)	
018	07FE		BCR	15,14	
.	.				
.	.				
.	.				
100	0000000A				*a* = 10
104	00000003				*b* = 3
108	FFFFFFF7				*c* = -9
10C	0000000D				*x* = 13
110					*y*

Load multiple

When loading several registers at once, it may be convenient to use the Load Multiple instruction. This instruction utilizes the Register and Storage (RS) format, which is similar to the RX format except that bits 12 to 15 of the instruction no longer refer to an index.

Machine format [RS] :

98	R_1	R_3	B_2	D_2
0	7 8 11 12	15 16	19 20	31

Assembler format: LM $R_1,R_3,D_2(B_2)$

Meaning: Load register R_1 through R_3 from consecutive full words in memory, beginning at $D_2(B_2)$. The counting from R_1 to R_3 is done positively with register 0 following register 15. The second operand must lie on a full-word boundary or it is an error.

For example, the statement

      LM   14,2,24(11)

will produce the same result as the five consecutive statements

      L   14,24(0,11)
      L   15,28(0,11)
      L   0,32(0,11)
      L   1,36(0,11)
      L   2,40(0,11)

Store multiple

Machine format [RS] :

90	R_1	R_3	B_2	D_2
0	7 8 11 12	15 16	19 20	31

Assembler format: STM $R_1,R_3,D_2(B_2)$

Meaning: Same as the Load Multiple instruction, except that the data are transmitted from the registers to the memory. The contents of the general registers remains unchanged.

EXERCISES

1. Write a program to calculate $a + [b/(c + d)] \rightarrow f$, where $a = 16$, $b = -74$, $c = 31$, and $d = -107$.

2. Same as Exercise 1 except $(a + b)/(c + d) \rightarrow f$.

4

Assembler language and the translation process

In Chapter 3 we introduced some features of assembler language: (1) the use of mnemonic abbreviations for the operations, (2) the use of decimal instead of hexadecimal operands, (3) the use of a variable format for the statement, and (4) the use of comment cards. Here we introduce some additional features of assembler language.

Programs written in assembler language are translated into machine language by a computer program called the assembler. The input to the assembler is a sequence of assembler language statements, usually punched on cards. This is called the *source program*. The output from the assembler is the source program in machine language form. This is called the *object program* or the object code. The process is indicated schematically in Figure 4-1. The assembler program runs in a computer. Normally, it runs in the computer for which it is translating programs, but this is not necessary. One could have an assembler program running in computer A to generate object code to run on computer B.

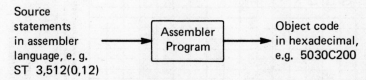

Figure 4-1. The assembly process.

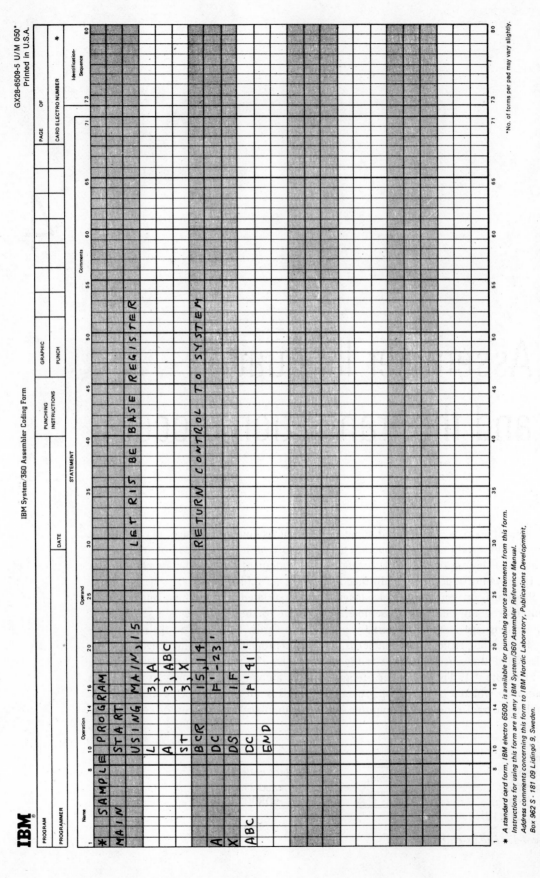

Figure 4-2. *Sample program written on coding paper. (Assembler Coding Form, Form GX28-6509, © by International Business Machines Corporation, reproduced by permission.)*

66

```
*    SAMPLE PROGRAM
MAIN     START
         USING MAIN,15          LET R15 BE BASE REGISTER
         L     3,A
         A     3,ABC
         ST    3,X
         BCR   15,14            RETURN CCNTROL TO SYSTEM
A        DC    F'-23'
X        DS    1F
ABC      CC    F'41'
         END
```

Figure 4-3. Listing of the deck for sample program. This is the input to the assembler.

The object program produced by the assembler may be used in several ways. One way is to load the object code into the memory immediately after the translation is completed, and then execute it. The loading is done by another program, usually called a *loader*. On the other hand, the object code may be saved to be executed at a later time—in this case it would be saved on magnetic tape or disk, or punched into cards as an *object deck*.

Figure 4-2 shows a sample assembler language program as written on coding paper, Figure 4-3 shows a listing of the cards after punching, and Figure 4-4 shows the corresponding assembler listing. In Figure 4-4 the right part of each line shows the source statement as fed to the assembler, and the left part of the line shows the corresponding locations and object code produced by the assembler. In the simple case, the assembler generates object code beginning at location 000000 and puts each succeeding item into the next location that is appropriate for that item. More on this later.

```
                                                                              PAGE    1

LOC     OBJECT CODE     ADDR1 ADDR2 STMT    SOURCE STATEMENT                  F15OCT70   6/25/72

                                    1  *   SAMPLE PROGRAM
000000                              2 MAIN    START
000000                              3         USING MAIN,15        LET R15 BE BASE REGISTER
000000  5830 F010             0G010 4         L     3,A
C00004  5A30 F018             00018 5         A     3,ABC
000008  5030 F014             00014 6         ST    3,X
00000C  07FE                        7         BCR   15,14          RETURN CONTROL TO SYSTEM
00000E  G000
000010  FFFFFFE9                    8 A       DC    F'-23'
000014                              9 X       DS    1F
000018  00000029                   10 ABC     DC    F'41'
                                   11         END
```

```
                              CROSS-REFERENCE                                    PAGE    1

SYMBOL    LEN   VALUE   DEFN    REFERENCES                                       6/25/72

A        00004 000010 00008    0004
ABC      C0004 030018 C0010    0005
MAIN     00001 C00000 C0002    0003
X        00004 C00014 00009    0006


NO STATEMENTS FLAGGED IN THIS ASSEMBLY
*STATISTICS*      SOURCE RECORDS (SYSIN) =    11
*OPTIONS IN EFFECT*   LIST, NODECK, LOAD, NORENT, XREF, NOTEST, ALGN, OS, NOTERM, LINECNT =  55
     28 PRINTED LINES
```

Figure 4-4. Assembler output for sample program. Solid line indicates a page break in the printer output.

SYMBOLIC ADDRESSES

The quantities MAIN, A, X, and ABC in the sample program are called *symbolic addresses* or *symbols*. The symbol ABC is *defined* by its appearance in the same field of a statement. The *value* of the symbol is the address of the first byte of object code produced by the corresponding statement. The assembler, as a part of the translation process, constructs for itself a *symbol table* showing the value of each symbol defined in the program. For the sample program the symbol table is as follows[1]:

Symbol	Value
MAIN	000000
A	000010
X	000014
ABC	000018

In this case the assembler assigned to the symbol A the value 000010_H, and so on.

Symbolic addresses are used to make it easier to refer to locations in memory. For example, instead of referring to a word in memory with an explicit address as in

    L   3,16(0,15)

we can refer to the word by its symbolic name, thus:

    L   3,A

These two forms are equivalent, provided that the symbol A has been defined appropriately, and both forms will cause the assembler to generate the same object code, in this case 5830F010. This saves the user a significant amount of work.

Symbols consist of strings of one to eight characters. The first character must be a letter and the following characters can be letters or digits. (The characters $, #, and @ are considered to be letters.) The following are valid symbols:

    ABCDEFGH
    A
    LOOP293
    X1234567

Symbols may not contain blanks, punctuation, or special characters.

---

[1] Assembler F prints the symbol table following the listing of the assembler statements and the object code. ESP does not print the symbol table.

MACHINE VERSUS ASSEMBLER INSTRUCTIONS

The sample program includes two kinds of instructions. The first kind is *machine instructions*, such as Load and Add. They appear in the listing both as assembler language statements and as object code. All machine instructions have executable object code.

The second kind is instructions to the assembler, such as START, CSECT, USING, DC, DS, and END. These are called *assembler instructions*.[2] The programmer uses assembler instructions to talk to the assembler. Some assembler instructions produce object code, for example, DC, and some do not, for example, START. Some assembler instructions are described next.

Define constant instruction

Two assembler language instructions, Define Constant (DC) and Define Storage (DS), allow symbols to be associated with data.

Name	Operation	Operand	Comments
Symbol or blank	DC	One or more constants	

An example of a DC instruction is statement 8 in the sample program:

A   DC   F'-23'

This statement tells the assembler to (1) convert the operand to internal form and store it in the appropriate location and (2) associate the symbol A with this location. In the operand field, the letter F and the single quotes indicate that the number inside the quotes, -23, is to be converted to full-word fixed-point form, FFFFFFE9, and stored in the next available full-word location. This means that if the assembly process has left as the next available location a byte whose address is not exactly divisible by 4, then bytes will be skipped in order to put the object code on the next full-word boundary. This *alignment* of data onto the appropriate boundary is automatic for F-type operands, but not for all types of operands, as will be discussed later.

An example of automatic alignment is shown in statements 7 and 8 from Figure 4-4, thus:

Loc	Object Code	Stmt	Source Statement		
00000C	07FE	7		BCR	15,14
00000E	0000				
000010	FFFFFFE9	8	A	DC	F'-23'

---

[2] Assembler instructions are also sometimes called "pseudoinstructions," as contrasted to "real" or machine instructions. However, since there are other categories of instructions, for example, instructions to the executive system; a system of names that suggests that there are only two categories of instructions is not entirely adequate.

The object code for   BCR   15,14 is 07FE and it occupies bytes 00C and 00D, leaving as the next available location byte 00E. But the next statement has an F-type operand that requires full-word alignment, and 00E is not a full-word boundary, so bytes 00E and 00F will be skipped and the constant −23 will be assembled at location 010.

A DC instruction may have several operands; for example, the statement

TABLE   DC   F'1,22,333,4444'

is entirely equivalent to the sequence of four statements

TABLE   DC   F'1'
           DC   F'22'
           DC   F'333'
           DC   F'4444'

A word that does not have a symbol associated with it can be referred to by an expression. For example, in the instruction

L   4,TABLE+12

the effective address of the second operand is TABLE+12 bytes, so the effect will be to load 4444 into register 4. The addition implied by the expression

TABLE+12

is performed by the assembler at *assembly time*, and the result is used in the construction of the object code. This is quite different from the addition in

A   3,ABC

which is performed at *execution time*.

Assembler language also allows X-type constants in which the constant is written in hexadecimal. The length may be up to 256 bytes, and there is no automatic boundary alignment. There may be only one X-type constant per statement. For example,

Loc	Object Code	Stmt	Source Statement		
000004	07FE	4		BCR	15,14
000006	000000FF	5	A	DC	X'000000FF'
00000A	0000				
00000C	000000FF	6	B	DC	F'255'
000010	C1C2	7	C	DC	X'C1C2'
000012	FFFFFFE3	8	D	DC	X'FFFFFFE3'
000016	0000				
000018	FFFFFFE3	9	E	DC	F'-29'
00001C	10000000	10	F	DC	X'10000000'
000020	10000000	11	G	DC	F'268435456'
000024	0AB1	12	H	DC	X'AB1'
		13		END	

Note that

      A   DC   X'000000FF'

and

      B   DC   F'255'

generate the same object code, 000000FF, but A is not aligned on a full-word boundary, while B is aligned. The implied length in bytes of an X-type constant is half the number of hex digits given, except that if an odd number of hex digits is given the constant is padded on the left with a hex 0, as in H of the previous table. Note that some constants, for example, X'10000000', are much easier to write in hexadecimal than in decimal.

Define storage instruction

Name	Operation	Operand	Comments
Symbol or blank	DS	One or more operands of the form nF	

The Define Storage (DS) instruction associates the symbol in the name field with the corresponding location in the memory, but it differs from the DC instruction in that it does not generate any object code; it only reserves space. For example,

      QRS   DS   3F

will allocate space for three full words, 12 bytes, beginning at the next available full-word boundary; it will associate the symbol QRS with the first of these 12 bytes, but it will not generate any contents. Normally, DS instructions are used to define areas into which something will be put by the program. If one attempts to read QRS without first storing something in it, one will read the contents left in that location by the previous user—in general, this is worthless jibberish as far as the present program is concerned.

ERRORS ASSOCIATED WITH SYMBOLS

Each symbol used to define a location in a program should appear in the name field of exactly one statement. If it appears in the name field of two or more statements, that is an error, and the symbol is *multiply defined*. If it does not appear in the name field of any statement but is used as an address, such as ANS in

    ST   6,ANS

then the symbol is *undefined*, which is also an error. In each case the assembler will produce an error message.

End instruction

Name	Operation	Operand	Comments
Blank	END	Symbol or blank	

This instruction tells the assembler to terminate the assembly process. It must be the last assembler language statement in the program, although control cards and data may follow the END card. The operand may specify the point where execution is to begin. If the operand is blank, execution will begin at the beginning of the program.

Start instruction

Name	Operation	Operand	Comments
Symbol or blank	START	Initial value of location counter or blank	

The START instruction identifies the beginning of the program named in the name field. If the name field is blank, the program is considered to be unnamed. The operand gives the initial value of the location counter; this value should be divisible by 8. If the operand field is blank (as is frequently the case), the initial value of the location counter is zero, and assembly will begin at location 0.

CONTROL SECTIONS

A *control section* is a program, subprogram, or section of data that can be relocated.[3] In this text, most programs will be written as single control sections, so for our purposes a control section is usually a program, and the beginning of it can be identified with a START statement.

However, there are more general cases. Assembler F allows the generation of object modules for two or more control sections in one assembly. Each object module contains, among other things, object code, or text, and an external symbol dictionary that contains the information the linkage editor needs to complete the cross referencing between control sections. The control sections are separable; that is, the user can later use the linkage editor to delete or add control sections without hurting the other control sections, and the linkage editor can use the external symbol dictionary to make the necessary linkages between sections.

If one wishes the assembler to produce more than one control section from an assembly, he divides the assembler language program into sections with CSECT instructions.

Name	Operation	Operand	Comments
Symbol or blank	CSECT	Blank	

A CSECT instruction identifies the beginning or continuation of the control section named in the name field. If the name field is blank, the control section is considered to be unnamed. The CSECT instruction can also be used to begin a program.

LOCATION COUNTER AND THE ASSEMBLY PROCESS

One important part of the assembly process is the assignment of values to all the symbols in the program. This is done with the aid of a counter in the assembler program named the *location counter* (LC). This counter keeps track of the location associated with the object code being generated.

Consider the assembly of the program shown in Figure 4-4. Assembly begins with the location counter containing 000. Statement 1, the comment statement, is listed (printed) but not otherwise used by the assembler. Next is statement 2:

```
MAIN      START
```

Since LC = 000, the symbol MAIN is defined to have the value of 000. This statement does not cause any object code to be created, so LC remains 000. Next is statement 3:

```
USING     MAIN,15
```

---

[3] For more on relocation, see Chapter 5.

This tells the assembler to use R15 as a base register and to assume that at execution time this register will contain the value of the symbol MAIN, that is, 000. Since USING does not cause any object code to be generated, the contents of LC remain unchanged. (More on the USING instruction in the next section.) Next is statement 4:

        L   3,A

The assembler can generate the object code for this statement as 5 8 3 0 F _ _ _, where the blanks represent a displacement that cannot be calculated yet because the value of the symbol A is still not known. This will have to be filled in later. This process continues for statements 5, 6, and 7. After statement 7 has been processed, LC = 00E. Next is statement 8:

        A   DC   F'-23'

An F-type operand in a DC statement requires full-word alignment, and 00E is not a full-word boundary. Therefore, the assembler will advance LC to the next full-word boundary, 010, and it will assemble -23 = FFFFFFE9 there, giving the symbol A the value 010. At the conclusion of this step, LC = 014. Next is statement 9:

        X   DS   1F

The F-type operand requires full-word alignment, but LC is already on a full-word boundary so no adjustment is required. The DS instruction reserves space by advancing LC by four (bytes), but it does not generate any object code. At the conclusion of this step, LC = 018.

The assembly process continues for each additional statement until the END card is encountered. At this time the assembler knows the value of the symbol A and all the other symbols used in the program. Now the assembler program can go back, calculate, and fill in the displacements that were earlier left blank. After this is done, the object code is complete, as shown in Figure 4-4.

ESTABLISHING A BASE REGISTER

In any discussion of the translation of symbolic addresses into base-displacement form it is necessary to distinguish two separate programs and two separate times. One program is the *problem program*; the other program is the assembler. At *assembly time,* the program being executed is the assembler, the input to the computer is the problem program in source language form, that is, in assembler language, and the output from the computer is the object code. Next the object code is loaded into the memory for execution. At *execution time* the program being executed is the problem program, which resides in the memory in machine language form. The original assembler language statements and the assembler program are no longer present. The computer input and output, if any, are the data associated with the problem program.

At assembly time it is necessary to tell the assembler (1) what register to use for a base register in constructing the object code, and (2) what value to assume that register will contain at execution time. But note that at assembly time the base register does *not* contain the base address. Tasks (1) and (2) are done by the USING instruction, one form of which is

Name	Operation	Operand	Comments
Blank	USING	v,r	

where v is a symbol and r specifies a register. This tells the assembler (1) to use register r as a base register and (2) to assume that at execution time register r will contain the address corresponding to symbol v. Thus all addresses can be expressed as a base address (corresponding to the value of the symbol v) and a displacement from that address. USING is an assembler instruction, and it does not generate any object code.

In the sample program the first three statements are

```
MAIN      START
          USING     MAIN,15
          L         3,A
            .

            .

            .
```

The USING instruction tells the assembler to use register 15 as a base register and to assume that at execution time R15 will contain the address of MAIN. By examining the object code in Figure 4-4, one can observe that the assembler did as instructed and constructed the object code for   L   3,A   as 5830F010. The effective address of the second operand of this instruction is

$$
\begin{aligned}
EA &= \text{displacement} + \text{contents of base register} \\
&= 010 + C(R15) \\
&= 010 + 000 \\
&= 010
\end{aligned}
$$

which is the address of A, as required.

The USING instruction is operative entirely at assembly time; it has no effect at execution time. So the next problem to consider is how to put the (promised) base address into the specified register at execution time. There are several ways to do this.

Method 1. It is conventional for the executive system to transfer control to a program, such as MAIN, by loading the address of that program into register 15 and then branching to that address. (More on branching in Chapter 7.) Thus we can assume that upon beginning execution of MAIN, the address of MAIN is in R15. This is precisely what we earlier told the assembler to assume would be the case; so nothing further need be done to set the base register.

Method 2. Sometimes R15 will need to be used later for another purpose, for example, for another branch address, so it cannot be used to hold a base address throughout the program. This can be handled by using the same base address but keeping it in another register, thus:

```
METH2        START
             USING       METH2,12
             LR          12,15
               .
               .
               .
```

The statement   USING   METH2,12   tells the assembler at assembly time that at execution time R12 will contain the address of METH2. Then at execution time the statement   LR   12,15   keeps the promise made earlier by copying the contents of R15 into R12. Both the USING and LR statements must appear early in the program, before the appearance of any RX instruction that uses a symbolic address.

Method 3. A more general method of loading a base register with a base address at execution time is

```
METH3        START
             BALR        12,0
             USING       *,12
               .
               .
               .
```

BALR is an executable machine instruction. Here we consider only the form   BALR r,0. This instruction puts the updated instruction address (the address of the next instruction) into register r. This is a special case of the Branch and Link, register-to-register instruction described in Chapter 10. The assembler instruction   USING   *,r tells the assembler at assembly time to assume that register r contains the value of the symbol *, where the asterisk means the current value of the location counter. Thus USING   *,r   tells the assembler to assume that the contents of r corresponds to the address of the next statement following the USING statement.

A version of the previous sample program using this method of obtaining addressability is shown in Figure 4-5. In this figure the BALR instruction has the effect of putting 000002 into R12, so we have the following:

Symbol	Value of the Symbol (= distance from the Beginning of the Program)	Displacement from Base Address
A	010	00E
X	014	012
ABC	018	016

```
LOC   OBJECT CODE    ADDR1 ADDR2  STMT   SOURCE STATEMENT                        F150CT70   6/25/72

                                    1 *   SAMPLE PROGRAM
000000                              2 MAIN     START
C00000 05C0                         3          BALR 12,0
C00002                              4          USING *,12
000002 5830 C00E          00010     5          L    3,A
C00006 5A30 C016          00018     6          A    3,ABC
C0000A 5030 C012          00014     7          ST   3,X
00000E C7FE                         8          BCR  15,14
000010 FFFFFFE9                     9 A        DC   F'-23'
000014                             10 X        DS   1F
000018 0C000029                    11 ABC      DC   F'41'
                                   12          END
```

```
                                  CROSS-REFERENCE                                 PAGE    1

                                                                                    6/25/72

SYMBOL   LEN  VALUE  DEFN    REFERENCES

A        00004 000010 C0009    0C05
ABC      00004 000018 00011    0006
MAIN     C0001 C00000 C0002
X        0C004 000014 C0010    0C07
```

```
NO STATEMENTS FLAGGED IN THIS ASSEMBLY
*STATISTICS*     SOURCE RECORDS (SYSIN) =    12
*OPTICNS IN EFFECT*   LIST, NODECK, LOAD, NORENT, XREF, NOTEST, ALGN, OS, NOTERM, LINECNT =   55
   28 PRINTED LINES
```

Figure 4-5. Obtaining addressability with BALR and USING. Solid line indicates a page break in the printer output.

Note statement 5 in Figure 4-5:

    000002   5830C00E   L   3,A

The effective address of the second operand of this instruction is

$$EA = \text{displacement } + \text{ contents of base register}$$
$$= 00E + C(R12)$$
$$= 00E + 002$$
$$= 010_H$$

which is the address of symbol **A**. For the convenience of the user, the assembler listing also shows this number to the right of the object code under the heading ADDR2. In Figure 4-5, note that the USING statement does not generate any object code.

Some restrictions associated with base-displacement addressing as used in the 360 are as follows:

1. Displacements are positive integers in the range 000 to $FFF_H = 4095_{10}$. Negative displacements are not allowed. This means that no symbol which is to be addressed using a given base register can have a value less than the value of the base symbol; that is, such a symbol cannot occur earlier in the program.

2. The USING instruction must occur before any instruction requiring a base address.

The result of requirements 1 and 2 is that a USING instruction usually occurs at or near the beginning of a program, and the base address it refers to is either the next available address, as in   USING   *,12, or another address at or near the beginning of the program, as in   USING   MAIN,15.

3. For programs larger than 4095 bytes all the addresses in the program cannot be referred to with displacements from a single base address, so multiple base registers must be used.[4]

Example:

Write a program to calculate

$$f \leftarrow \frac{a * x^2}{c} + b * x$$

where $a = 6$
$b = -7$
$c = 8$
$x = -3$

and leave the result in memory. Ignore the remainder from the division. To save a multiplication, we rewrite the expression as

$$f \leftarrow \left(\frac{a * x}{c} + b \right) * x$$

The solution is

```
PROG      CSECT
          BALR      12,0
          USING     *,12
          L         3,A
          M         2,X
          D         2,C
          A         3,B
          M         2,X
          ST        3,F
          BCR       15,14
F         DS        1F
A         DC        F'6'
B         DC        F'-7'
C         DC        F'8'
X         DC        F'-3'
          END
```

---

[4]For details of using multiple base registers, see *Assembler Language*, Form GC28-6514.

EXERCISES

1. Rewrite the program on page 61 in assembler language using symbolic addresses and the assembler language instructions described in this chapter.

2. Fill in the blanks in the following assembler listing.

Object Code		Source Statement		
Loc	Contents	Name	Operation	Operand
000		PROG	START	
000			USING	PROG,15
000	5830F030		L	3,A
004	5850F034			
___	5B50F03C	___	___	___
___	___		M	4,B
___	___		AR	5,3
___	___		ST	5,C
			.	
			.	
			.	
030	00000006	A	DC	F'6'
034	___	B	DC	F'-27'
___	___	C	DS	1F
___	___	ONE	DC	F'1'
			END	

3. Translate the following assembler language program into object code.

Object Code		Source Statement		
Location	Contents	Name	Operation	Operand
000		ABC	CSECT	
			SR	5,5
			BALR	10,0
			USING	*,10
		JJ	A	5,X
			ST	5,Y
			BCR	15,14
		Y	DS	3F
		X	DC	F'-11'
			END	

Fill in the symbol table for this assembly

Symbol	Value of Symbol

What is base register for this assembly? What is base address for this assembly?

4. Write an assembler language program to compute

$$f = ax^4 + bx^3 + cx^2 + dx + e$$

and

$$g = a + \frac{b}{c + d * e}$$

where $a = +13$, $b = -21$, $c = +74$, $d = +20$, $e = -3$, and $x = +3$. Use method 3 to establish addressability. Ignore remainders.

5. Write an assembler language program to implement the Fortran statement $J = I + M * N - (K * 1)$, and leave the result in memory. Let $I = 13$, $M = 9$, $N = -7$, and $K = 16$.

5

Relocation, loading, and execution

In this chapter we consider the steps leading to actual execution of the object code that was produced by the assembler.

NEED FOR RELOCATION

The output of the assembler consists of the object code plus some tables.[1] Suppose that the assembler happens to construct the object code for Figure 4-5 as consecutive bytes beginning at location 004CB0 in memory. Then the memory at the end of assembly might look as in Figure 5-1. The object code might be executed in the place where it was constructed, in this case at 004CB0, but generally this is not done. In general, the object code is moved or *relocated* before execution. There are several reasons for this.

    1. *Subroutines.* Suppose that we want to use the assembler twice, first to assemble a main program and second to assemble a subprogram, and then we want to execute the two

---

[1]The tables contain information that is needed when linking together the outputs of two or more assemblies and when loading the object code into memory. For further details, see *OS Assembler [F] Programmer's Guide,* Form GC26-3756, and J. J. Donovan, *Systems Programming* (New York: McGraw-Hill, 1972).

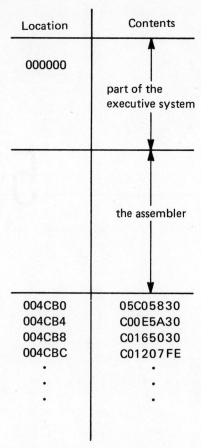

Location	Contents
000000	part of the executive system
	the assembler
004CB0	05C05830
004CB4	C00E5A30
004CB8	C0165030
004CBC	C01207FE
.	.
.	.
.	.

Figure 5-1. A possible memory map at the end of assembly of the program in Figure 4-5.

programs together. If the assembler always constructs the object code at a fixed location, then the object code from the second assembly will lie on top of, and destroy, the object code from the first assembly. This can be avoided by moving the object code elsewhere after each assembly. The "elsewhere" might be another part of main memory, magnetic disk, magnetic tape, or punched cards. After the two assemblies were completed, the two sections of object code would be brought back into main memory by the *loader* program. It is possible that one of the two might be loaded for execution at the same location where it was assembled, but clearly they both cannot be put there. At least one, and in general both, of the programs will be loaded and executed at a location different from where it was constructed.

2. *Size.* Another reason for relocation is related to memory size. Consider a computer with a small memory and only one user at a time. Suppose that the size of the main memory is 10 units, the executive system takes 1 unit, the assembler takes 7 units, and the loader takes 1 unit. During assembly the memory contains

> executive system   1 unit
> assembler   7 units

leaving 2 units for the object code that the assembler is to construct. This limits the size of the object code per assembly to 2 units. This limit can be avoided by using the assembler serially to create several 2-unit sections of object code which are stored on disk or tape. After this, the executive system can remove the assembler program from memory and bring in the loader program. Then the memory contains

executive system	1 unit
loader	1 unit

leaving 8 units for object code. Thus the size limit on programs is 8 units, provided the program can be assembled in pieces that are each no bigger than 2 units.

3. *Multiple users.* The memories of most large computers contain several problem programs at once, and each problem program can consist of a main program plus subprograms. One reason for doing this is that some of the problem programs may be real-time programs, which must be continuously present in memory so that they can rapidly respond to messages that arrive over wires from other equipment. Other reasons for multiple occupancy of memory are related to efficiency, particularly the efficient use of input-output devices.[2]

RELOCATION

As discussed, a computer memory usually contains the object code for several programs at once, and most of them are in locations different from where they were constructed.

To simplify the assembly process, it is common to design assemblers to produce object code that is independent of the location where the program will eventually be loaded and run. This avoids the necessity of telling the assembler where the program will eventually be loaded and executed (which is usually unknown at assembly time), and it avoids the necessity of assembling more than one version, for example, a version to run at 1000, a version to run at 5000, and so on. There are several ways to do this.

One scheme is for the assembler to produce object code with absolute addresses starting at 0000, as if the object code were always to be loaded into the memory at location 0000. Later, when the executive system decides where to put the program in memory for a particular run, for example, at 003AC0, then another operation is needed, the addition of 003AC0 to all addresses that refer to main memory. This adjustment of the addresses is called *relocation,* and the amount added is called the *relocation amount.* This adjustment can be done by the loader program. An example of this is as follows. Here we use a fictitious machine with an accumulator. The machine is word addressed, and the word size is six decimal digits. The instruction format in decimal is

$$\underbrace{X \ X}_{\text{operation}} \ \underbrace{X \ X \ X \ X}_{\substack{\text{absolute} \\ \text{address of} \\ \text{operand}}}$$

[2] For more on buffering and the efficiency problems related to input-output devices, see Donovan, *op. cit.*, or C. W. Gear, *Computer Organization and Programming* (New York: McGraw-Hill, 1969).

The program segment in Figure 5-2 adds $X = 23$ to $Y = 99$ and stores the result in Z, where X, Y, and Z are 100, 101, and 102 words beyond the beginning of the program, respectively. The object code as assembled is shown in column 2. If this program segment is to be loaded and run beginning at location 0200, then all addresses that refer to main memory must be increased by 0200. This is shown in column 3. If, on another occasion, the same program segment is to be loaded and run beginning at location 4300, then all addresses must be increased by 4300, as shown in column 4.

This scheme has two disadvantages. First, many words have to be modified, and the modification has to be done again for each place the program is to be loaded. Second, some of the words, such as the word resulting from

$$X \qquad DC \qquad +23$$

do not contain main memory addresses and should not be modified. Hence the assembler needs to tell the loader which words are relocatable and thus need to be adjusted, and which words are absolute and thus do not need to be adjusted.

Another scheme is used on the 360. Main memory addresses are composed of three parts: a displacement, an index, and a base. The effective address is

$$EA = C(\text{index reg.}) + C(\text{base reg.}) + \text{displacement}$$

Using 360 assembler and machine language, the previous example would look as shown in Figure 5-3. For this example we assume that register 15 is to be used as a base register and that prior to execution R15 will be set to the address at which the program is actually

Col. 1	Col. 2		Col. 3		Col. 4	
Assembler Language	Object code as assembled		Object code as loaded at 0200		Object code as loaded at 4300	
	Loc	Contents	Loc	Contents	Loc	Contents
LOAD X	0000	500100	0200	500300	4300	504400
ADD Y	0001	600101	0201	600301	4301	604401
STORE Z	0002	700102	0202	700302	4302	704402
.	.		.		.	
.	.		.		.	
.	.		.		.	
X DC +23	0100	000023	0300	000023	4400	000023
Y DC +99	0101	000099	0301	000099	4401	000099
Z DS	0102	——	0302	——	4402	——

Figure 5-2. Relocation of object code for a fictitious machine.

| Col. 1 | Col. 2 | | Col. 3 | | Col. 4 | |
| Assembler Language | Object code as assembled | | Object code as loaded at 3AC0 | | Object code as loaded at 6F00 | |
	Loc	Contents	Loc	Contents	Loc	Contents
L 3,X	0000	5830F100	3AC0	5830F100	6F00	5830F100
A 3,Y	0004	5A30F104	3AC4	5A30F104	6F04	5A30F104
ST 3,Z	0008	5030F108	3AC8	5030F108	6F08	5030F108
.	.		.		.	
.	.		.		.	
.	.		.		.	
X DC F'23'	0100	00000017	3BC0	00000017	7000	00000017
Y DC F'99'	0104	00000063	3BC4	00000063	7004	00000063
Z DS 1F	0108	———	3BC8	———	7008	———

Figure 5-3. Relocation of 360 object code.

loaded. Also, we assume that the index is always 0.[3] Column 2 shows the object code as produced by the assembler. It was produced as if it were to be loaded and run at location 0000. Column 3 shows the object code as it would have to be loaded if it were run at location 3AC0. Note that all the code is the same as in column 2. All the addressing adjustments are handled by the assumption that register 15 contains 0000 in column 2 and 3AC0 in column 3. For example, the effective address of the second operand of the first instruction as assembled (column 2) is

$$EA = C \text{ (base reg.)} + \text{displacement}$$
$$= 0000 + 0100$$
$$= 0100$$

which correctly refers to the location of X. As loaded at 3AC0 (column 3), the effective address of the second operand of the first instruction is

$$EA = C(\text{base reg.}) + \text{displacement}$$
$$= 3AC0 + 0100$$
$$= 3BC0$$

which also correctly refers to the location of X. Thus we see that this scheme handles the

---

[3]Figure 5-3 is simplified by the absence of CSECT, BALR, USING, and so on, but the conclusions reached here also apply to the more general case.

relocation problem without requiring a modification of each instruction. This is an advantage over the previous scheme. In column 4 the same thing is repeated except that the program is loaded at location 6F00.

In summary, there are several ways of handling the relocation problem. There is no single best way, and successful computer systems have been built using various schemes. In the sequel we shall confine our attention to the base-displacement system as used in the 360 computer.

ABSOLUTE AND RELOCATABLE SYMBOLS

In Figure 5-3, the symbol X is a *relocatable symbol*; that is, its value depends on the relocation amount. For example, in column 2 the value of X is 0100 and in column 3 the value of X is 3BC0. The symbols we have used so far have all been relocatable.

There are also *absolute symbols*. An absolute symbol can be created with the Equate Symbol assembler instruction.

Name	Operation	Operand	Comments
Symbol	EQU	Expression	

The Equate Symbol instruction assigns to the symbol on the left the value of the expression on the right. If the expression is relocatable, then the symbol will be relocatable. If the expression is absolute, then the symbol will be absolute. For example, if we include in the program of Figure 5-3 the additional statements

```
D1      EQU     X
D2      EQU     X+4
```

then D1 will have the same value as X and D2 will have the value of X plus 4, which in this case is the same as the value of Y. Then the first two arithmetic statements could be written

```
L       3,D1
A       3,D2
```

As a second example, we write

```
AAA     EQU     3
```

Here the value of the expression is absolute, so AAA is defined to be an absolute symbol with value 3. If this EQU statement were inserted into the program of Figure 5-3, then we could write the first three arithmetic statements as

```
L       AAA,X
A       AAA,Y
ST      AAA,Z
```

It is sometimes convenient to designate registers symbolically; then if a change in register usage becomes necessary, it can be done by changing one statement instead of many.

INSTRUCTION COUNTER, INSTRUCTION LENGTHS, AND FLOW OF CONTROL

When a program is being executed, the program and its data lie in the memory. The program may lie in one contiguous section of memory and the data may lie in another contiguous section, or the program and data may be broken into several pieces, as indicated in Figure 5-4. The flow of control can pass from one section of program to another by means of branch instructions.[4] Within each section of program, the instructions lie in contiguous bytes and there are no unused bytes between instructions. There is no such requirement within areas of memory devoted to data, so unused bytes may occur between data items.

At execution time, the computer hardware maintains a counter to keep track of what instruction is being executed. This is usually called the instruction counter; it contains the instruction address. When the computer is to begin execution of a section of

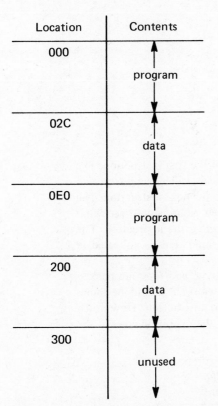

Location	Contents
000	program
02C	data
0E0	program
200	data
300	unused

Figure 5-4. Example of memory allocation for program and data.

---

[4] Branching is discussed in detail in Chapter 7.

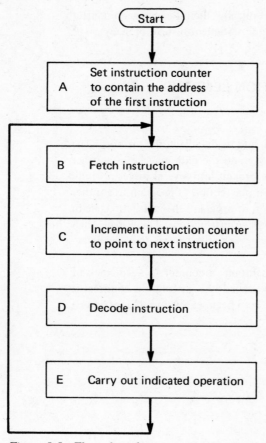

Figure 5-5. Flow chart for instruction fetching and execution.

program, the instruction counter is set to contain the address of the first instruction. The instruction itself is then fetched from memory and put in a register called the *instruction register.* The instruction counter is then incremented to point to the next instruction. The present instruction, which is in the instruction register, is then examined to see what operation is to be performed. This examination is called *decoding* the instruction. The required operation is then carried out. Then the cycle is repeated. This is indicated in Figure 5-5.

In the 360 computer, instructions are 2, 4, or 6 bytes long, and they are packed into contiguous bytes in the memory. Thus the instruction counter should be incremented by 2, 4, or 6 depending on the length of the current instruction. How much should be added can be determined from the first four bits of the operation code of the current instruction, as indicated in the table.

First Hex Digit of Operation Code	*Instruction Format*	*Instruction Length*
0 to 3	RR	16 bits or 2 bytes
4 to 7	RX	32 bits or 4 bytes
8 to B	RS or SI	32 bits or 4 bytes
C to F	SS	48 bits or 6 bytes

For example, suppose that a portion of memory and its contents look as shown in the following table, and that location 03E is known to contain the first byte of an instruction. We could tell the computer to begin execution with the instruction at 03E. Then the computer could find the length of each instruction and the address of the first byte of the next instruction, one after another, as follows:

Byte Location	Byte Contents	Implications
03E	5C	Op code 5C indicates that instruction length is 4 bytes, so next instruction will begin at 042.
03F	80	
040	50	
041	24	
042	1A	Op code 1A indicates that instruction length is 2 bytes.
043	93	
044	50	Op code 50 indicates that instruction length is 4 bytes.
045	90	
046	50	
047	28	
048	07	Op code 07 indicates that instruction length is 2 bytes.
049	FE	

Note that it is not possible to tell which bytes are op codes and which are not, unless you know where to begin. For example, we might erroneously tell the computer to begin execution at byte 040. The contents beginning at byte 040 is 50241A93.... The first byte, 50, appears to be the op code for a store instruction, so these four bytes would be interpreted thus:

$$5\ 0\ 2\ 4\ 1\ A\ 9\ 3$$

$$\text{ST} \qquad 2,2707(4,1)$$

This instruction is spurious, and the computer may or may not recognize this fact. The most likely result would be that the effective address of the second operand, C(R4) + C(R1) + 2707, would be illegal (because of improper alignment or because it lies outside the region of memory assigned to this program) and an interruption would occur. If the effective address happens to be legal, then the computer would execute this spurious instruction and go on to the next instruction, which happens to be 50905028 = ST 9,40(0,5). This is one of the original legal instructions, so execution will continue normally, leaving the user with a mystery to solve when the answers come out wrong.

It is unusual for the flow of control, having once gone wrong, to right itself and resume normal execution, as shown in this example. The more normal result of an error in flow of control is that an interruption will occur immediately or within a few bytes. But if one or two spurious instructions have been executed, the results may be rather mysterious at first glance.

TERMINATION OF EXECUTION

The flow chart in Figure 5-5 appears to describe an infinite loop; no means of stopping are readily apparent. There are two ways to get stopped. One way is to allow a Stop or Halt instruction in the instruction repertoire and to include this in the program. When this Stop instruction is executed (at box E), execution of the problem program is terminated. This method is not normally used at large computer installations.

A second and more common way to terminate execution of a program is to branch to another program. This does not stop the computer as a whole; it only stops the execution of the program we are considering at the moment. Frequently, the branch is to an executive program that will do some record keeping and then cause another problem program to begin execution. In this case, the amount of computer time wasted between the execution of successive problem programs may only be milliseconds. Henceforth, we shall use this method, usually writing BCR 15,14 to return control to the executive program.

EXERCISES

1. Generate object code for the following program by hand.

Pl	START	
	BALR	12,0
	USING	*,12
	L	3,A
	A	3,C
	AR	3,3
	ST	3,B
	BCR	15,14
A	DC	F'−5'
B	DS	1F
C	DC	F'24'
	END	

Assume this program is loaded and executed at 06A2B0. What are the addresses of A, B, and C as assembled? As executed? What are the contents of R12 after the execution of the BALR instruction? What is the effective address of the second operand of the load instruction at execution time? What is the contents of the byte at 06A2C2? At 06A2C4?

2. There is no simple direct way for the user to load object code into the computer. However, one can use the assembler for this purpose by feeding the object code in as X-type constants in DC statements.

a. Write an assembler language program to calculate

$$\frac{X}{Y} + \frac{Z}{W} \to A$$

where $X = 13, Y = -4, Z = 75$, and $W = -39$.

b. Translate this assembler language program into object code by hand.

c. Load this object code into the computer by means of an assembler language program consisting of one START or CSECT statement, one END statement, and a number of DC statements with X-type operands. No other kinds of statements are allowed.

d. Execute this program, obtain a postexecution dump, and verify that the program was loaded and executed correctly.

6

Mechanics of running
a program

In this chapter we describe the details of running and debugging a program written in 360 Assembler Language on a 360 computer.

One method is to use the IBM-supplied Assembler F running under the executive system named *Operating System 360*. This has both advantages and disadvantages. Among the advantages are the following. Assembler F is available at most 360 installations. Assembler F implements all the features of the 360 Assembler Language. Operating System 360 (hereinafter referred to as O.S.) is quite versatile, allowing the user to do a large variety of things with his job. For example, he may wish to write the program in sections on several different days, assemble the sections separately, and save some of the object code on disk and some as punched object decks. Later he may wish to link the sections with each other and with other programs and finally load and execute the whole job. All this can be done under O.S.

Among the disadvantages of this method are the following. The executive system O.S. is much more versatile than necessary for a novice user, and the control cards it requires are numerous and elaborate. Assembler F is slow in assembly, although the code it produces runs at full machine speed. Also, this method does not provide a trace of execution, and it does not provide any simplified input-output method.

To overcome these disadvantages, a number of assembler systems have been written specifically for use by beginners who are writing and debugging short programs. One such system, named ESP, is described in Appendix A. A number of other similar systems are available at various installations. If one of them is available at the reader's installation, he will have to obtain instructions on its use locally.

In the remainder of this chapter we describe the use of Assembler F running under O.S. The rules given here are explained only minimally—the reader is expected to follow them, or analogous rules for his own installation, without understanding them completely. A complete discussion of the pertinent subject matter is beyond the scope of this text.[1]

The reader is warned that getting a program into and out of a computer is a sometimes frustrating job, requiring adherence to a lot of little rules. He should not be surprised if he has trouble with the details the first few times.

CONTROL CARDS

To run a simple assembler language program under O.S./360 and Assembler F, the deck makeup is of the form shown in Figure 6-1. The details of the control cards differ somewhat from one installation to another. The reader should consult the staff at his computer installation for the exact local rules.

One version of the control card and deck arrangement in more detail is the following:

```
┌─ column 1
│
//jobname          JOB       accounting information
//stepname         EXEC      ASMFCLG
//ASM.SYSIN        DD        *
                 }  assembler language statements
/*
//GO.SYSPRINT      DD        SYSOUT=A
//GO.SYSUDUMP      DD        SYSOUT=A
//GO.SYSIN         DD        *                    ┐
                 }  data deck                     │ Omit all of
/*                                                │ this if there
                                                  ┘ is no data deck.
```

The statements beginning with a slash in column 1 are job control statements.[2,3] The first card, the JOB card, names the job and provides accounting information and other parameters. The second card, the EXECUTE card, says to execute the cataloged procedure ASMFCLG.[3] A cataloged procedure is a group of job control statements. When O.S. executes the statement

//stepname   EXEC   ASMFCLG

---

[1] See, for example, J. J. Donovan, *Systems Programming* (New York: McGraw-Hill, 1972), and G. D. Brown, *System/360 Job Control Language* (New York: Wiley, 1970).

[2] See *IBM System/360 Operating System Job Control Language User's Guide,* Form GC28-6703.

[3] *OS Assembler [F] Programmer's Guide,* Form GC26-3756.

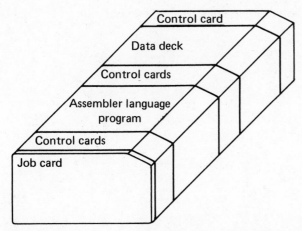

Figure 6-1. Deck arrangement for running an assembler language program under Operating System 360.

O.S. will expand this job control statement into a number of job control statements. For this particular cataloged procedure, the statements will be expanded into three groups of statements, or steps. The first step is an assembly step. The input to the assembly, that is, the deck of assembler language statements, is the part of the deck beginning after

    //ASM.SYSIN   DD   *

and ending before

        /*

The output from the assembly step is the object code, which is usually put not in main memory but on a secondary storage device, such as a disk. The second step of the cataloged procedure is the linkedit step, which combines the object code from this assembly and from other sources, such as previous assemblies (here there were no other sources), to form the object code from one job. This object code is then loaded into the memory and executed in the third step or "go" step. The statement

    //GO.SYSPRINT   DD   SYSOUT=A

says that the execution output, SYSPRINT, is to be transmitted to a device in the output class SYSOUT=A, that is, to a printer. The statement

    //GO.SYSUDUMP   DD   SYSOUT=A

says that SYSUDUMP, the diagnostic information that may be generated if errors occur during execution, should be transmitted to the same device so it will appear on the same piece of paper with the execution output. The execution input, that is, the data deck, begins after

> //GO.SYSIN   DD   *

and ends before

> /*

INPUT-OUTPUT UNDER O.S. [4]

There are several ways to perform input-output operations in an assembler language program. One way is to use the input-output instructions that can be executed by the 360 hardware, but this is complicated and beyond the scope of this text. Another way is to use input-output subprograms written in a higher-level language, such as Fortran. One of these is called by the assembler language program each time a card is to be read or a line is to be printed. A third way is to use the macros OPEN, CLOSE, GET, PUT, and DCB to perform the input-output. Here we briefly describe this third method.

> This description of input-output macros is very brief in view of the enormous amount of material that cound be discussed. Here we give only one way to accomplish a particular task instead of describing the technique in more general terms and is done in the other chapters. The reader who wants to understand the full generality of these methods should refer to
>
> > *IBM System/360 Operating System Introduction,* Form GC28-6534
> > *IBM System/360 Operating System Data Management Services,* Form GC26-3746
> > *IBM System/360 Operating System Data Management Macro Instructions,* Form GC26-3794
>
> The novice assembler language programmer is advised not to compose his own input-output statements but to use the standard ones for his computer installation, if possible. Presumably they will be rather similar to these examples.

Each of the statements OPEN, CLOSE, GET, PUT, and DCB is a *macro instruction.* A macro instruction is one that the assembler will *expand* to produce several machine language instructions instead of only one. The assembler does this by looking up the general definition of the macro in a *macro library* and then tailoring the general definition of the macro to fit this particular case. [5] Not all assemblers can expand macros; for example, Assembler F can, but ESP cannot. Assembler F will expand the statement

> OPEN   (XX,INPUT)

---

[4] This material on input-output is included here for completeness. The reader may wish to return to this section again after reading Chapter 8 on character manipulation.

[5] The macro library, usually kept on disk, is a collection of macro definitions supplied by IBM. See *IBM System/360 Operating System Data Management Macro Instructions,* Form GC26-3794.

as follows:

```
CNOP    0,4
BAL     1,*+8
DC      AL1(128)
DC      AL3(XX)
SVC     19
```

Here we are not concerned with what these particular assembler language statements do.[6] The point is only that a macro instruction is expanded into a sequence of assembler language statements and these are then translated into object code. In the example program the assembler language instruction

```
PRINT     NOGEN
```

is included to suppress the listing of the macro expansions since some of them are rather long and fairly meaningless at this point. This does not affect the expansion of the macro into object code; it just suppresses the printing of the expansion.

The four macros OPEN, CLOSE, GET, and PUT are executable. Their expansion results in subroutine calls that use and do not restore the contents of general registers 0, 1, 14, and 15. If the user needs the contents of these registers later, then he must save and restore them himself. In the example program this is done with STM and LM instructions.

A *data set* is a collection of machine-readable data, for example, a group of cards in a card reader, a magnetic tape with its information stored at a particular density, or the like. To transmit data from a data set to main memory, one writes

```
GET       dcbname,areaname
```

where dcbname is the name of a DCB statement elsewhere in the program that describes the data set, and areaname refers to an area in memory where the data are to be stored. In the example program the statement

```
GET     XX,CARD
```

reads bytes into main memory beginning at address CARD in accordance with the parameters specified by the DCB statement named XX. After the data movement has been completed, execution resumes with the statement following the GET.

The macro DCB expands to produce a table of information describing the way the data in a data set are stored. The mnemonic DCB stands for Data Control Block. In the example program the input data set is specified by the statement

```
XX    DCB     DSORG=PS,RECFM=FB,MACRF=GM,DDNAME=SYSIN
```

---

[6]CNOP is an assembler instruction, Conditional No Operation. See *Assembler Language*, GC28-6514. BAL is a machine instruction, Branch and Link. See Chapter 10. SVC is a machine instruction, Supervisor Call. See *Principles of Operation*, GA22-6821.

The possible operands of a DCB statement are very numerous. For details, see the IBM manuals mentioned previously. The DCB macro is nonexecutable, so it should be placed in a nonexecutable part of the program.

Before attempting to read from a data set, that data set must be *defined* by a DCB statement as just shown, and it must be *opened* by a statement of a form

> OPEN   (dcbname,option)

For example,

> OPEN   (XX,INPUT)

says open the data set described by the DCB statement named XX as an input data set. OPENing corresponds in part to initializing the data set and the device it is on to some standard condition, for example, positioning a magnetic tape to the beginning of the data.

To perform output, one must define an output data set by a DCB statement; for example,[7]

> YY   DCB   DSORG=PS,RECFM=FBA,MACRF=PM,   X
>   BLKSIZE=1064,LRECL=133,DDNAME=SYSPRINT

This says, among other things, that the output data set contains 133 byte records (LRECL=133); these will be appropriate for transmission to a printer that uses the first byte for carriage control (blank means single space, 1 means advance to the top of the next page) and prints the following 132 bytes on a line.

Before printing on a data set, one must open it as an output data set, for example, by the statement[8]

> OPEN   (YY,OUTPUT)

To print one line, one writes a statement of the form

> PUT   dcbname,areaname

For example, the statement

> PUT   YY,LINE

in conjunction with the DCB statement named YY says to transmit 133 bytes from the main memory, beginning at address LINE, to the data set described by the DCB. Control

---

[7]An assembler language statement may be continued on a second card by punching a nonblank character in column 72 and then continuing the statement at column 16 of the following card, leaving columns 1 through 15 blank.

[8]Several data sets may be opened in one statement, as shown in Figure 6-2.

then returns to the statement following the PUT, but the printing may not have been done yet. This is because the output data are not printed line by line as they are generated; the output is stored in a buffer. In the example program the record size is 133 bytes (LRECL=133) and the buffer size is 1064 bytes (BLKSIZE=1064), so eight lines will be accumulated before any are printed. After all the PUT statements have been executed, one should *close* the data set with the statement

       CLOSE   (YY)

to force the printing of the contents of a partially full buffer. Otherwise, if an interruption occurs while the buffer contains some still-to-be-printed line images, these line images will be destroyed and the user may never see up to eight lines from the end of his output.

REGISTER USAGE CONVENTIONS

At the beginning of execution, register 15 contains the entry point address. This corresponds to the beginning of the program unless another entry point was specified by an operand on the END statement. Hence R15 can be used as a base register until another base register is established.

At the beginning of execution, R14 contains the address to which control should be returned at the end of execution of the problem program, and R13 contains the address of an 18-word area in which the register contents can be saved.

The normal way to end execution of a program is with

       BCR   15,14

However, the input-output macro instructions alter and do not restore the contents of registers 14, 15, 0, and 1, so the user must save and restore the contents of R14 himself. In the example program we save[9] the registers at the beginning with

       STM   14,12,12(13)

and restore them just before branching back to the system with

       LM   14,12,12(13)

SAMPLE PROGRAM

A sample program is shown in Figures 6-2 and 6-3. Figure 6-2 is a listing of the deck; Figure 6-3 shows the computer output for this deck. The first part of the program

---

[9] This method of saving and restoring register contents is compatible with the O.S. conventions for register usage with subprograms. For a more general discussion of register usage with subprograms and the establishment of save areas, see Chapter 10.

```
***************************************************************************************************************
//D227J    JOB     'U9329,TIME=2,SIZE=128K',BREARLEY,MSGLEVEL=(1,1)
//STEP1    EXEC    ASMFCLG
//ASM.SYSIN  DD  *
*   SAMPLE PROGRAM FOR ASSEMBLER F
SAMPLE     CSECT
           STM     14,12,12(13)    SAVE REGISTER CONTENTS
           BALR    12,0
           USING   *,12
           PRINT   NOGEN           SUPPRESS MACRO EXPANSIONS
           OPEN    (XX,INPUT,YY,OUTPUT)
           L       2,A
           A       2,B
           ST      2,C
           GET     XX,CARD
           MVC     CARD+4(1),DOLLAR
           PUT     YY,LINE
           CLOSE   (YY)
           DC      X'00000000'     ILLEGAL INSTRUCTION
           LM      14,12,12(13)    RESTORE REGISTER CONTENTS
           BCR     15,14
A          DC      F'-23'
B          DC      F'4'
C          DS      1F
LINE       DC      C' '            CARRIAGE CONTROL CHARACTER
CARD       DC      80C' '
           DC      52C'*'
DOLLAR     DC      C'$'
XX         DCB     DSORG=PS,RECFM=FB,MACRF=GM,DDNAME=SYSIN
YY         DCB     DSORG=PS,RECFM=FBA,MACRF=PM,BLKSIZE=1064,          X
           LRECL=133,DDNAME=SYSPRINT
           END
/*
//GO.SYSPRINT  DD  SYSOUT=A
//GO.SYSUDUMP  DD  SYSOUT=A
//GO.SYSIN  DD  *
ABCDEFGHI
/*
```

Figure 6-2.   *Listing of a deck for Assembler F running under Operating System.*

```
***************************************************************************************************************
                  ~
//D227J    JOB     'U9329,TIME=2,SIZE=128K',BREARLEY,MSGLEVEL=1
//STEP1    EXEC    ASMFCLG
XX         PROC    LKEDPGM=IEWLF440                                     00000010
XXASM      EXEC    PGM=IEUASM,PARM='LOAD,NODECK',REGION=64K,TIME=(1,0)  00000020
XXSYSGO  DD  DSN=&LOADSET,UNIT=SPOOL,SPACE=(400,(140,140)),            Z00000030
IEF653I SUBSTITUTION JCL - DSN=&LOADSET,UNIT=SPOOL,SPACE=(400,(140,140)),
XX         DCB=(RECFM=FB,LRECL=80,BLKSIZE=0400),DISP=(NEW,PASS)         00000040
XXSYSLIB    DD   DSNAME=SYS1.MACLIB,DISP=SHR,UNIT=2314,VOL=SER=OS201L   00000050
XXSYSPRINT DD SYSOUT=A,DCB=(RECFM=FBM,LRECL=121,BLKSIZE=1936,BUFNO=1)   00000060
XXSYSPUNCH DD SYSOUT=B,DCB=(RECFM=FB,LRECL=80,BLKSIZE=640,BUFNO=1)      00000070
XXSYSUT1  DD     DSNAME=&SYSUT1,SPACE=(1700,(400,50)),UNIT=SPOOL        00000080
IEF653I SUBSTITUTION JCL - DSNAME=&SYSUT1,SPACE=(1700,(400,50)),UNIT=SPOOL
XXSYSUT2  DD     DSNAME=&SYSUT2,SPACE=(1700,(400,50)),UNIT=SPOOL        00000090
IEF653I SUBSTITUTION JCL - DSNAME=&SYSUT2,SPACE=(1700,(400,50)),UNIT=SPOOL
XXSYSUT3  DD     DSNAME=&SYSUT3,SPACE=(1700,(400,50)),UNIT=SPOOL        00000100
IEF653I SUBSTITUTION JCL - DSNAME=&SYSUT3,SPACE=(1700,(400,50)),UNIT=SPOOL
//ASM.SYSIN  DD  *
```

(1)

```
                                      EXTERNAL SYMBOL DICTIONARY                      PAGE    1
SYMBOL    TYPE ID  ADDR   LENGTH LD ID                                             17.22   7/01/72

SAMPLE    SD   01 000000  0001AC
```

(2)

```
                                                                              PAGE    1

LOC   OBJECT CODE     ADDR1 ADDR2 STMT   SOURCE STATEMENT                  F15OCT70   7/01/72

                                   1 *  SAMPLE PROGRAM FOR ASSEMBLER F
000000                             2 SAMPLE  CSECT
000000  90EC D00C          0000C   3         STM     14,12,12(13)   SAVE REGISTER CONTENTS
000004  05C0                       4         BALR    12,0
000006                             5         USING   *,12
                                   6         PRINT   NOGEN          SUPPRESS MACRO EXPANSIONS
                                   7         OPEN    (XX,INPUT,YY,OUTPUT)
```

(3)

Figure 6-3.   *Output from deck of Figure 6-2 run under Assembler F and O.S. Page boundaries of the original printer output are indicated by solid lines and circled numbers. Some pages are omitted.*

```
000016 5820 C052        00058    15          L      2,A
00001A 5A20 C056        0005C    16          A      2,B
00001E 5020 C05A        00060    17          ST     2,C
                                 18          GET    XX,CARD
000030 D200 C063 C0E3 00069 000E9  23        MVC    CARD+4(1),DOLLAR
                                 24          PUT    YY,LINE
                                 29          CLOSE  (YY)
00004E 00000000         35          DC     X'00000000'   ILLEGAL INSTRUCTION
000052 98EC D00C        0000C    36          LM     14,12,12(13)  RESTORE REGISTER CONTENTS
000056 C7FE             37          BCR    15,14
000058 FFFFFFE9         38 A        DC     F'-23'
00005C 00000004         39 B        DC     F'4'
000060                  40 C        DS     1F
000064 40               41 LINE     DC     C' '           CARRIAGE CONTROL CHARACTER
000065 4040404040404040 42 CARD     DC     80C' '
000085 5C5C5C5C5C5C5C5C 43          DC     52C'*'
0000E9 5B               44 DOLLAR   DC     C'$'
                        45 XX       DCB    DSORG=PS,RECFM=FB,MACRF=GM,DDNAME=SYSIN
                        99 YY       DCB    DSORG=PS,RECFM=FBA,MACRF=PM,BLKSIZE=1064,         X
                                           LRECL=133,DDNAME=SYSPRINT
                       153          END
```

RELOCATION DICTIONARY   PAGE   1

POS.ID   REL.ID   FLAGS   ADDRESS   7/01/72

  01   01   08   00000D
  01   01   08   000011   ④
  01   01   08   000049

                          CROSS-REFERENCE   PAGE   1

SYMBOL   LEN VALUE   DEFN   REFERENCES   7/01/72

A   00004 000058 00038   0015
B   00004 00005C 00039   0016
C   00004 000060 00040   0017   ⑤
CARD   00001 000065 00042   0020 0023
DOLLAR   00001 0000E9 00044   0023
LINE   00001 000064 00041   0026
SAMPLE   00001 000000 00002
XX   00004 0000EC 00049   0011 0019
YY   00004 00014C 00103   0013 0025 0033

NO STATEMENTS FLAGGED IN THIS ASSEMBLY
STATISTICS   SOURCE RECORDS (SYSIN) =   28   SOURCE RECORDS (SYSLIB) = 2689
OPTIONS IN EFFECT   LIST, NODECK, LOAD, NORENT, XREF, NOTEST, ALGN, OS, NOTERM, LINECNT = 55
   54 PRINTED LINES

```
IEF373I STEP /ASM      / START 72183.1721
IEF374I STEP /ASM      / STOP  72183.1722 CPU   0MIN 09.59SEC MAIN  64K LCS   OK

END OF STEP D227J  , ASM   , CPU TIME= 0000009.59SEC,      ERT = 0000037.09SEC
              REGION ALLOCATED = 0064K MAIN  0000K LCS   DISK EXCP = 00000410          ⑥
              REGION USED      = 0064K MAIN  0000K LCS   RETURN CODE= 00000000

XXLKED    EXEC  PGM=&LKEDPGM,PARM=(XREF,LIST,NCAL),REGION=64K,        X00000110
IEF653I SUBSTITUTION JCL - PGM=IEWLF440,PARM=(XREF,LIST,NCAL),REGION=64K,
XX             TIME=(0,30)                                            00000120
XXSYSLIN DD    DSNAME=&LOADSET,DISP=(OLD,DELETE)                      00000130
IEF653I SUBSTITUTION JCL - DSNAME=&LOADSET,DISP=(OLD,DELETE)
XX        DD   DDNAME=SYSIN,DCB=BLKSIZE=400                           00000140
XXSYSLMOD DD DSN=&GOSET(GO),UNIT=SPOOL,DISP=(MOD,PASS),              X00000150
IEF653I SUBSTITUTION JCL - DSN=&GOSET(GO),UNIT=SPOOL,DISP=(MOD,PASS),
XX             SPACE=(TRK,(25,1))                                     00000160
XXSYSPRINT DD  SYSOUT=A,DCB=(RECFM=FBM,LRECL=121,BLKSIZE=605,BUFNO=1) 00000170
XXSYSUT1 DD DSN=&SYSUT1,UNIT=SPOOL,SPACE=(1024,(50,20))               00000180
IEF653I SUBSTITUTION JCL - DSN=&SYSUT1,UNIT=SPOOL,SPACE=(1024,(50,20))
```

F44-LEVEL LINKAGE EDITOR OPTIONS SPECIFIED XREF,LIST,NCAL
         DEFAULT OPTION(S) USED - SIZE=(90112,12288)

                                                                  ⑦
                          CROSS REFERENCE TABLE

CONTROL SECTION   ENTRY

  NAME   ORIGIN LENGTH   NAME LOCATION   NAME LOCATION   NAME LOCATION   NAME LOCATION

SAMPLE   00   1AC

Figure 6-3. (Continued)

101

LOCATION REFERS TO SYMBOL IN CONTROL SECTION   LOCATION REFERS TO SYMBOL IN CONTROL SECTION

ENTRY ADDRESS   00
TOTAL LENGTH   1B0

****GO   DOES NOT EXIST BUT HAS BEEN ADDED TO DATA SET

IEF373I STEP /LKED   / START 72183.1722
IEF374I STEP /LKED   / STOP 72183.1723 CPU   0MIN 00.44SEC MAIN 64K LCS   OK

END OF STEP D227J   , LKED   , CPU TIME= 000000.44SEC,   ERT = 0000008.04SEC   ⑧
          REGION ALLOCATED= 0064K MAIN 0000K LCS   DISK EXCP = 00000012
          REGION USED   = 0064K MAIN 0000K LCS   RETURN CODE= 00000000

XXGO   EXEC PGM=*.LKED.SYSLMOD,TIME=(0,30)   00000190
//GO.SYSPRINT DD   SYSOUT=A
//GO.SYSUDUMP DD   SYSOUT=A
//GO.SYSIN DD   *

ABCD$FGHI   ***

                              └ OUTPUT PRODUCED BY THIS PROGRAM

JOB D227J   STEP GO   TIME 172317   DATE 72183   PAGE 0001

COMPLETION CODE   SYSTEM = 0C1   ⑨

PSW AT ENTRY TO ABEND FFE50000 700436A0   INTERRUPTION ADDRESS

TCB 018DC0   RBP   000194C0   PIE 00000000   DEB 00018C4C   TIO 00019BF8   CMP 800C1000   TRN 00000000
              MSS   01020BA8   PK-FLG E0850517 FLG 00007B7B   LLS 0001D698   JLB 00000000   JPQ 0001DAC8
              FSA   01052768   TCB 00000000   TME 00000000   JST 00018DC0   NTC 00000000   OTC 00021430
              LTC   00000000   IQE 00000000   ECB 00019CE4   STA 20000000   D-PQE 000248C0 SQS 000188B0
              NSTAE 00000000   TCT 00019D28   USER 00000000 DAR 00000000   RESV 00000000   JSCB 0001D5B8

ACTIVE RBS

PRB 01D228   RESV 00000000   APSW 700436A0   WC-SZ-STAB 00040082   FL-CDE 0001D388   PSW FFE50000 700436A0
              Q/TTR 00000000   WT-LNK 00018DC0

SVRB 0197A8   TAB-LN 001801F8 APSW F3F0F1C3   WC-SZ-STAB 0012D002   TQN 00000000   PSW 00040033 5000EB9A
              Q/TTR 0000580D   WT-LNK 0001D228
              RG 0-7 00000030   00052FC8   FFFFFFED   5C019CE8   000218C8   00021430   00019C64   00022CB0
              RG 8-15 00019CC0   00019D28   00019CE8   00000000   40043656   00052768   40043694   9008B996
              EXTSA   00021BE   8F052FA0   00000000   00000000   FF030000   00019824   0001982C   E2E8E2C9
                      C5C1F0F1   C9C5C1C0   C1C2C5D5   C4F30C10

SVRB 0194C0   TAB-LN 000803C8 APSW F1F0F5C1   WC-SZ-STAB 0012D002   TQN 00000000   PSW FF040001 400A9B50
              Q/TTR 00005D07   WT-LNK 0001S7A8
              RG 0-7 00000000   00019808   8000EAB2   0000F308   00018DC0   000197A8   04018DC0   000197A8
              RG 8-15 00018DC0   4000EA22   00018DC0   8F052FA0   00019C3C   0001982C   4000EC24   00000000
              EXTSA   E2E8E2C9   C5C1F0F1   0018002C   002C003C   0040004C   0054005C   0068006C   007C007C
                      00000000   00000000   0012C002   00000000

LOAD LIST

        NE 0001DCA0   RSP-CDE 0201DAC8   NE 0001DDD0   RSP-CDE 010262F8   NE 0001DEE8   RSP-CDE 01026228
        NE 0001DEF0   RSP-CDE 010261F8   NE 0001D210   RSP-CDE 010261C8   NE 0001D408   RSP-CDE 010262C8
        NE 0001DAC0   RSP-CDE 01026268   NE 0001E038   RSP-CDE 01026298   NE 0001F628   RSP-CDE 0101D0D8
        NE 00000000   RSP-CDE 01026358

CDE

        01D388   ATR1 0B   NCDE 000000   ROC-RB 0001D228   NM GO   USE 01   EPA 043650   ATR2 20   XL/MJ 01D378
        01DAC8   ATR1 30   NCDE 01D0D8   ROC-RB 00000000   NM IGC0A05A   USE 02   EPA 04F960   ATR2 28   XL/MJ 01CE88
        0262F8   ATR1 B0   NCDE 026328   ROC-RB 00000000   NM IGG019CD   USE 01   EPA 0AA268   ATR2 20   XL/MJ 0262E8
        026228   ATR1 B0   NCDE 026268   ROC-RB 00000000   NM IGG019CJ   USE 01   EPA 0A9DE0   ATR2 20   XL/MJ 026218
        0261F8   ATR1 B0   NCDE 026228   ROC-RB 00000000   NM IGG019BA   USE 01   EPA 0A9C50   ATR2 20   XL/MJ 0261E8
        0261C8   ATR1 B0   NCDE 0261F8   ROC-RB 00000000   NM IGG019BB   USE 01   EPA 0A9B28   ATR2 20   XL/MJ 026188
        0262C8   ATR1 B0   NCDE 0262F8   ROC-RB 00000000   NM IGG019CC   USE 01   EPA 0AA088   ATR2 20   XL/MJ 026288
        026268   ATR1 B0   NCDE 026298   ROC-RB 00000000   NM IGG019CI   USE 01   EPA 0A9EF0   ATR2 20   XL/MJ 026258
        026298   ATR1 B0   NCDE 0262C8   ROC-RB 00000000   NM IGG019CH   USE 01   EPA 0AA008   ATR2 20   XL/MJ 026288
        01D0D8   ATR1 30   NCDE 01D388   ROC-RB 00000000   NM IGG019AC   USE 01   EPA 052AD8   ATR2 20   XL/MJ 01CB70
        026358   ATR1 B0   NCDE 026398   ROC-RB 00000000   NM IGG019AQ   USE 01   EPA 0AA5D8   ATR2 20   XL/MJ 026348

                                                                                      PAGE 0003

              00000000 00000000 00000000 2B000001   31052738 40000005 08052740 00000780   ⑪
              08052758 70000001 92043744 60000005   86051880 00000780 00000000 00000000
        UCB 001C08 D000FFA8 01330020 01480100 00F1F3F3   30C02008 24480004 00400600 E2C3D9F0
                     F0F10804 03340100 00000000 00000000   00000000 31000500 0E000000 00002850

        Figure 6-3. (Continued)

                                                                                           102

```
MSS                 ************ SPQE ************   *************** DQE ***************   ******* FQE ********
                    FLGS  NSPQE    SPID    DQE       BLK      FQE       LN       NOQE       NFQE         LN

         020BA8     00    023FE8   251   010368      00043000 00043000 00000800 00000000   00000000     00000650
         023FE8     00    01FF08   252   023768      00052800 00052BF0 00000800 0001CB30   00052800     000003B0
                                                                                           00000000     000002D8
                                                     0004F800 0004F800 00000800 0001C878   00000000     00000160
                                                     00050000 00050000 00000800 00000000   00000000     000001A0
         01FF08     C0    000000   000   022C18
         022C18     60    000000   000   01E4F8      00052000 00052000 00000800 0001D358   00000000     000006B8
                                                     00051800 00051800 00000800 0001D218   00000000     00000078
                                                     00050800 00050800 00001000 00000000   00000000     000007A8

D-PQE   00024800   FIRST 0001DBF0   LAST 0001DBF0
PQE  01DBF0   FFB 00043800   LFB 00043800   NPQ 00000000   PPQ 00000000
              TCB 00021430   RSI 00010000   RAD 00043000   FLG 0000

FBQE 043800   NFB 0001DBF0   PFB 0001DBF0   SZ 0000C000


QCB TRACE

MAJ 024CA0   NMAJ 0001D0A0   PMAJ 00012898   FMIN 00024900   NM  SYSDSN

MIN 01E160   FQEL 0001FFD8   PMIN 0001E5A8   NMIN 0001E678   NM  FF  SYS1.MACLIB

             NQEL 00000000   PQEL 8001E160   TCB  00021430   SVRB 00018A18

MAJ 01BEB0   NMAJ 00000000   PMAJ 0001D0A0   FMIN 0001BE98   NM  SYSIEA01

MIN 01BE98   FQEL 0001CB20   PMIN 0001BEB0   NMIN 00000000   NM  EO  IEA

             NQEL 00000000   PQEL 0001BE98   TCB  00018DC0   SVRB 000194C0


SAVE AREA TRACE

INTERRUPT AT 0436A0

REGS AT ENTRY TO ABEND          CONTENTS OF REGISTER 2

   FLTR 0-6   0000000000000000   000000000001A488      000000B000030FE4   000191D800000068

      REGS 0-7    00000030   00052FC8   FFFFFFED   05C019CE8      000218C8   00021430   00019C64   00022CB0
      REGS 8-15   00019CC0   00019D28   00019CE8   00000000       40043656   00052768   40043694   9008B996

LOAD MODULE   GO
```

FIRST BYTE OF THIS PROGRAM   CARD   PAGE 0004

```
043640                                          90ECD00C 05C00700 4510C00E 0004373C   *..........0.............*      12
043660    8F04379C 0A135820 C0525A20 C0565020   C05A4110 C0E64100 C05F58F0 103005EF   *.........W...0...........*
043680    D200C063 C0E34110 C1464100 C05E58F0   103005EF 4510C046 8004379C 0A140000   *K...T.A...0.............*
0436A0    000098EC D00C07FE FFFFFFE9 00000004   FFFFFFED 40C1C2C3 C458C6C7 C8C94040   *.........Z....... ABCD.FGHI *
0436C0    40404040 40404040 40404040 40404040   40404040 40404040 40404040 40404040   *                            *
          LINE 0436E0 SAME AS ABOVE
043700    40404040 405C5C5C 5C5C5C5C 5C5C5C5C   5C5C5C5C 5C5C5C5C 5C5C5C5C 5C5C5C5C   *    .*******************.*
043720    5C5C5C5C 5C5C5C5C 5C5C5C5C 5C5C5C5C   5C5C5C5C 5C5C5C5C 5C5B0000 00000000   *.******************.....*
043740    2DC00000 00280001 01007EC8 00281C7E   01051878 07804000 04000001 04000001   *..........H.............*
043760    90000000 00545000 C001903C 12052AD8   00AA5D8 0B000001 00090780 00005000   *.........Q...Q..........*
043780    00052710 00051800 00051800 00000050   00000001 00000000 000AA088 00000100   *........................*
0437A0    2D000000 004A0012 01007EC8 0028008F   00050FA8 00000001 04000001 04000001   *..........H.............*
0437C0    94000000 E2E8E2D7 D9C9D5E3 02000050   00000001 0B000001 00000428 00000000   *....SYSPRINT............*
0437E0    00000000 00000000 00000001 00000085   00000001 00000000 00000000 00024670   *........................*

LOAD MODULE   IGC0A05A

04F960    418D0D99 18114313 0000IA81 41330001   95FF3000 47806068 1BEE1BFF 1B001811   *.T..................*
04F980    43E30000 43030001 8CE00004 88F0001C   8C000004 8810001C 1A2044E0 60701A1E   *.T.................*
04F9A0    41818001 44F06076 F3840069 D069DC07   D0962C6 41FFF001 44F0607C 418F8004   *.....0..3......F..0..0..*
04F9C0    413E3003 47F06010 41330001 47F060E2   D2008000 3002D200 D0692000 D2008000   *.......0.....O.SK...K...K..*
04F9E0    D0695050 D08C5000 D12094FC D1235800   D1201A10 5800D120 41110003 5010D064   *.........J..J.........*
04FA00    94FCD067 D703D06C D06C1810 54006290   1901478D 60BC1B10 401D06C 5813D064   *.....P.................*
04FA20    4A10D06C 1B005D00 66784000 D06A1211   4770611C 4810D06A 12114770 60E85850   *.....................Y..*
04FA40    D08C5860 D12407F5 41200121 45B06236   5820D120 413062C4 48A0D06A 4BA0D06C   *...J..5..J.......J...D...*
04FA60    88A00002 45B0623E 46A06104 9640D112   455062DA 948FD112 47F060DE 18A15810   *.........J......J..O.....*
04FA80    D12048ID D06C5010 D0704120 D0714580   62364810 D06C8810 00011A31 5820D120   *J........J............J.*
04FAA0    45B0623E 5020D120 9640D112 455062DA   948FD112 4810D06C 12114770 61984700   *.J...J.....J.......J.....*
04FAC0    615E4110 0001191A 47B061A6 18125B10   6678051F 10002000 47736IA6 4810D06E   *.........J........N.....*
04FAE0    41110001 4010D06A 41220020 5020D120   46A0615E 47F061B0 1B114010 D06C46A0   *.........J...O..........*
04FB00    611E47F0 60D44810 D06E1211 4780619E   5810D120 4800D06E 89000005 1B105010   *...0.M......J...........*
04FB20    D0704120 D0714810 D06E0610 12114770   6202D2D3 D09F629D 41306294 45B0623E   *...........K...........*
04FB40    D20DD0AA 62A29640 D1124550 62DA948F   D112D701 D06ED06E 12AA4780 600447F0   *K....J...J.P..........M.0*
04FB60    619ED204 D09F629D 41306297 45B0623E   9260D0AB 5810D120 5B106678 5010D070   *..K......................*
04FB80    4120D071 413D629A 45B0623E D20DD0B2   62A247F0 61E64130 628047F0 65744180   *.......K....O.W....0....*
04FBA0    D09995FF 30004780 627C1800 43030000   1B114313 00011A80 44106284 F384D070   *................3......*
04FBC0    D070DC07 D07062C6 41111001 4410628A   41330002 41220004 47F0623E 41330001   *....F...........0.......*
04FBE0    07FB0040 D2000070 20000200 8000D070   FFFFFFE0 0B02FF0C 02FF1302 FFD3C9D5   *....K...K..........LIN*
04FC00    C5E240E2 C1D4C540 C1E240C1 C2D6E5C5   0002FF09 0312031B 03240330 03390342   *ES SAME AS ABOVE.........*
04FC20    034B03FF 0903FF12 03F1B03 FF2403FF   3003FF39 03FF4203 FF0098E0 D08012EE   *........................*
```

Figure 6-3. (Continued)

```
04FC4J   47806310  D27CF000  D09441FF  007D50F0     D084411F  007D1910  47006330  1BFE40F0     *....K.O.........O.............. O*
04FC60   D090D203  E000D090  41FE0004  50F0D084     41100048  92201005  58F10008  58F0F030     *..K.........O..........1...OO.*
04FC80   05EF411J  DJ4858E0  100858F0  EJ3405EF     41100J01  4800D05C  9560D098  47406348     *.............O................*
04FCA0   47206346  1A011A01  1A019240  0098D277     D099D098  41100038  190147B0  636C4000     *.............K................*
04FCCO   DO5C9140  D1120715  47F060E2  4810D05E     41110001  4010D05E  92F1D098  D203D105     *... J...O.S........ ....1..K.J.*
04FCEJ   63AE4E1J  DO78F333  D1OAD07C  96FOD1OD     D2J1D05C  63B247F0  62DA98E0  D08012EE     *......3.J....OJ.K......O.......*
04FD00   0785411E  0004191F  078547F0  62FCD7C1     C7C5FFFF  07FEF0F1  F2F3F4F5  F6F7F8F9     *...........O..PAGE...0123456789*
04FD20   C1C2C3C4  C5C69120  D1384710  64C69101     D1384710  6684918J  D13947F0  6616910C     *ABCDEF.J...F..J.......J..O....*
04FD40   D1384750  64D29120  D1394710  64D29118     D1394750  64E29110  D1384710  64EE9102     *J...K.J....K.J...S..J.........*
04FD60   D1394710  64EE58E4  007C13EE  45506504     47F06418  47F06434  947FE020  58100010     *J.......U.......O...O.........*
04FD80   58B010C8  58BBJ028  188E18AE  47FJ668C     470J640C  94FE401D  D20BD098  652CD203     *....H........O......O....K....K.*
04FDA0   D124D128  455062DA  4550639A  9879D080     12774780  646A1B97  41000000  89000018     *J.J..........................*
04FDCO   16091817  41110000  0A0A58E0  D0609180     E0024780  64A24110  D070D070B  10001000     *........................P.....*
04FDE0   41E0656C  58F0D060  41FF0004  41300J04     92FF1000  42301001  50E01004  50FJ1008     *.....O.....................O..*
```

```
                                                                                    PAGE 0011
051760   20080332  J000001D  20080335  JOJOJ1CF     00000000  00000000  02091005  02091100     *.........................*
051780   00000000  00740D09  82000404  0001FD00     00000EE1  28C9C5C6  F3F7F5C9  4040D1D6     *....................IEF375I. JO*
0517AO   C24061C3  F2F9F1C4  C3D2D261  40E2E3C1     D9E34JF7  F2F1F8F3  48F1F3F1  F63CC9C5     **B .C291DCKK. START 72183.1316.IE*
0517CO   C6F3F7F6  C94040D1  D6C24061  C3F2F9F1     C4C3D2D2  6140E2E3  D6074040  F7F2F1F8     **F376I  JOB .C291DCKK. STOP  7218*
0517EO   F34BF1F3  F1F840C3  D7E44040  40F0D4C9     D540F1F6  48F8F9E2  C5C30000  00000000     **3.1318 CPU   OMIN 16.89SEC......*
```

(19)

END OF DUMP

```
COMPLETION CODE - SYSTEM=OC1  USER=0000
IEF242I ALLOC. FOR D227J   GO     STEP1    AT ABEND
IEF237I 335    ALLOCATED TO PGM=*.DD
IEF237I 335    ALLOCATED TO SYSPRINT
IEF237I 335    ALLOCATED TO SYSUDUMP
IEF237I 133    ALLOCATED TO SYSIN
IEF285I   SYS72143.T152143.RV000.D227J.GOSET           PASSED
IEF285I   VOL SER NOS= SCR004.
IEF285I   SYS72183.T152143.SV000.D227J.R0000133        SYSOUT
IEF285I   VOL SER NOS= SCR004.
IEF285I   SYS72183.T152143.SV000.D227J.R0000134        SYSOUT
IEF285I   VOL SER NOS= SCR004.
IEF285I   SYS72183.T152143.RV000.D227J.S0000135        SYSIN
IEF285I   VOL SER NOS= SCRJO1.
IEF285I   SYS72183.T152143.RV000.D227J.S0000135        DELETED
IEF285I   VOL SER NOS= SCR001.
IEF373I STEP /GO      / START 72183.1723
IEF374I STEP /GO      / STOP  72183.1723 CPU   OMIN 00.87SEC MAIN  16K LCS    OK

END OF STEP D227J  , GO    , CPU TIME= 0000000.87SEC,    ERT = 0000008.02SEC
          REGION ALLOCATED= J064K MAIN  0000K LCS   DISK EXCP = 00000003
          REGION USED    = 0016K MAIN  0000K LCS   RETURN CODE= 00000193

IEF285I   SYS72183.T073124.RV003.C.LOADSET            KEPT
IEF285I   VOL SER NOS= SCR005.
IEF285I   SYS72183.T152143.RVJ00.D227J.GOSET          DELETED
IEF285I   VOL SER NOS= SCR004.
IEF375I JOB /D227J    / START 72183.1721
IEF376I JOB /D227J    / STOP  72183.1723 CPU   OMIN 10.90SEC
```

(20)

Figure 6-3. (Continued)

calculates $A + B \rightarrow C$ or $-23 + 4 \rightarrow C$. The answer can be found in the dump to be $FFFFFFED_H = -19_{10}$. The second part of the program reads 80 characters from a card, replaces the fifth character with a dollar sign, and prints the result. The condition of the character string after the insertion of the dollar sign can be seen in two places: in the line printed by the   PUT   instruction and in the dump.

For this example the complete output is 20 pages long. The length is caused by several things. One is the expansion of the cataloged procedure ASMFCLG into a large number of job control statements which are printed in the listing in three groups. The statements in the expansions of the cataloged procedure have XX in columns 1 and 2. Another cause of additional length is the printing of a number of tables and messages to aid the user in following the progress of his program through assembly and execution. Some page-by-page comments on the output are as follows, where the page numbers refer to circled numbers in Figure 6-3.

Page   1. Listing of job card. Listing of job control statements for expansion of first step of cataloged procedure ASMFCLG, the assembler (ASM) step.

Page 2. External symbol dictionary. In this case the program contains only one control section, named SAMPLE.

Page 3. Listing of assembler language source statements and object code. The assembler instruction   PRINT   NOGEN   suppresses the listing of the macro expansions, but not the expansions themselves. For example, the MVC instruction at statement 23 has object code beginning at 000030, but the next two instructions, PUT at statement 24 and CLOSE at statement 29, are macro instructions whose expansions are not shown; so the next complete line shown in the listing corresponds to the DC instruction, statement 35, with object code beginning at 00004E.

Page 4. Relocation dictionary.

Page 5. Cross-reference table. This is also called the symbol table. It shows, for example, that the symbol CARD is defined in statement 42 to have the value 000065, and that symbol CARD is used in statements 23 and 20 (which is not shown because it is part of a macro expansion). An undefined symbol would be flagged in this table.

Page 6. Messages associated with the end of the first step (ASM) and the job control statements for the expansion of the second step (LKED) of the cataloged procedure ASMFCLG.

Page 7. Linkage editor cross-reference table. This is not particularly significant here since object code from other sources was not used in this job.

Page 8. Messages associated with the end of the second step (LKED) and the job control statements for the expansion of the third step, the execute or GO step, of the cataloged procedure ASMFCLG. The middle of this page also contains the single line of execution output from this program

ABCD$FGHI   · · ·   ******· ·

Pages   ABEND dump.
9-19.   This program contains a deliberate error to force a dump to be printed. The error is statement 35, DC X'00000000', which constitutes an illegal operation code. The ABEND dump that results is quite lengthy, and much of it is not needed to debug a simple program. However, some of it is quite important. On page 9, line 2, we find

COMPLETION CODE   SYSTEM = 0C1

This completion code is of the form 0Cx, where x is a hexadecimal digit that indicates the interruption code. In this case the interruption code is 1, indicating an operation-type interruption, as expected.[10]

On page 9, line 10, we find

APSW   700436A0

---

[10] For a list of the 16 interruption codes, see *Principles of Operation.* For all system completion codes, see *IBM System/360 Operating System Messages and Codes,* Form GC28-6631.

The right-hand six hexadecimal digits give the address where the interruption occurred.

The object code for this program as it lies in memory after the interruption has occurred is shown following the heading

LOAD MODULE   GO

at the bottom of page 11. The numbers in the left column are absolute hexadecimal addresses; the other numbers are the contents in hexadecimal of the corresponding bytes. Each line of the dump shows the contents of 32 bytes. At the right end of the line the same 32 bytes are printed as characters, except that only letters, digits, and blanks are printed correctly; all special characters and all bytes that do not correspond to a printable character are printed as periods. In this example the object code begins at location 043650 with contents 90ECD00C05C0 . . ., which can be seen to correspond to the first part of the object code generated by the assembler. Thus this program was relocated by 043650 bytes. To find where in this program the interruption occurred, we subtract, thus:

$$
\begin{array}{ll}
0436A0 & \text{absolute address of interruption} \\
-\ \underline{043650} & \text{relocation amount} \\
000050 & \text{relative address of interruption}
\end{array}
$$

This address, 000050, corresponds to the updated instruction address at the time the byte at relative address 00004E was discovered to be illegal as an operation code.

At the bottom of page 11 are shown the contents of the registers at termination. The sum

$$C = A + B = -23 + 4 = -19_{10} = \text{FFFFFFED}_H$$

is shown both in register 2 and in the dump of main memory at the location corresponding to symbol C, namely

$$
\begin{array}{ll}
043650 & \text{relocation amount} \\
+\ \underline{\quad 60} & \text{relative address of } C \text{ within program} \\
0436B0 & \text{absolute address of } C
\end{array}
$$

The string of characters beginning at CARD lies at address

$$
\begin{array}{l}
043650 \\
+\ \underline{\quad 65} \\
0436B5
\end{array}
$$

and contains the bytes C1 C2 C3 C4 5B C6 C7 . . ., which correspond to the graphics   A   B   C   D $ F   G   . . ..

The listing of load module GO takes a fraction of a page. The following pages, 13 to 19, contain listings of system-supplied modules, which were also in the memory as a part of the execution of this job. For example, the load modules with names IGG are related to opening and closing data sets. These are not significant to us in this example.[11]

Page 20. Messages associated with the end of the GO step. Some systems also give charge information (dollars or seconds) here.

The program in Figure 6-3 contains no error that the assembler can detect; hence the statement on page 5 of Figure 6-3:

NO STATEMENTS FLAGGED IN THIS ASSEMBLY

Figure 6-4 shows the result of an assembly in which the assembler did detect an error. The error is in statement 40

C   DC   1F

where the operand is illegal for the operation given. The error is flagged under the offending statement and there is an error message on page 6 of Figure 6-4. The error can be fixed either by changing DC to DS or by providing the required constant. No object code was generated for the offending statement and the location counter was not advanced, so the symbol C has the same value as the symbol LINE, that is, 000060, as shown in the cross-reference table (symbol table) on page 5 of Figure 6-4.

After an assembly in which an error is detected, execution will be attempted or not depending on the severity of the error. In this case execution was not attempted. The various error messages that Assembler F can produce and their severity codes are listed in *Assembler [F] Programmer's Guide,* Form GC26-3756.

SNAP DUMPS

Some programming errors are hard to find using only the assembler listing and a postexecution dump. Sometimes they are more easily found if the registers and/or main storage can be looked at one or more times during execution of the program. When running under O.S., one can obtain this information by using the SNAP macro. This produces a dump somewhat like the ABEND dump, but with the difference that execution resumes after the dump.

An example using two SNAP statements to produce two SNAP dumps is shown in Figures 6-5 and 6-6. Statement 20 of Figure 6-6 is

SNAP   DCB=ZZ,PDATA=(PSW,REGS,SA),STORAGE=(SAMPLE2,WW)

---

[11]For further information on ABEND dumps, see *IBM System/360 Operating System Programmers Guide to Debugging,* Form GC28-6670.

```
       LOC   OBJECT CODE     ADDR1 ADDR2  STMT   SOURCE STATEMENT                                    FO1OCT71  1/09/73

                                            1 * SAMPLE PROGRAM WITH SOURCE LANGUAGE ERROR
     000000                                  2 SAMPLE  CSECT
     000000 90EC DOOC              0000C      3         STM    14,12,12(13)   SAVE REGISTER CONTENTS
     000004 05C0                              4         BALR   12,0
     000006                                   5         USING  *,12
                                              6         PRINT  NOGEN          SUPPRESS MACRO EXPANSIONS
                                              7         OPEN   (XX,INPUT,YY,OUTPUT)
     000016 5820 C052              00058     15         L      2,A
     00001A 5A20 C056              0005C     16         A      2,B
     00001E 5020 C05A              00060     17         ST     2,C
                                             18         GET    XX,CARD
     000030 D200 C05F C0DF 00065 000E5      23         MVC    CARD+4(1),DOLLAR
                                             24         PUT    YY,LINE
                                             29         CLOSE  (YY)
     00004E 00000000                        35         DC     X'00000000'    ILLEGAL INSTRUCTION
     000052 98EC D00C              0000C     36         LM     14,12,12(13)   RESTORE REGISTER CONTENTS
     000056 07FE                             37         BCR    15,14
     000058 FFFFFFE9                         38 A       DC     F'-23'
     00005C 00000004                         39 B       DC     F'4'
                                             40 C       DC     1F

            *** ERROR ***
     000060 40                               41 LINE    DC     C' '           CARRIAGE CONTROL CHARACTER
     000061 4040404040404040                 42 CARD    DC     80C' '
     000081 5C5C5C5C5C5C5C5C                  43        DC     52C'*'
     0000E5 5B                               44 DOLLAR  DC     C'$'
                                             45 XX      DCB    DSORG=PS,RECFM=FB,MACRF=GM,DDNAME=SYSIN
                                             99 YY      DCB    DSORG=PS,RECFM=FBA,MACRF=PM,BLKSIZE=1064,    X
                                                               LRECL=133,DDNAME=SYSPRINT
                                            153         END
```

③

```
                                   CROSS-REFERENCE                                         PAGE    1

    SYMBOL    LEN   VALUE   DEFN     REFERENCES                                             1/09/73

    A         00004 000058 00038    0015
    B         00004 00005C 00039    0016
    C         00001 000060 00040    0017
    CARD      00001 000061 00042    0020  0023
    DOLLAR    00001 0000E5 00044    0023
    LINE      00001 000060 00041    0026
    SAMPLE    00001 000000 00002
    XX        00004 0000E8 00049    0011  0019
    YY        00004 000148 00103    0013  0025  0033
```

⑤

```
                                      DIAGNOSTICS                                          PAGE    1

    STMT   ERROR CODE    MESSAGE                                                           1/09/73

      40   IEU107     NEAR OPERAND COLUMN   3--INVALID OPERAND


       1 STATEMENT  FLAGGED IN THIS ASSEMBLY
       8 WAS HIGHEST SEVERITY CODE
    *STATISTICS*    SOURCE RECORDS (SYSIN) =    28     SOURCE RECORDS (SYSLIB) = 2787
    *OPTIONS IN EFFECT*   LIST, NODECK, LOAD, NORENT, XREF, NOTEST, ALGN, OS, NOTERM, LINECNT = 55
      59 PRINTED LINES
```

⑥

Figure 6-4.   Assembler F listing for a program that contains a source language error. Page boundaries in the original printer output are indicated by solid lines and circled numbers. Some pages are omitted.

This is an executable statement, which causes the printing of a SNAP dump.[12] The operand   PDATA=(PSW,REGS,SA)   says that the dump is to include the program status word (which among other things gives the updated instruction address at the time the SNAP macro is executed), the registers, and the save area trace. The operand STORAGE=(SAMPLE2,WW)   says to list the contents of main memory from SAMPLE2 to WW, which are symbols in this program. The SNAP macro also requires a

---

[12]For details, see *Supervisor Services and Macro Instructions,* Form GC28-6646.

```
//D227I  JCB   'U9329,TIME=2,SIZE=128K',BREARLEY,MSGLEVEL=(1,1)
//STEP1  EXEC  ASMFCLG
//ASM.SYSIN  DD  *
*   SAMPLE PROGRAM FCR ASSEMBLER F ILLUSTRATING USE OF SNAP MACRO
SAMPLE2  CSECT
         STM   14,12,12(13)
         BALR  12,0
         USING *,12
         PRINT NOGEN          SUPPRESS MACRO EXPANSIONS
         CPEN  (XX,INPUT,YY,OUTPUT,ZZ,OUTPUT)
         L     2,A
         A     2,B
         ST    2,C
         SNAP  CCB=ZZ,PCATA=(PSW,REGS,SA),STORAGE=(SAMPLE2,WW)
         GET   XX,CARD
         MVC   CARD+4(1),DOLLAR
         PUT   YY,LINE
         CLOSE (YY)
         SNAP  CCB=ZZ,PCATA=(PSW,REGS,SA),STORAGE=(SAMPLE2,WW)
         LM    14,12,12(13)
         BCR   15,14
A        CC    F'-23'
B        CC    F'4'
C        CS    1F
LINE     DC    C' '           CARRIAGE CCNTRCL CHARACTER
CARD     CC    80C' '
         CC    52C'*'
DOLLAR   CC    C'$'
XX       CCB   CSORG=PS,RECFM=FB,MACRF=GM,DDNAME=SYSIN
YY       CCB   DSCRG=PS,RECFM=FBA,MACRF=PM,BLKSIZE=1064,       X
               LRECL=133,DDNAME=SYSPRINT
ZZ       CCB   CCNAME=SNAPDUMP,CSORG=PS,RECFM=VBA,MACRF=(W),   X
               BLKSIZE=1632,LRECL=125
WW       CS    1F
         END
/*
//GO.SYSFRINT  DD   SYSCUT=A
//GO.SNAPDUMP  DD   SYSCUT=A
//GO.SYSLDUMP  CD   SYSCLT=A
//GO.SYSIN  CD   *
ABCDEFGHI
/*
```

Figure 6-5. Listing of a deck containing two SNAP instructions.

```
LOC   OBJECT CODE    ADDR1 ADDR2  STMT  SOURCE STATEMENT                                    F15OCT70  6/29/72

                                    1 *    SAMPLE PROGRAM FOR ASSEMBLER F ILLUSTRATING USE OF SNAP MACRO
000000                              2 SAMPLE2  CSECT
000000 90EC D00C       0000C        3          STM   14,12,12(13)
000004 05C0                         4          BALR  12,0
000006                              5          USING *,12
                                    6          PRINT NOGEN          SUPPRESS MACRO EXPANSIONS
                                    7          OPEN  (XX,INPUT,YY,OUTPUT,ZZ,OUTPUT)
00001A 5820 C09A       000A0       17          L     2,A
00001E 5A20 C09E       000A4       18          A     2,B
000022 5020 C0A2       000A8       19          ST    2,C
                                   20          SNAP  DCB=ZZ,PDATA=(PSW,REGS,SA),STORAGE=(SAMPLE2,WW)
                                   35          GET   XX,CARD
000058 D200 C0AB C12B 000B1 00131  40          MVC   CARD+4(1),DOLLAR
                                   41          PUT   YY,LINE
                                   46          CLOSE (YY)
                                   52          SNAP  DCB=ZZ,PDATA=(PSW,REGS,SA),STORAGE=(SAMPLE2,WW)
00009A 98EC D00C       0000C       67          LM    14,12,12(13)
00009E 07FE                        68          BCR   15,14
0000A0 FFFFFFE9                    69 A         DC    F'-23'
0000A4 00000004                    70 B         DC    F'4'
0000A8                             71 C         DS    1F
0000AC 40                          72 LINE      DC    C' '           CARRIAGE CONTROL CHARACTER
0000AD 4040404040404040            73 CARD      DC    80C' '
0000FD 5C5C5C5C5C5C5C5C            74          DC    52C'*'
000131 58                          75 DOLLAR    DC    C'$'
                                   76 XX        DCB   DSORG=PS,RECFM=FB,MACRF=GM,DDNAME=SYSIN
                                  130 YY        DCB   DSORG=PS,RECFM=FBA,MACRF=PM,BLKSIZE=1064,       X
                                                      LRECL=133,DDNAME=SYSPRINT
                                  184 ZZ        DCB   DDNAME=SNAPDUMP,DSORG=PS,RECFM=VBA,MACRF=(W),   X
                                                      BLKSIZE=1632,LRECL=125
00024C                            235 WW        DS    1F
                                  236          END
```

ABCDSFGHI   ***

Figure 6-6. Part of the output for the deck of Figure 6-5, which contains two SNAP instructions.

```
JOB D227I          STEP GO          TIME 222941   DATE 72181                          PAGE 0001

PSW AT ENTRY TO SNAP    FFE50033 500705FA

SAVE AREA TRACE

INTERRUPT AT 0705FA

REGS AT ENTRY TO SNAP

     FLTR 0-6      0001EFC0000000D8      00019C2800123714        00001C984000EA22    0012373800000000

     REGS 0-7      00000040   900705DC   FFFFFFED   5C01F290      00020F48   00022D90   0001F428   00024AD8
     REGS 8-15     0001F268   0001D7A0   0001F290   00000000      40070586   0007F768   000068A0   00000000

STORAGE

0705A0                                             90ECD00C 05C00700 4510C012 000706E4   *.............K..................U*
0705C0   0F070744 8F07C7A4 0A135820 C09A5A20       C09E5020 C0A20700 4510C03E 000084A4   *.................................*
0705E0   000707A4 00000000 00C705EC 000705B0       800707FC 92801014 0A334110 C12E4100   *............................A...*
070600   C0A758F0 103005EF D200C0A8 C12B4110       C18E4100 C0A658F0 103005EF 4510C06E   *...0....K...A...A........0......*
070620   80070744 0A140700 4510C08E 000084A4       000707A4 00000000 0007063C 000705B0   *.................................*
070640   000707FC 92801014 0A3398EC D00C07FE       FFFFFFE9 00000004 FFFFFFED 40404040   *.................Z..........     *
070660   40404040 40404040 40404040 40404040       40404040 40404040 40404040 40404040   *                                 *
         LINE 070680 SAME AS ABOVE
0706A0   40404040 40404040 40404040 405C5C5C       5C5C5C5C 5C5C5C5C 5C5C5C5C 5C5C5C5C   *             .....................*
0706C0   5C5C5C5C 5C5C5C5C 5C5C5C6C 5C5C5C5C       5C5C5C5C 5C5C5C5C 5C5C5C5C 5C5C5C5C   *.................................*
0706E0   5C5B0000 00000000 2D000000 002D0000       01007EC8 00281C7E 0107E878 07804000   *................H.......Y.....*
070700   C0000001 04000001 90000000 00685000       0001EE8C 1207F8E8 000AA5D8 0B000001   *.............8Y...Q....*
070720   00090780 00005000 0007F710 00000000       00000000 00000050 00000001 00000000   *...........7.................*
070740   000AA088 00000100 2D000000 007D0000       00007EC8 00281C7E 0207DFA8 00004000   *.................H...........*
070760   00000001 0400C001 94000000 002C0050       0001E48C 920AA720 000AA4D8 0B000001   *............U........Q....*
070780   00090428 30040048 +207F660 0007E3D8       00070FB0 00000000 00000001 00000000   *........6....TQ...........*
0707AC   000AA268 00000100 2D000000 00B00000       01007EC8 00281577 00000001 00004000   *.................H...........*
0707C0   00000001 04000001 54000000 00400020       0001C5F4 920A9C50 000A9B28 0B000001   *..............E4............*
0707E0   00000660 30040048 41C7F608 010AA268       000AA268 0000007D 00000001 41110000   *............6..................*

END OF DUMP
```

```
JOB D227I          STEP GO          TIME 222943   DATE 72181                          PAGE 0001

PSW AT ENTRY TO SNAP    FFE50033 7007064A

SAVE AREA TRACE

INTERRUPT AT 07064A

REGS AT ENTRY TO SNAP

     FLTR 0-6      0001EFC0000000D8      00019C2800123714        00001C984000EA22    0012373800000000

     REGS 0-7      000C0030   8007062C   FFFFFFED   5C01F290      00020F48   00022D90   0001F428   00024AD8
     REGS 8-15     0001F268   0001D7A0   0001F290   00000000      40070586   0007F768   4007061C   90088996

STORAGE

0705A0                                             90ECD00C 05C00700 4510C012 000706E4   *.............K..................U*
0705C0   0F070744 8F0707A4 0A135820 C09A5A20       C09E5020 C0A20700 4510C03E 000084A4   *.................................*
0705E0   000707A4 00000000 000705EC 000705B0       800707FC 92801014 0A334110 C12E4100   *............................A...*
070600   C0A758F0 103005EF D200C0A8 C12B4110       C18E4100 C0A658F0 103005EF 4510C06E   *...0....K...A...A........0......*
070620   80070744 0A140700 4510C08E 000084A4       000707A4 00000000 0007063C 000705B0   *.................................*
07064C   800707FC 92801014 0A3398EC D00C07FE       FFFFFFE9 00000000 FFFFFFED 40C1C2C3   *.................Z........ABC*
070660   C45B8C6C7 C8C94040 40404040 40404040       40404040 40404040 40404040 40404040   *D.FGHI                      *
070680   40404040 40404040 40404040 40404040       40404040 40404040 40404040 40404040   *                            *
0706A0   40404040 40404040 40404040 405C5C5C       5C5C5C5C 5C5C5C5C 5C5C5C5C 5C5C5C5C   *             .....................*
0706C0   5C5C5C5C 5C5C5C5C 5C5C5C5C 5C5C5C5C       5C5C5C5C 5C5C5C5C 5C5C5C5C 5C5C5C5C   *.................................*
0706E0   5C5B0000 00000000 2D000000 002D0000       01007EC8 00281C7E 0107E878 07804000   *................H.......Y.....*
070700   00000001 04000001 90C00000 00685000       C001EE8C 1207F8E8 000AA5D8 0B000001   *.............8Y...Q....*
070720   00090780 00005000 0007F710 0007E8D0       0007E8D0 00000050 00000001 00000000   *...........7...Y...Y..........*
070740   000AA088 00000100 2D000000 007D0000       01007EC8 0028008F 0007DFA8 00004000   *.................H...........*
070760   00000001 04000001 94000000 E2E8E2D7       D9C9D5E3 02000050 00000001 0B000001   *...........SYSPRINT...........*
070780   00000428 00000000 00C00000 00000000       00000001 00000085 00000001 00000000   *.............................*
0707A0   00000000 00000100 2D000000 00B00000       04007EC8 00280579 00000001 00004000   *.................H...........*
0707C0   00000001 04000001 54000000 00400020       0001C5F4 920A9C50 000A9B28 0B000001   *..............E4............*
0707E0   00000660 30040048 41C7F608 010AA268       000AA268 0000007D 00000001 41110000   *............6..................*

END OF DUMP
```

Figure 6-6.   (Continued)

corresponding DCB macro (here named **ZZ**) to denote the output data set. SNAP also requires a DD card

        //GO.SNAPDUMP   DD   SYSOUT=A

Figure 6-6 contains two SNAP macros (statements 20 and 52) and two SNAP dumps. The single line of execution output appears before the two SNAP dumps, even though the assembler language program indicates the execution output should come between them. This occurs because the execution output is put into one data set (SYSPRINT) and all the dumps are put into another data set (SNAPDUMP); then, in this case, all of SYSPRINT is printed followed by all of SNAPDUMP.

CONCLUSION

In this chapter we have described some of the mechanical details of executing a program using Assembler F and Operating System, including input-output macros and the obtaining of debugging information. This was only a brief introduction to the subject, not a complete treatment. The reader who wishes to learn more should consult the appropriate manuals.

The reader should not be content with merely reading this chapter. He should actually run problems using Assembler F or a student assembler if he has access to one. At this stage the problems that can be run will be somewhat limited. But some rather substantial programs can be written after we cover branching and loops in Chapter 7.

EXERCISES

1. Run the program for Exercise 4, Chapter 4, on the computer, obtain a postexecution dump, and answer the following questions.
   a. Where was the program loaded?
   b. What was the contents of base register after setting?

c. Fill in the following table in hexadecimal:

Variable Name	Address as Assembled	Address as Executed	Contents as Assembled	Contents After Execution	OK? Yes or No. (if no, explain)
a					
b					
c					
d					
e					
f					
g					
x					

d. For the first RX instruction in the program, carry out the calculation of the effective address of the second operand at execution time and show that it is correct.

2. Introduce an error into the program of Exercise 1, such as changing the spelling of DC to DG, and rerun it.
   a. Find and explain all assembly-time error messages.
   b. Find and explain all execution-time error messages.

3. Show by several methods that in Figure 6-6 the first SNAP dump corresponds to the first SNAP instruction and the second SNAP dump corresponds to the second SNAP instruction, and not vice versa. How many distinct ways can you show this?

4. Here is the object code from an assembly

   05805890 800E5C80 800E5090 800E07FE 00000017 FFFFFF1F

   Reconstruct the assembler language source program as far as possible, inventing symbolic addresses where needed. Explain what will happen when this program is executed.

7

Branching, loops, and arrays

An important feature of any computer language is a *branch* statement, a statement that allows the flow of control to follow one of two or more paths, depending upon some condition. For example, the Fortran language contains a logical IF statement that allows one of two branches to be chosen, depending on whether a logical expression is true or false. The Fortran language also contains an arithmetic IF statement that allows one of three branches to be chosen, depending on whether an arithmetic expression is negative, zero, or positive.

In the 360, branching is done by the instruction Branch on Condition. An example is shown in Figure 7-1. In this example the statement   BC   2,PLUS   says to branch to PLUS if the result of the previous addition is positive. If the result is zero or negative, then take the next instruction in sequence, the one named ELSE. The instruction   BC   15,JJ   says to branch unconditionally, that is, always branch, to JJ. This is analogous to the unconditional branch statement in Fortran, the GO TO statement.

The 360 computer remembers the result of one of the recent operations in a four-state (two-bit) memory called a condition code. Some instructions set the condition code and some do not. Thus the present state of the condition code sometimes represents the result of the most recent operation, and sometimes it represents the result of an

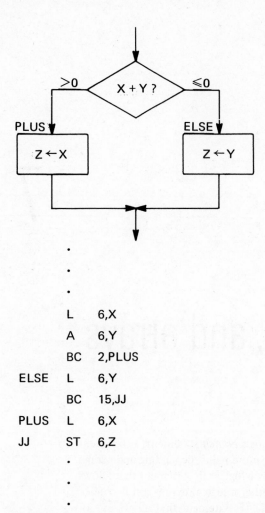

```
              L    6,X
              A    6,Y
              BC   2,PLUS
ELSE          L    6,Y
              BC   15,JJ
PLUS          L    6,X
JJ            ST   6,Z
```

Figure 7-1. Program segment illustrating the Branch on Condition instruction. Symbols X, Y, and Z are presumed to be defined elsewhere in the program.

operation several instructions earlier. For example, after fixed-point arithmetic the condition code will represent the following:

Condition Code (Binary) (Decimal)	00 0	01 1	10 2	11 3
After fixed-point add, subtract	Result $= 0$	Result < 0	Result > 0	Overflow occurred
After fixed-point multiply, divide	Condition code remains unchanged			
After load, store	Condition code remains unchanged			

The condition code can be tested by a branch on condition instruction. There are two formats.

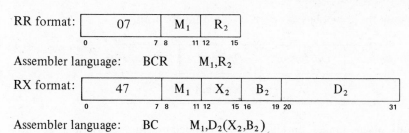

RR format:

Assembler language: BCR M_1,R_2

RX format:

Assembler language: BC $M_1,D_2(X_2,B_2)$

Meaning: The first operand lies in bit positions 8 to 11 of the instruction and is called a *mask*. The mask indicates what condition codes are to be examined. If any of these codes are found to be true, then the normal flow of control is altered by branching to the address indicated by the second operand. If none of the condition codes indicated by the mask is true, then no branch occurs and the next instruction in sequence is executed.

In machine language the mask is a four-bit integer lying in bits 8 to 11 of the instruction. In assembler language the mask is written as a decimal integer in the range 0 to 15. Some examples are as follows:

Mask bit position	8	9	10	11
Weight	8	4	2	1
Example 1 (mask = 2)	0	0	1	0
Example 2 (mask = 12)	1	1	0	0

The correspondence between mask bits and the four condition codes (CC) is as follows:

Mask bit position	8	9	10	11
Condition code	0	1	2	3

In example 1, when the mask contains a 1 in bit position 10 as in   BC   2,symbol, then branching will occur whenever CC = 2, for example, after a fixed-point addition whose result is > 0. In example 2, when the mask value is $1100_2 = 12_{10}$ as in BC   12,symbol, then branching will occur when CC = 0 or CC = 1. This corresponds to branching after a fixed-point addition whose result is 0 or < 0. The meanings of the various masks are not easy to remember, so tables similar to the table on page 114 are provided in *Principles of Operation* and on the reference data card, Form GX20-1703.

Another convenience is that the assembler provides *extended mnemonics*. For example, the assembler will accept a statement of the form

Name	Operation	Operand	Comments
	BP	Symbol	

and generate exactly the same object code as it would for the form

Name	Operation	Operand	Comments
	BC	2,symbol	

The mnemonic BP means Branch on Plus. Other extended mnemonics useful after fixed-point arithmetic instructions are as follows:

Extended Form			Ordinary Form		Meaning
BO	symbol	=	BC	1,symbol	Branch on Overflow
BM	symbol	=	BC	4,symbol	Branch on Minus
BZ	symbol	=	BC	8,symbol	Branch on Zero
BNP	symbol	=	BC	13,symbol	Branch on Not Plus
BNM	symbol	=	BC	11,symbol	Branch on Not Minus
BNZ	symbol	=	BC	7,symbol	Branch on Not Zero

These are all RX instructions. In each case where "symbol" appears, the operand may also be written in the explicit displacement-index-base form, D(X,B).

There are two special cases. A mask value of $1111_2 = 15_{10}$ means always branch, and a mask value of $0000_2 = 0_{10}$ means never branch—this is also called a "no operation." The extended forms are

B	symbol	=	BC	15,symbol	Branch Unconditionally
BR	R_2	=	BCR	15,R_2	Branch Unconditionally
NOP	symbol	=	BC	0,symbol	No Operation
NOPR	R_2	=	BCR	0,R_2	No Operation

Note that most of the extended mnemonics are for the RX format. For example, there is no extended mnemonic for an RR branch on plus.

Example: Write a program segment to raise $X = C(R2)$ to the nth power, where $n = C(R5)$. Leave the result in register 7. Assume that all products will be single length.

The strategy we shall use is to repeatedly multiply a product, initially 1, by X, each time decrementing n by 1. When n gets to zero, the product will be X^n. A table describing the sequence of results for the case $X = 3$ and $n = 4$ is as follows:

	Product	C(R5)
Before first trip through loop	1	4
After first trip through loop	3	3
After second trip through loop	9	2
After third trip through loop	27	1
After fourth trip through loop	81	0

A flow chart and program that correspond to this table are shown in Figure 7-2.

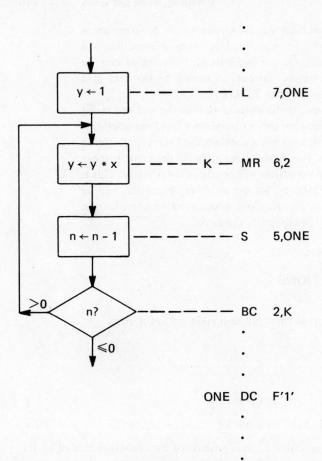

Figure 7-2. A program segment containing a loop.

LOOPS

The repetitive execution of a portion of a program is called *looping*. In general, a loop contains three parts:

1. The initialization part. This portion is usually executed only once. It initializes variables, sets up counters, and so on, in preparation for the repetitive part that follows.

2. The repetitive part.

3. The end test. This causes the flow of control to return to the repetitive part again and again until some condition occurs, such as a counter reaching a certain value or a certain value becoming negative.

In the example in Figure 7-2, the initialization part is the statement L, the repetitive part is the statements MR and S, and the end test is the statement BC.

The number of times a loop is to be traversed may be known to the programmer at the time he writes the program; for example, he may want to write a loop that will multiply a number by itself exactly nine times. On the other hand, the number may be unknown to the programmer, or not immediately obvious, as would be the case in a program to find the largest power of 13 that is less than 1,000,000.

It is easy to make errors in writing loops. If the initialization or the end test is not quite right, then the loop may be traversed one time more or one time less than intended. To avoid this, it is frequently helpful to construct a table showing the values of pertinent quantities each time through the loop, as in the previous example. If the error is more serious, the end test may fail completely, and execution will continue indefinitely. This is called an *infinite loop,* but it is not really infinite. Sooner or later, execution will be terminated by some secondary error (such as an overflow, protection, or specification interruption), by the executive system, or by the computer operator.

MORE FIXED-POINT INSTRUCTIONS

Some other fixed-point instructions that set the condition code are as follows:

Compare

RR version: CR R_1,R_2 op code 19

RX version: C $R_1,D_2(X_2,B_2)$ op code 59

Meaning: Compare the first operand, that is, the contents of the register indicated by R_1, with the second operand and set the condition code as follows:

Operands are equal   CC = 0
First operand $<$ second operand   CC = 1
First operand $>$ second operand   CC = 2

CC = 3 is not used. The comparisons are arithmetic. Neither of the operands is changed.

Load and test

RR version: LTR R_1,R_2 op code 12

Meaning: Same as   LR R_1,R_2; that is, copy the contents of the register indicated by R_2 into the register indicated R_1, except also set the condition code as indicated in the following table. (The instruction LR does not change the condition code.)

Load complement

RR version: LCR R_1,R_2 op code 13

Meaning: Similar to   LTR R_1,R_2 except copy the two's complement of the second operand into the first operand location. (The two's complement of a number is obtained by subtracting that number from zero.) Because the two's complement number system is not symmetric about zero, the most negative number, -2^{31} = X'80000000' cannot be complemented. Attempting to complement this most negative number will give an overflow interruption. The resulting condition codes are indicated in the table.

Load positive

RR version: LPR R_1,R_2 op code 10

Meaning: Similar to LCR except the absolute value of the second operand is copied into the first operand location.

Load negative

RR version: LNR R_1,R_2 op code 11

Meaning: Similar to LCR except the negative of the absolute value of the second operand is copied into the first operand location. Overflow cannot occur.

The condition codes resulting from these instructions are as follows:

Condition code	0	1	2	3
Mask bit	8	9	10	11
Weight	8	4	2	1
Compare (A:B)	A=B	A<B	A>B	—
Load and Test	=0	<0	>0	—
Load Complement	=0	<0	>0	overflow
Load Negative	=0	<0	—	—
Load Positive	=0	—	>0	overflow

An instruction that is frequently useful in connection with branching is Load Address.

Load address

Machine format [RX]:

41	R_1	X_2	B_2	D_2
0 7	8 11	12 15	16 19	20 31

Assembler format: LA $R_1,D_2(X_2,B_2)$

Meaning: The address of the second operand (calculated by the usual rules for address arithmetic) is inserted into the low-order 24 bits of the register indicated by R_1. The left-hand 8 bits of the register are set to zero.

This instruction does *not* refer to storage. That is,

    LA   6,12(0,10)

says "take the contents of register 10, add 12, insert this number in register 6." [On the other hand, the Load instruction *does* refer to storage and

$$L \qquad 6,12(0,10)$$

says "take the contents of register 10, add 12, go to storage, get the corresponding four-byte word, insert this word in register 6."]

The LA instruction is useful for initializing a register. For example, the statement

$$LA \qquad 6,300$$

which is equivalent to

$$LA \qquad 6,300(0,0)$$

tells the computer to construct an effective address,

$$EA = 300 + 0 + 0 = 300$$

and insert this number in register 6.

The LA instruction can also be used to increment a register. The statement

$$LA \qquad 6,4(0,6)$$

will have the effect

$$R6 \leftarrow 4 + C(R6) + 0$$

The LA instruction is also used to load an address into a register prior to branching with a BCR instruction. For example, the two instructions

$$LA \qquad 6,HAT$$
$$BCR \qquad 11,6$$

result in the same branching as the single instruction

$$BC \qquad 11,HAT$$

EXERCISES

```
1. START     SR      2,2
             L       3,ONE
             L       4,TH
   LOOP      A       2,ONE
             AR      3,2
             CR      3,4
             BC      12,LOOP
             ST      2,X
             ST      3,Y
             BCR     15,14
   ONE       DC      F'1'
   TH        DC      F'13'
   X         DS      1F
   Y         DS      1F
```

Execution of this program segment begins at START. Make a table showing the contents of registers 2, 3, and 4 as execution progresses. Find the contents of X and Y at the end of execution.

```
2. BEGIN     SR      2,2
             L       3,A
   K         A       3,B
             BCR     4,14
             A       2,D
   J         BC      15,K
   A         DC      F'8'
   B         DC      F'-2'
   D         DC      F'-1'
```

Execution of this program segment begins at BEGIN. Make a table showing the contents of registers 2 and 3 each time statement J is executed. What will be the contents of registers 2 and 3 when the branch to the address in register 14 occurs?

3. In a loop the end test does not necessarily have to be performed last. Rewrite the example of Figure 7-2, putting the end test before the multiplication.

4. Write a program to calculate the thirteenth power of 3. Leave the result in register 7.

5. Write a program to find the largest integer N such that $13^N < 1,000,000$. Leave N in register 7 and leave 13^N in register 9.

6. Write a program to find the largest power of 9 that will fit correctly in a 32-bit full word. Before writing the program, write a one-paragraph description of how a product could fail to fit in a four-byte word and how this can be tested for.

7. Let N and S be defined recursively as follows:

$$N_0 = 0$$

$$S_0 = 0$$

$$N_{i+1} = N_i + 1$$

$$S_{i+1} = S_i + N_{i+1}$$

a. Calculate N_9 by hand.

b. Write a program to calculate N_9. It is not necessary to keep all the values of N and S calculated to date; it can be done by keeping just the latest values.

ARRAYS

A one-dimensional array is a vector, indicated in mathematical notation as

$$(a_1, a_2, a_3, \ldots, a_n)$$

where each a_i is an *element* of the array and i is a subscript or *index*. For example, the one-dimensional array

$$(16, 13, -9, 75, 0, 0, 16)$$

has seven elements, and the elements are integers.

The usual way to store a one-dimensional array in a computer memory is to store the individual elements consecutively and contiguously in some part of the memory. For example, in the 360, full-word integers require four bytes of memory, so the array of full-word integers in the previous paragraph might be stored in successive full-word locations, beginning at location 006A08, as follows:

Algebraic Notation for the Element	Address (Hex)	Contents (Decimal)	Addressable in Assembler Language as
a_1	006A08	16	A
a_2	006A0C	13	A+4
a_3	006A10	-9	A+8
a_4	006A14	75	A+12
a_5	006A18	0	A+16
a_6	006A1C	0	A+20
a_7	006A20	16	A+24

In assembler language this could be achieved by defining a seven-word area of memory with the statement

```
A       DS      7F
```

and then filling the array with appropriate numbers at execution time. Or the area might be both defined and filled at assembly time by the statement

```
A       DC      F'16,13,-9,75,0,0,16'
```

A two-dimensional array may be indicated pictorially as a rectangular arrangement:

$$a_{11} \quad a_{12} \quad a_{13} \quad a_{14}$$
$$a_{21} \quad a_{22} \quad a_{23} \quad a_{24}$$
$$a_{31} \quad a_{32} \quad a_{33} \quad a_{34}$$

where the first subscript indicates the row number (here there are three rows) and the second subscript indicates the column number (here there are four columns). There are two standard ways to store a rectangular array into a (linear) memory. One is called "by columns" and is as indicated[1]:

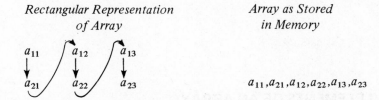

Rectangular Representation of Array   *Array as Stored in Memory*

$$a_{11}, a_{21}, a_{12}, a_{22}, a_{13}, a_{23}$$

The other way to store an array is called "by rows" and is as indicated:

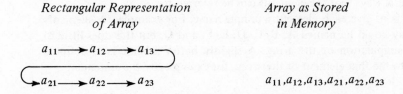

Rectangular Representation of Array   *Array as Stored in Memory*

$$a_{11}, a_{12}, a_{13}, a_{21}, a_{22}, a_{23}$$

Both these schemes may be extended to arrays of dimensionally higher than 2. The "by-columns" scheme is extended by allowing the leftmost index to vary most rapidly. In this scheme the elements of a $2 \times 2 \times 3$ array would be stored in the following order:

```
1 1 1
2 1 1
1 2 1
2 2 1
1 1 2
2 1 2
1 2 2
2 2 2
1 1 3
2 1 3
1 2 3
2 2 3
```

---

[1] In the Fortran language, arrays are treated as stored by columns, in the PL/I language as stored by rows.

The "by-rows" scheme can be extended to higher dimensions by allowing the rightmost index to vary most rapidly. In this scheme the elements of a $2 \times 2 \times 3$ array would be stored in the following order:

```
1  1  1
1  1  2
1  1  3
1  2  1
1  2  2
1  2  3
2  1  1
2  1  2
2  1  3
2  2  1
2  2  2
2  2  3
```

REFERENCING ELEMENTS OF AN ARRAY

In referring to elements of an array in assembler language, one cannot refer to "a_3." However, there are several ways that the elements can be referred to.

A primitive way is to give each element a unique name. For example, the elements of a seven-element array could be named A, B, C, D, E, F, and G, but this does little to facilitate systematic manipulation of the array. A slightly better scheme is to define a symbol to correspond to the first element of the array, for example, by the statement

```
A     DS     7F
```

or

```
A     DC     F'16,13,-9,75,0,0,16'
```

and then refer to the other elements with arithmetic expressions, such as A+8, meaning "the value of the symbol A plus 8 bytes." Thus one could add the third and fifth elements of array A and store the sum in the fifth element with the statements

```
L      2,A+8
A      2,A+16
ST     2,A+16
```

A disadvantage of this scheme is that the meaning of the expression A+16 is fixed at assembly time. It cannot be changed at execution time, as would be desirable, for example, if one wished to search through a whole array for an element with a particular value.

INDEXING

The most versatile way to refer to individual elements of an array is by use of an index register. Recall that an RX operand of the form $D_2(X_2,B_2)$ refers to an area in memory whose address is

$$D_2 + C(X_2) + C(B_2)$$

where an index field or a base field of zero means to add zero, not the contents of register 0. In the examples up to now, the index has always been 0. Using symbolic addresses, we have written RX instructions such as

    ST   6,ANS

for which the assembler generated an appropriate base and displacement and an index of 0. On the other hand, if we write

    ST   6,ANS(11)

the assembler will generate object code with base and displacement fields corresponding to ANS as before, and it will also generate an index field containing $11_{10} = B_H$. Later on, at execution time, if we can cause the contents of the index register to vary appropriately we can make the effective address step through the array.

For example, Figure 7-3 shows a program to define a 100-word area and set it to zero (at execution time, not at assembly time). There are some small differences between the flow chart and the assembler language versions of the program. The flow chart is written in a flow chart notation wherein the array elements are denoted a_1, a_2, a_3, . . ., a_{100} and the index begins at 1 and steps by one. The assembler language version is written using register 11 for an index, and the contents of R11 begin at 0 and are stepped by four, because the addresses of consecutive full words differ by four bytes. The sequence of events is indicated in the table:

Trip Through Loop	C(R11) at Execution of Store Instruction	Effective Address of the Store Instruction
First	0	A + 0
Second	4	A + 4
Third	8	A + 8
.	.	.
.	.	.
.	.	.
One hundredth	396	A + 396

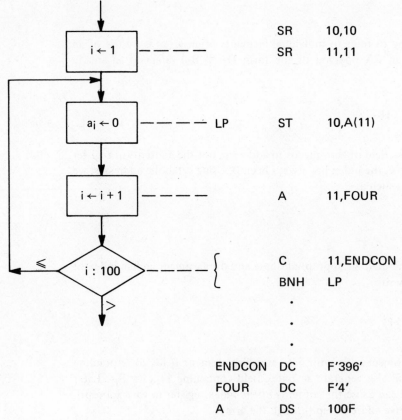

	SR	10,10
	SR	11,11
LP	ST	10,A(11)
	A	11,FOUR
	C	11,ENDCON
	BNH	LP
ENDCON	DC	F'396'
FOUR	DC	F'4'
A	DS	100F

Figure 7-3.   A program segment to set to zero a 100-word array.

An assembler listing for the program of Figure 7-3 is shown in Figure 7-4. Note that the object code for   ST   10,A(11)   is 50ABC022, and the index field is B, as expected. Part of the ABEND dump caused by the deliberate illegal instruction is also shown in Figure 7-4. Note that the 400_{10} bytes from 5266C through 527FB were set to zero, as expected.

To refer to an element of a multidimensional array, one must calculate an offset within the array using the subscripts and the dimensions of the array. For example, in a 2 $\times$ 2 $\times$ 3 array that is stored by columns, the offset from the beginning of the array to element (i, j, k) is

$$4 * [(i - 1) + 2 * (j - 1) + 4 * (k - 1)]$$

or, in general,

$$w * [(i - 1) + d_1 * (j - 1) + d_1 * d_2 * (k - 1)]$$

where w is the width of each item in the array (four bytes in the preceding example) and d_1 and d_2 are the first and second dimensions of the array. For an element whose subscripts are not known until execution time, the program must calculate this offset at execution time.

```
LOC   OBJECT CODE    ADDR1 ADDR2   STMT    SOURCE STATEMENT                           F15OCT70   7/14/71

000000                              1  INDEX    CSECT
000000  05C0                        2           BALR  12,0
000002                              3           USING *,12
000002  1BAA                        4           SR    10,10
000004  1BBB                        5           SR    11,11
000006  50AB C022          00024    6  LP       ST    10,A(11)
00000A  5AB0 C01E          00020    7           A     11,FOUR
00000E  59B0 C01A          0001C    8           C     11,ENDCON
000012  47D0 C004          00006    9           BNH   LP
000016  00000000                   10           DC    X'00000000'
00001A  0000
00001C  0000018C                   11  ENDCON   DC    F'396'
000020  00000004                   12  FOUR     DC    F'4'
000024                             13  A        DS    100F
                                   14           END
```

SAVE AREA TRACE

INTERRUPT AT 052660

```
REGS AT ENTRY TO ABEND

   FLTR 0-6    0F00000004017A48     1001B3D468000000          0000400001FFFFFF     8B000000FF07F0E0

   REGS 0-7    FD000008   000617F8   0001F2E0   5C01D510      000184D0   000182F0   0001BF64   00018DF0
   REGS 8-15   0001D4E8   00017308   00000000   00000190      4005264A   00061768   0000CEC8   01052648
LOAD MODULE    GO

052640                   05C01BAA 1BBB50AB     C0225AB0 C01E59B0 C01A47D0 C0040000   *..............................*
052660   00000000 0000018C 00000004 00000000   00000000 00000000 00000000 00000000   *..............................*
052680   00000000 00000000 00000000 00000000   00000000 00000000 00000000 00000000   *..............................*
         LINES 0526A0-0527C0 SAME AS ABOVE
0527F0   00000000 00000000 00000000 00000000   00000000 00000000 00000000 600047F0   *.............................0*
```

Figure 7-4. Assembler listing and part of the dump for the program of Figure 7-3.

MORE INSTRUCTIONS FOR BRANCHING

The Branch on Condition instruction described previously is quite sufficient, in conjunction with the arithmetic instructions, for the construction of any kind of loop. However, certain kinds of loops are so common that the 360 includes special branch instructions to implement them in one instruction, instead of in the two or more instructions that would otherwise be needed. The instructions are BXLE, BXH, and BCT.

Branch on index low or equal

Machine format [RS]: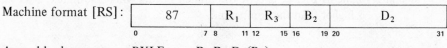

Assembler language: BXLE $R_1,R_3,D_2(B_2)$

Meaning: The register indicated by R_1 is considered to contain an index; the register indicated by R_3 contains an increment. There is a comparand register, which is odd and is either one larger than R_3 or equal to R_3. The branch address is indicated by $D_2(B_2)$. The effect of the instruction is to add the increment to the index to form a sum. If the sum is less than or equal to the comparand, then branch to the branch address. If the sum is greater than the comparand, do not branch. In either case, store the sum in the index before going on to the next instruction. (Note that the branch address is determined before the index is incremented.)

For example, let

$$C(R2) = 0 \qquad \text{index}$$
$$C(R4) = 4 \qquad \text{increment}$$
$$C(R5) = 20 \qquad \text{comparand}$$

Then the instruction   BXLE   2,4,QRS   in a suitable loop will cause the index to assume the following sequence of values:

$$0, 4, 8, 12, 16, 20$$

On the next trip the index will be incremented to 24 and the branch will not be taken.

If R_3 is odd, the increment and the comparand are in the same register. For example, let

$$C(R2) = -10 \qquad \text{index}$$
$$C(R5) = +2 \qquad \text{increment and comparand}$$

Then the instruction   BXLE   2,5,XYZ   will cause the index to take on the following sequence of values:

$$-10, -8, -6, -4, -2, 0, +2$$

The exit from the loop will occur on the next trip after the index is incremented to +4.

Branch on index high

Machine format [RS]:

86	R_1	R_3	B_2	D_2
0	7 8	11 12	15 16 19 20	31

Assembler language: BXH $R_1,R_3,D_2(B_2)$

Meaning: Same as BXLE, except the branch occurs when the index, after incrementing, is higher than the comparand.

For example, let

$$C(R2) = 10 \qquad \text{index}$$
$$C(R5) = -2 \qquad \text{increment and comparand}$$

Then the instruction   BXH   2,5,LOOP   will cause the index to take on the following sequence of values:

10, 8, 6, 4, 2, 0

On the next trip, the index will be incremented to −2 and the branch will not be taken.

Using the BXLE instruction, the example of Figure 7-3 would become

```
        SR      10,10
        SR      11,11       index
        LA      8,4         increment
        LA      9,396       comparand
LP      ST      10,A(11)
        BXLE    11,8,LP
        .
        .
        .
```

Here the loop contains only two instructions versus the four instructions in the version of Figure 7-3. This is a worthwhile saving in programmer effort, execution time, and bytes needed for program storage.

Branch on count

Machine format [RR]:

06	R_1	R_2

0   7 8   11 12   15

Assembler language: BCTR R_1,R_2

Machine format [RX]:

46	R_1	X_2	B_2	D_2

0   7 8   11 12   15 16   19 20   31

Assembler language: BCT $R_1,D_2(X_2,B_2)$

Meaning: The contents of the register indicated by R_1 is reduced by 1. When the result is zero, normal instruction sequencing occurs. When the result is not zero, branch to the address indicated by the second operand. In BCTR, if $R_2 = 0$, then count without branching.

EXERCISES

1. Write a flow chart and a program to store the integers 1, 2, 3, . . ., 100 into 100 consecutive full words in the memory. Run it on the computer, obtain a postexecution dump, and verify that it did what was intended. In the dump find the contents of the variable(s) used for loop control and explain its value.

   a. Use BC for loop control.

b. Use BCT for loop control.

c. Use BXH or BXLE for loop control.

2. Generate object code by hand for the following program.

Loc	Object Code	Source Statement		
		PR	CSECT	
			BALR	12,0
			USING	*,12
			LA	2,8
			LA	3,20
			LA	4,TABLE
			SR	5,5
			SR	6,6
		K	A	6,4(5,4)
			BXLE	5,2,K
			BCR	15,14
		TABLE	DC	F'16,13,19,-1,-21,16,3,16,-9'
			END	

3. For the program of Exercise 2, make a table showing the contents of registers 2, 3, 4, 5, and 6 as execution proceeds.

4. PQR is a 3 × 4 array of 32-bit integers. Assume it is stored in memory so that element   PQR (1,1)   is at address 006A30. Construct a memory map showing the address of each element of PQR. What is the absolute address of element   PQR (2,3)?

a. Assume that the array is stored by rows.

b. Assume that the array is stored by columns.

5. ABC is a 3 × 5 array of 32-bit integers stored in memory with element   ABC (1,1) at symbolic address ABC. Write a program segment to find the biggest element in array ABC and leave it in register 7. Assume the array is stored by rows or by columns as you prefer. Which is easier? Explain why.

6. Write a program segment to find the biggest element in the jth column of array ABC (as defined in Exercise 5), where $1 \leqslant j \leqslant 5$, and $j = C(R6)$ when execution of this program segment begins. Is it easier by rows or by columns? Why?

7. Write a complete program to define a 3 × 4 × 2 array named FIL and fill it with integers

$$m = i + j + k$$

where i = value of the first subscript

j = value of the second subscript

k = value of the third subscript

For example, FIL (1,1,1) ← 3 and FIL (3,3,2) ← 8, and, in general, FIL (i,j,k) ← i + j + k. Run it on the computer, obtain a postexecution dump, and verify that the array was properly filled.

8

Character manipulation

A computer can manipulate characters such as A, B, C, . . . Z, ?, :, =, \$, (,), and so on, in addition to numbers. The computer can input characters from an input device such as a card reader or a keyboard, and it can output characters to an output device such as a printer, typewriter, or card punch. Some computer jobs consist almost entirely of character manipulation—other jobs are partly numeric, partly character manipulation. Even a job that appears to be entirely numerical may involve character manipulation if the computer has to translate statements that the programmer wrote, convert decimal numbers to internal form, and so on.

CHARACTER CODES

Inside a computer, a character is represented by a string of bits. Many computers built in the 1950s and 1960s used six-bit codes. The codes varied somewhat from one computer to another. Six-bit codes can represent $2^6 = 64$ different characters. This was sufficient for the capital letters A to Z, the digits 0 to 9, and some special symbols. But these codes were somewhat limited; for example, they could not be expanded to also include the lowercase alphabet. The word lengths of computers are usually an integral multiple of the character size. For example, the IBM 704, 709, 7090, and 7094 computers had 36-bit words and used six-bit character codes, so six characters could be packed into one word without any leftover space.

The IBM System/360/370 series of computers uses an eight-bit code for characters, and characters are stored one character per byte or four characters per word. The eight-

Hexadecimal	Punched Cards	Graphic	Hexadecimal	Punched Cards	Graphic
40	no punches	space	A2	11-0-2	s
4A	12-8-2	¢ cent sign	A3	11-0-3	t
4B	12-8-3	. period	A4	11-0-4	u
4C	12-8-4	< less than	A5	11-0-5	v
4D	12-8-5	(left parenthesis	A6	11-0-6	w
4E	12-8-6	+ plus	A7	11-0-7	x
4F	12-8-7	I logical or	A8	11-0-8	y
50	12	& ampersand	A9	11-0-9	z
5A	11-8-2	! exclamation point	C1	12-1	A
5B	11-8-3	$ dollar sign	C2	12-2	B
5C	11-8-4	* asterisk	C3	12-3	C
5D	11-8-5	) right parenthesis	C4	12-4	D
5E	11-8-6	; semicolon	C5	12-5	E
5F	11-8-7	¬ logical not	C6	12-6	F
60	11	− minus	C7	12-7	G
61	0-1	/ slash	C8	12-8	H
			C9	12-9	I
6B	0-8-3	, comma			
6C	0-8-4	% percent	D1	11-1	J
6D	0-8-5	_ underscore	D2	11-2	K
6E	0-8-6	> greater-than	D3	11-3	L
6F	0-8-7	? question mark	D4	11-4	M
			D5	11-5	N
7A	8-2	: colon	D6	11-6	O
7B	8-3	# number sign	D7	11-7	P
7C	8-4	@ at sign	D8	11-8	Q
7D	8-5	' apostrophe	D9	11-9	R
7E	8-6	= equals			
7F	8-7	" quotation mark	E0	0-8-2	no graphic
81	12-0-1	a	E2	0-2	S
82	12-0-2	b	E3	0-3	T
83	12-0-3	c	E4	0-4	U
84	12-0-4	d	E5	0-5	V
85	12-0-5	e	E6	0-6	W
86	12-0-6	f	E7	0-7	X
87	12-0-7	g	E8	0-8	Y
88	12-0-8	h	E9	0-9	Z
89	12-0-9	i			
			F0	0	0
91	12-11-1	j	F1	1	1
92	12-11-2	k	F2	2	2
93	12-11-3	l	F3	3	3
94	12-11-4	m	F4	4	4
95	12-11-5	n	F5	5	5
96	12-11-6	o	F6	6	6
97	12-11-7	p	F7	7	7
98	12-11-8	q	F8	8	8
99	12-11-9	r	F9	9	9

Figure 8-1. EBCDIC codes for the printable characters. All of these characters can be punched on an IBM Model 029 Keypunch except the lower case alphabet.

bit code allows $2^8 = 256$ different characters. Codes are assigned for the digits 0 to 9, the upper and lowercase alphabets, and a number of special symbols, with considerable space left over for future expansion. The code is named Extended Binary-Coded-Decimal Interchange Code, or EBCDIC.[1] Figure 8-1 shows the correspondence between the printed character (also called the graphic) and its internal representation for the EBCDIC code. For example, the graphic A is represented inside the computer by the bit string 1100 0001 , which is usually written in hexadecimal as C1. Figure 8-1 also shows the corresponding punched card code. For example, the letter A is represented by punches in the 12 and 1 rows of a column.

Figure 8-1 shows 88 printable characters plus two nonprintable ones—40_H is the standard space character and $E0_H$ is a special control character. The remaining $256 - 90 = 166$ bit combinations do not correspond to printable characters, but each of them does have a corresponding card code.[2] For example, BC_H corresponds to the card code 12-11-0-4-8. Thus a 12-11-0-4-8 punch read from a card column will result in the byte BC_H stored in memory. The translation between the external (punched card) code and the internal (eight-bit) code is done by the 360 hardware as a part of the input operation; the programmer does not have to write additional instructions to cause the translation to occur. On output, if one transmits to a printing device a byte that does not have a corresponding graphic, one will get a blank or other printed character, depending on the software at that particular installation.

There are $2^{12} = 4096$ different patterns that can be punched into the 12 punch positions of a card column. Of these, only 256 correspond to a byte; the other $4096 - 256 = 3840$ combinations are illegal. One word of caution is in order. Note that

$$\text{graphic ``blank''} = \text{no punches} = 40_H$$

is not the same thing as

$$\text{graphic ``zero''} = 0 \text{ punch} = F0_H$$

and note that neither corresponds to the byte 00_H.

DEFINE CONSTANT AND DEFINE STORAGE FOR CHARACTERS

The general form of a DC (Define Constant) statement is

Name	*Operation*	*Operand*
[symbol]	DC	$\begin{bmatrix}\text{duplication}\\\text{factor}\end{bmatrix}$ type[length] constant

---

[1] The 360 also allows another eight-bit code called USASCII-8. The USASCII stands for USA Standard Code for Information Interchange, which is a seven-bit code. The "-8" indicates that this is an eight-bit extension of the seven-bit code. The 370 allows only EBCDIC.

[2] See *Principles of Operation,* Form GA22-6821, p. 150.3, or *Reference Data,* Form GX20-1703, or Appendix B.

where the brackets indicate optional quantities. The type code for characters is C. For a C-type operand, the constant is a string of characters contained in single quotes. The meaning of a DC statement with a C-type operand is that each character of the string is to be translated into one byte of the object code, unless overridden by an explicit length or duplication factor, as discussed later, and the symbol, if present, is to be associated with the first byte.

The examples that follow show DC statements and the corresponding object code. Locations are not shown. C-type constants do not have any automatic alignment, so in each case the assembler assembles the constant at the next available byte.

Object Code	Name	Operation	Operand
C1C2C3	Y	DC	C'ABC'

An explicit length may be specified by a length specification of the form Ln, where n is a decimal integer indicating the length of the constant in bytes.[3] If the explicit length is larger than the constant, then the constant will be padded on the right with blanks, thus:

C1C2C3404040	Z	DC	CL6'ABC'

If the explicit length is smaller than the constant, then the constant will be truncated on the right, thus:

C1C2	W	DC	CL2'ABCD'

A duplication factor may be used to repeat a string, thus:

C1C2C1C2C1C2	Q	DC	3CL2'ABCDE'

Note that the length is applied first and the duplication factor is applied last.

The general form of a DS (Define Storage) statement is

Name	Operation	Operand		
[symbol]	DS	$\begin{bmatrix} \text{duplication} \\ \text{factor} \end{bmatrix}$ type	[length]	[constant]

This is the same form as for the DC statement, except here the constant is optional. The meaning of the DS statement is that it reserves space for the operand but does not cause the generation of any object code. The constant, if present, is used only to indicate the amount of space to be reserved; the constant is not assembled. The symbol, if present, is associated with the first byte of the reserved area.

---

[3] For ESP, the maximum length is 64 bytes. For Assembler F, the maximum length is 256 bytes.

Some examples are as follows:

	Statement		Effect
F	DS	23C	Reserves 23 bytes, associates the symbol F with the first byte
C	DS	C'ABC'	Reserves 3 bytes, etc.
H	DS	6CL3	Reserves 18 bytes, etc.

In the two consecutive statements

A	DS	0C
B	DS	80C

the first statement reserves 0 bytes for symbol A; that is, it does not advance the location counter. Then the second statement reserves 80 bytes for B. Thus A and B both refer to the same address.

Another example with 0 duplication factor is the two consecutive statements

X	DS	0F
Y	DS	13C

Here the first statement does not reserve any space because the duplication factor is 0; but it may advance the location counter because F-type operands have automatic full-word alignment. Thus the 13-byte string is forced to begin on a full-word boundary, and X and Y refer to the same address.

A portion of an assembler listing is shown next. Only the first eight bytes of the long constants are shown.

Location	Object Code	Name	Operation	Operand
00005C	00000004	B	DC	F'4'
000060		C	DS	1F
000064	40	LINE	DC	C' '
000065		CARD	DS	80C
0000B5	5C5C5C5C5C5C5C5C		DC	52C'*'
0000E9	5B	DOLLAR	DC	C'$'
0000EC		SAVE	DS	15F

Note that the object code for the DS statements is blank. The reader can verify that the location counter did advance as required by the lengths of the operands. At SAVE, the location counter was advanced two extra bytes for alignment.

A PROGRAM TO LIST A DECK

A simple example of character manipulation is a program to read six cards and print the card images. The input data is to be 80 bytes wide and the printed line is to contain 132 bytes (plus 1 byte for carriage control). We can handle the length difference by printing the contents of card columns 1 to 80 as columns 1 to 80 of the printed line and then can fill out the rest of the printed line (columns 81 to 132) with an arbitrary string, for example, 20 asterisks, followed by 'bbbCARDbIMAGEb', followed by 18 asterisks.[4] The first byte of the 133-byte string transmitted to the printer should be the carriage-control byte, followed by the contents of card column 1, the contents of card column 2, and so on. This can be accomplished by overlapping the two areas in memory, thus:

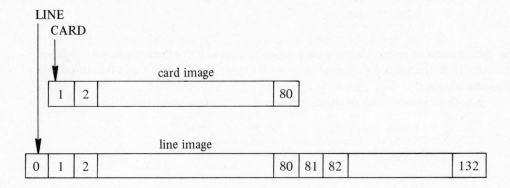

This can be done by the following set of consecutive statements:

```
LINE    DC    C'b'          CARRIAGE CONTROL CHARACTER
CARD    DS    80C
        DC    20C'*'
        DC    C'bbbCARDbIMAGEb'
        DC    18C'*'
```

where the 52 bytes beyond the card image are arbitrary.

The ESP and Assembler F versions of this program are slightly different. The ESP version is shown in Figure 8-2. The GET statement causes 80 bytes to be transmitted from the card reader to the 80-byte region beginning at CARD, that is, locations 00001D through 00006C. The PUT statement causes 133 bytes beginning at LINE, that is, locations 00001C through 0000A0, to be transmitted to the printer. The byte at 00001C is used for carriage control, and since it is 40_H = blank, the printer will single space. The remaining 132 bytes, locations 00001D through 0000A0, will be printed. The first 80 bytes to be printed are the bytes that were read from the card reader; the last 52 bytes in the printed line are as defined in statements 13, 14, and 15 of the program. The placement of the data deck with respect to the program is shown on page 198.

The GET and PUT statements destroy the contents of registers 0, 1, 14, and 15, as was mentioned in Chapter 6, so the programmer must save and restore any of these registers that he needs later. In this case, all that really needs to be saved is C(R14), the

---

[4]We denote a blank in a character string by b.

```
/ESP    000     U9329.S000.P01.BREARLEY,E=500,T=50,A=1,P=10                              PAGE      1
  LOC  OBJECT         ADDR1 ADDR2 STMT SOURCE STATEMENT              VERSION 2 1/1/69    DATE 04-26-72

000000                            1 MAIN       CSECT
000000 90EC D00C                  2            STM    14,12,12(13)   SAVE REGISTERS
000004 05C0                       3            BALR   12,0
000006                            4            USING  *,12
000006 4130 0006                  5            LA     3,5
00030A 5100 C017     0001D        6 LOOP       GET    CARD
00030E 5200 C016     0001C        7            PUT    LINE
000012 4630 C004           0000A  8            BCT    3,LOOP
000015 98EC D00C                  9            LM     14,12,12(13)   RESTORE REGISTERS
00001A 07FE                      10            BCR    15,14
00001C 40                        11 LINE       DC     C' '           CARRIAGE CONTROL CHARACTER
00001D                           12 CARD       DS     80C
00006D 5C                        13            DC     20C'*'
000081 404040C3C1D9C440          14            DC     C'   CARD IMAGE '
00008F 5C                        15            DC     18C'*'
000000                           16            END

    NO  ERRORS/WARNINGS FOUND IN THIS ASSEMBLY
```

Figure 8-2.   ESP program to read and print six cards.

link back to the system, but we show a more general method. At the beginning of the program we save all the register contents except C(R13) with the statement STM   14,12,12(13). This statement depends on the convention (true in both ESP and O.S.) that upon entry to the user's program register 13 will contain the address of an 18-word "save area" in which the register contents can be saved for later retrieval.[5]

READING BEYOND THE END OF THE DATA DECK

The preceding program is supposed to read exactly six cards from the card reader, print six lines, and then return control to the system by executing the statement BCR   15,14. If the data deck contains more than six cards, the surplus cards will simply remain unread. This is quite legitimate. If the data deck contains fewer than six cards, the behavior depends on whether the program uses ESP or Assembler F.

In ESP an attempt to read beyond the end of the data deck will lead to abnormal termination of execution plus a printed message "337." Before termination actually occurs, all the instructions prior to the pertinent GET statement will have been executed completely; in particular, all prior PUT statements will have been executed and all the corresponding lines will have been printed. No printed data will be lost. In ESP the user may not regain control after attempting to read beyond the end of the data deck. However, in spite of this limitation, running off the end of the data is a legitimate way to end execution in some cases.

An Assembler F version of this program is shown in Figure 8-3. This is different from the ESP version in several respects. Each GET or PUT statement refers to a DCB statement that describes the data to be transmitted.[6] Also, there is an OPEN statement to open each data set, and there is a CLOSE statement for the output data set. The DCB statement for the input data set is

XX   DCB   DSORG=PS,RECFM=FB,MACRF=GM,DDNAME=SYSIN,   X
               EODAD=ENDDATA

---

[5]For more on save areas, see Chapter 10.
[6]See pages 96–99.

```
 LOC   OBJECT CODE    ADDR1 ADDR2  STMT   SOURCE STATEMENT                                          F15OCT70  6/15/72

000000                                 1 MAIN     CSECT
000000 90EC D00C            0000C       2          STM    14,12,12(13)    SAVE REGISTERS
000004 05C0                             3          BALR   12,0
000006                                  4          USING  *,12
000006 4130 0006            0C006       5          LA     3,6
                                        6          PRINT  NOGEN
                                        7 BEGIN    OPEN   (XX,INPUT,YY,OUTPUT)
                                       15 LOOP     GET    XX,CARD
                                       20          PUT    YY,LINE
000036 4630 C014            0001A      25          BCT    3,LOOP
                                       26 ENDDATA  CLOSE  (YY)            CLOSE OUTPUT DATA SET
000046 98EC D00C            0000C      32          LM     14,12,12(13)    RESTORE REGISTERS
00004A 07FE                            33          BCR    15,14           RETURN TO SYSTEM
                                       34 YY       DCB    DSORG=PS,RECFM=FBA,MACRF=PM,BLKSIZE=1064,                X
                                                          LRECL=133,DDNAME=SYSPRINT
                                       88 XX       DCB    DSORG=PS,RECFM=FB,MACRF=GM,DDNAME=SYSIN,EODAD=ENDDATA
00010C 40                             142 LINE     DC     C' '            CARRIAGE CONTROL CHARACTER
00010D                                143 CARD     DS     80C
00015D 5C5C5C5C5C5C5C5C               144          DC     20C'*'
000171 404040C3C1D9C440               145          DC     C'   CARD IMAGE '
00017F 5C5C5C5C5C5C5C5C               146          DC     18C'*'
                                      147          END
```

Figure 8-3. Assembler F program to read and print six cards.

which has an additional parameter of the form

> EODAD=name

This parameter indicates that if an attempt is made to read beyond the end of the data, then control is to be transferred to ENDDATA. This allows the program to resume execution. In this case all we do is CLOSE the output data set and terminate execution. It is necessary to CLOSE the output data set before terminating execution; otherwise, up to one buffer full of output information (in this case, up to eight lines) will not be printed.

With Assembler F this loss of several lines of output data can also occur as a result of other abnormal terminations, such as attempting to divide by zero. This can be quite annoying to a user who is trying to debug a program because the output makes it appear that execution has proceeded less far than was actually the case.

EXERCISES

1. Modify the program of Figure 8-3 to print one message if six data cards are successfully read, and another message if there are fewer than six cards in the data deck.

MOVING CHARACTERS

In the preceding program we transmitted data from the input area (the area that was filled from the card reader) to the output area (the area that is transmitted to the printer) by causing the two areas to overlap in memory. Another method is to use nonoverlapping areas of memory and to transmit the data from one area to the other with move instructions.

In the 360, strings of bytes can be moved from one part of the memory to another without transmitting the bytes through a register. The movement is directly from storage to storage, and the instructions utilize the Storage to Storage [SS] format.

Move characters

Machine format [SS] :

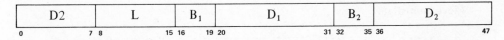

D2	L	B_1	D_1	B_2	D_2
0	7 8	15 16	19 20	31 32	35 36	47

Assembler format: MVC $D_1(l,B_1),D_2(B_2)$

Meaning: The second byte of the instruction, bits 8 to 15, indicates a machine-language length, L, which is related to the assembler-language length, l, by the relation $l = L + 1$, except that if $l = 0$, then L = 0. The range of the machine length L is 0 to 255. The range of the assembler length l is 0 to 256. The meaning of the instruction is move l bytes from the second operand location to the first operand location. Movement is storage to storage, one byte at a time, from left to right. General registers are not used except for bases.

An example using the MVC instruction is as follows:

Before: C(X) = F0 F0 F1 F5 F7 F9

           C(Y) = C1 C2 C3 C4

Execute: MVC   X(3),Y

After: C(X) = C1 C2 C3 F5 F7 F9

           C(Y) = C1 C2 C3 C4

This example uses symbolic operands. If the address of X was already in R2 and the address of Y was already in R5, then this move instruction could also have been written with explicit operands as   MVC   0(3,2),0(5).

In the next example, we show a program segment that reads a card, exchanges the contents of columns 1 to 10 and 21 to 30, leaving the other bytes as is, and then prints the card image:

```
              .
              .
         GET     CARD
         MVC     TEMP(10),CARD
         MVC     CARD(10),CARD+20
         MVC     CARD+20(10),TEMP
         PUT     LINE
              .
              .
              .
LINE     DC      C'b'
CARD     DS      80C
         DC      52C'b'
TEMP     DS      10C
              .
              .
              .
```

It was necessary to establish TEMP as a temporary 10-byte location while exchanging the byte strings.

Move immediate

Machine format [SI] :

92	I_2	B_1	D_1

0   7 8   15 16   19 20   31

Assembler format: MVI $D_1(B_1),I_2$

Meaning: Move the second operand, bits 8 to 15 of this instruction, to the first operand location.

This instruction utilizes the Storage and Immediate operand format [SI]. The immediate data are in the instruction itself, not elsewhere in memory. This is convenient when a one-byte constant is to be moved; it saves defining the constant with a DC statement. The immediate operand may be specified in decimal, hex, or character form.

For example, let C(XYZ) = F1 F2 F3 F4. To move a blank into the first byte of this string, write

      MVI   XYZ,64

or

      MVI   XYZ,X'40'

or

      MVI   XYZ,C'b'

The three forms are equivalent, and all three have the same object code, 9240XXXX, where the X's indicate the base and displacement digits.

In the following example, we illustrate the looping inherent in the MVC instruction. The statement

      MVC   AA(6),BB

which has a length specification of 6, has the same effect as the six consecutive statements

      MVC   AA+0(1),BB+0
      MVC   AA+1(1),BB+1
      MVC   AA+2(1),BB+2
           .
           .
      MVC   AA+5(1),BB+5

where each statement has a length specification of 1. If the source and destination fields are overlapped, thus:

        MVC   AA+1(6),AA

we obtain the same effect as if we wrote

        MVC   AA+1(1),AA+0
        MVC   AA+2(1),AA+1
                .
                .
                .
        MVC   AA+6(1),AA+5

Thus whatever byte is at AA+0 is propagated (copied) throughout the whole field. Sometimes this is a useful technique. For example, the statements

        MVI   G,X'40'
        MVC   G+1(20),G

have the effect of (1) storing a blank into G+0 and (2) propagating the blank through the string from G+0 to G+20, inclusive.

Move long

The MVC instruction can only move 256 bytes at a time. If one wishes to move more than 256 bytes, he must execute more than one MVC instruction. The 370, but not the 360, allows up to 16 million bytes to be moved by one instruction, Move Long.

Machine format [RR]:

OE	R₁	R₂
0 7	8 11	12 15

Assembler format: MVCL   R₁,R₂

The data are moved from the second operand (the source) to the first operand (the destination) one byte at a time, from left to right. The first operand is described by the contents of the even-odd register pair R_1, $R_1 + 1$. Thus

	R₁		R₁ + 1	
unused	address of first operand	unused	length of first operand
0 7	8 31	0 7	8 31

The second operand is described by the contents of the even-odd register pair R_2, $R_2 + 1$. Thus

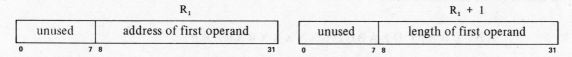

	R₂		R₂ + 1	
unused	address of second operand	padding character	length of second operand
0 7	8 31	0 7	8 31

Both R_1 and R_2 must be even; otherwise, a specification interruption will occur. The lengths of the first and second operands, l_1 and l_2, do not have to be equal as for the MVC instruction. There are four cases.

Case 1. $l_1 = l_2$. The number of bytes moved is $l = l_1 = l_2$. At the conclusion of execution of the MVCL instruction, the condition code will be 0.

Case 2. $l_1 < l_2$. Truncation will occur, that is, only l_1 bytes will be moved into the first operand location. After execution the condition code will be 1.

Case 3. $l_1 > l_2$. After all l_2 bytes have been moved from the second operand location to the first operand location, the remaining bytes of the first operand will be filled with the padding character. After execution the condition code will be 2.

Case 4. If the first and second operands do not overlap, or if the operands do overlap and the first byte of the first operand coincides with, or lies to the left of, the first byte of the second operand, then successful execution will occur as described under cases 1 to 3. If the operands overlap and the first byte of the first operand lies to the right of the first byte of the second operand, then destructive overlap is said to occur, data movement will not take place, and the condition code will be set to 3.

During execution of the MVCL instruction, the addresses in R_1 and R_2 are incremented and the counts in $R_1 + 1$ and $R_2 + 1$ are decremented. Thus, if the execution of this program is interrupted while an MVCL is being executed, and if execution of this program is later resumed without having destroyed the contents of R_1, $R_1 + 1$, R_2, and $R_2 + 1$, then execution of the MVCL can resume where it left off. When execution of the MVCL is completed, $count_1$ will be 0 in cases 1 to 3, $count_2$ will be 0 in cases 1 and 3, and $count_2$ will be greater than 0 in case 2. Also, the left-hand bytes of R_1 and R_2 will be set at 0; the left-hand bytes of $R_1 + 1$ and $R_2 + 1$ remain unchanged.

An example using MVCL is shown in Figure 8-4. The source string is

ABCDEABCDEABCDEABCDEABCDEA...

The destination string is

BBBBBBBBBBBBBBBBBBBBBBBBBB...

After executing an MVCL with source length 15, destination length 20, and padding character X, the destination string is

ABCDEABCDEABCDEXXXXXBBBBBB...

the counts in registers 5 and 7 have been decremented to zero, and the addresses in registers 4 and 6 have been incremented by 20_{10} and 15_{10}, respectively.

```
  LOC  OBJECT CODE    ADDR1 ADDR2  STMT   SOURCE STATEMENT                           F150CT70   2/09/73

C0C000                                1 HCB       CSECT
C0C0C0 05C0                           2           BALR  12,0
000002                                3           USING *,12
                                      4 *
C0C002 9847 C012          00014       5           LM    4,7,PP
C0C006 9047 C0&6          00088       6           STM   4,7,SAVE1
C0CCCA 0E46                           7           MVCL  4,6
C0C00C 9047 C096          C0098       8           STM   4,7,SAVE2
000010 47F0 C0A6          0C0A8       9           B     J
                                     10 *
000014 00000024                      11 PP        DC    A(DES)         DESTINATION ADDRESS
000018 CC000014                      12           DC    F'20'          DESTINATION LENGTH
00001C CC000056                      13           DC    A(SS)          SOURCE ADDRESS
000020 E7                            14           DC    C'X'           PADDING CHARACTER
00C021 00000F                        15           DC    AL3(15)        SOURCE LENGTH
000024 C2C2C2C2C2C2C2C2              16 DES       DC    50C'B'         DESTINATION STRING
000056 C1C2C3C4C5C1C2C3              17 SS        DC    10C'ABCDE'     SOURCE STRING
000088                               18 SAVE1     DS    4F
000098                               19 SAVE2     DS    4F
0000A8 C0000000C0C00                 20 J         DC    X'J0000C0CCC00'
                                     21           END
```

```
INTERRUPT AT 032FFA

REGS AT ENTRY TO ABEND

   FLTR 0-6       0001369880013678      00013628CC0C00D0          CC80C9C5C5E5C9C3   C000000000000000

   REGS 0-7    FD00C008   0005IFF8   00015148   5C015330      00032F88   00CC0C00   C0032F85   E7000000
   REGS 8-15   C0015308   000128C0   00015330   C0000000      40032F52   0005IF68   0000D59A   01032F50

LOAD MODULE   GO

032F 40                                   05C09847 C0129047 C0860E46 9047C096   *......D..K.....K................*
032F60   47F0C0A6 00032F74 00000014 00032FA6   E70J000F C1C2C3C4 C5C1C2C3 C4C5C1C2   *.0.............X...ABCDEA8CDEA8*
032F80   C3C4C5E7 E7E7E7E7 C2C2C2C2 C2C2C2C2   C2C2C2C2 C2C2C2C2 C2C2C2C2 C2C2C2C2   *CDEXXXX8888888888888888888888*
032FA0   C2C2C2C2 C2C2C1C2 C3C4C5C1 C2C3C4C5   C1C2C3C4 C5C1C2C3 C4C5C1C2 C3C4C5C1   *8E8888ABCDEA8CDEABCDEABCDEA*
032FC0   C2C3C4C5 C1C2C3C4 C5C1C2C3 C4C5C1C2   C3C4C5C1 C2C3C4C5 00032F74 00000014   *8CDEA8CDEA8CDEABCDEA8CDE........*
032FE0   00032FA6 E70J0C0F 00032F88 00C00000   00032F85 E70000J0 00000C00 000093AA   *.....X..............X..........*
```

Figure 8-4.   Example of Move Long instruction (370 only).

LOGICAL AND BYTE COMPARISONS

In Chapter 7 we considered the arithmetic comparison instructions C and CR. These instructions compare full words and interpret them arithmetically according to the rules of 32-bit two's complement arithmetic. Full words may also be compared as unsigned integers; this is called a "logical" comparison. The full-word logical comparison instructions are

RR format: CLR R_1,R_2 op code 15

RX format: CL $R_1,D_2(X_2,B_2)$ op code 55

Meaning: Compare the first operand with the second operand, treating both as unsigned integers, and set the condition code as follows:

Operands equal   CC = 0
First operand $<$ second operand   CC = 1
First operand $>$ second operand   CC = 2

CC = 3 is not used. Neither of the operands is changed.

Figure 8-5 shows four 32-bit words and their arithmetic and logical interpretations. Observe that $B = 100\ldots000_2 = 80000000_H$ is less than $C = 0111\ldots111_2 = 7FFFFFFF_H$ when interpreted arithmetically, so the following arithmetic comparison will *not* result in a branch:

```
L     2,B
C     2,C
BH    XYZ
```

On the other hand, B is greater than C when interpreted logically, so changing the comparison from arithmetic to logical *will* cause a branch to occur:

```
L     2,B
CL    2,C
BH    XYZ
```

The 360 can also compare strings of characters, including strings of length 1. The comparisons are based on the *collating sequence,* that is, the fact that the set of characters is an ordered set. The ordering is indicated by the hexadecimal equivalent of each character. Thus

¢ is less than %

because $C'¢' = 4A_H$
$ C'\%' = 6C_H$
$ 4A_H < 6C_H$

To compare a single byte to a constant, we can use the Compare Logical Immediate instruction.

Machine format [SI]:

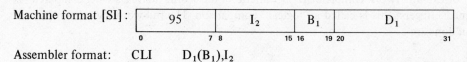

95	I_2	B_1	D_1
0	7 8	15 16 19 20	31

Assembler format: CLI $D_1(B_1),I_2$

Meaning: Compare the byte indicated by the first operand, $D_1(B_1)$, with the immediate

Symbol	Contents of 32 bit positions	Arithmetic interpretation	Logical interpretation
A	$1111\ldots11111$	-1	$+2^{32} - 1$
B	$1000\ldots00000$	-2^{31}	$+2^{31}$
C	$0111\ldots11111$	$+2^{31} - 1$	$+2^{31} - 1$
D	$0000\ldots00001$	$+1$	$+1$

Figure 8-5.   Arithmetic and Logical interpretation of 32-bit words.

operand, bits 8 to 15 of this instruction. The bytes are interpreted as unsigned integers in the range 0 to 255. Set the condition code as follows:

Operands equal	CC = 0
First operand low	CC = 1
First operand high	CC = 2

In assembler language, the immediate operand may be a decimal, hexadecimal, or character constant. For example,

```
DOLLAR    DC      C'$'
            .
            .
            .
          CLI     DOLLAR,C','
          BL      QRS
```

For the preceding comparison instruction, the first operand is $C'\$' = 5B_H$ and the second operand is $C',' = 6B_H$. Thus

first operand < second operand

so the branch will occur. The comparison instruction could also have been written as

```
          CLI     DOLLAR,X'6B'
```

or as

```
          CLI     DOLLAR,107
```

The three forms are equivalent, and all three have the same object code, 956BXXXX, where the X's indicate the base and displacement digits.

Example: Let XYZ be a character string of length 20, where each character is a decimal digit. We wish to replace all the leading zeros ($=F0_H$) by blanks ($=40_H$). For example,

```
              XYZ
Before:    F0 F0 F0 ... F0 F4 F0 F9

              XYZ
After:     40 40 40 ... 40 F4 F0 F9
```

Assume that the number of leading zeros is unknown at the time the program is written, but must be determined by examining the data at execution time. A program to do this is as follows:

```
            LA      5,XYZ+19      FOR END TEST
            LA      4,XYZ
LOOP        CLI     0(4),C'0'     IS BYTE A LEADING ZERO?
            BNE     NEXT
            MVI     0(4),C' '     INSERT LEADING BLANK
            LA      4,1(0,4)      MOVE POINTER
            CR      4,5           TEST FOR END OF STRING
            BL      LOOP
NEXT        .
            .
            .
```

Here we set the address of the first byte of the string into R4, and then step it through the string.

EXERCISE

1. What will the preceding program segment do if the string XYZ is entirely filled with zeros?

COMPARING STRINGS OF BYTES

Character strings can be compared by converting each character to its numeric equivalent and then comparing the numbers. For example, consider the comparison of CAT and CAMP to see which is closest to the front of the alphabet.

First string:	C	A	T	b	b
	C3	C1	E3	40	40
Second string:	C	A	M	P	b
	C3	C1	D4	D7	40

(Here we show the graphic above and the corresponding byte below.) Beginning at the left end of the strings, we compare the leftmost characters and find that they are equal, and then repeat for the second characters and find that they match also. We then compare the third characters and find that they do not match and the character in the second string is the smaller; that is, $D4 < E3$. Hence the second string lies closer to the beginning of the alphabet. In the 360 this can be done by the following instruction:

Compare logical

Machine format [SS]:

D5	L	B_1	D_1	B_2	D_2
0	7 8	15 16	19 20	31 32	35 36	47

Assembler format: CLC $D_1(l,B_1),D_2(B_2)$

Meaning: The first operand is the character string beginning at $D_1(B_1)$. The second operand is the character string beginning at $D_2(B_2)$. The meaning is compare the first operand to the second operand, byte by byte from left to right, that is, from low-numbered addresses to higher-numbered addresses. The comparison continues until unequal bytes are found or until $l = L + 1$ bytes have been compared. Then the condition code is set as follows:

Strings equal	CC = 0
First string low	CC = 1
First string high	CC = 2

CC = 3 is not used. Neither of the operands is changed.

Example:

```
X       DC      C'JOHNbbbb'
Y       DC      C'JOHNIE'
        .
        .
        .
        CLC     X(6),Y
        BC      4,ABC
        .
        .
        .
```

The comparison in the CLC will be continued until the fifth characters are compared, at which time C'b' will be discovered to be less than C'I', so

string X < string Y

the condition code will be set to 1, and the branch will be taken.

Compare logical long

The CLC instruction can compare strings up to 256 bytes long. The 370, but not the 360, allows strings up to 16 million bytes long to be compared by one instruction, Compare Logical Long. This instruction is similar to the MVCL instruction, just as CLC is similar to MVC.

Machine format [RR]:

OF	R_1	R_2
0 7	8 11	12 15

Assembler format: CLCL R_1,R_2

Meaning: The first operand is compared to the second operand and the condition code is set to indicate the result. The first operand is described by the contents of the even-odd register pair R_1 and $R_1 + 1$, and the second operand is described by the contents of R_2 and $R_2 + 1$ as for the MVCL instruction. The comparison is byte by byte from left to right and continues until an inequality is found or the longer field is exhausted. For purposes of the comparison, the shorter operand is padded on the right with the padding character, but the operands in storage remain unchanged. The condition code is set as follows:

Operands equal, or both fields have zero length	CC = 0
First operand low	CC = 1
First operand high	CC = 2

During execution the registers are incremented and decremented as for the MVCL instruction. If an inequality is discovered, the count and address fields identify the unequal bytes. If the comparison continues to the end of the longer operand, then the register contents are as for the MVCL instruction.

An example is shown in Figure 8-6. The first operand is

C O M P U T A T I O N

and the second operand is

C O M P U T A T I O N b b b b b b b b b

PAGE   1

```
 LOC   OBJECT CODE    ADDR1 ADDR2  STMT    SOURCE STATEMENT                              F15OCT70   2/09/73

000000                                1  TEST2     CSECT
000000 05C0                            2            BALR  12,0
000002                                 3            USING *,12
                                       4            PRINT DATA
000002 9825 C03A          003C         5            LM    2,5,C1
000006 9025 C04A          004C         6            STM   2,5,CA1
00000A 0F24                            7            CLCL  2,4
00000C 9025 C05A          005C         8            STM   2,5,CA2
000010 4780 C036          0038         9            BE    J
000014 00000001                       10  K         DC    X'00000001'
000018 C3D6D4D7E4E3C1E3                11  FIRST     DC    C'COMPUTATION'
000020 C9D6D5
000023 C3D6D4D7E4E3C1E3                12  SECOND    DC    C'COMPUTATION
000028 C9D6D54040404040
000033 40404040
000038                                13            DS    0F
000038 00000002                       14  J         DC    X'00000002'
00003C 00000018                       15  C1        DC    A(FIRST)            ADDRESS OF FIRST OPERAND
000040 0000000B                       16            DC    F'11'               LENGTH OF FIRST OPERAND
000044 00000023                       17            DC    A(SECOND)           ADDRESS OF SECOND OPERAND
000048 40                             18            DC    C' '                PADDING CHARACTER
000049 000014                         19            DC    AL3(20)             LENGTH OF SECOND OPERAND
00004C                                20  CA1       DS    4F
00005C                                21  CA2       DS    4F
                                      22            END
```

```
INTERRUPT AT 032FCA

REGS AT ENTRY TO ABEND

    FLTR 0-6    2740CCEC00000049   E48349D8E273040F           0CC0F0C02000C000   00000C0000000000

    REGS 0-7    FDCCC008   00051FFA   00032F83   C0000000    00032FC7   4CCF0000   00015480   0016EAB
    REGS 8-15   000153F0   00015200   00015418   000J0000    40032F92   0CC51F68   0000D59A   0C032F90

LOAD MODULE   GO

032F80                                                05C09825 C03A9025 C04A0F24 9025C05A   *......K..............*
032FA0   4780C036 00000001 C3D6D4D7 E4E3C1E3   C9D6D5C3 D6D4D7E4 E3C1E3C9 D6D54040   *........COMPUTATIONCOMPUTATION *
032FC0   40404040 40404CAC 00000002 00032FAB   000C0008 00032F83 40000014 00032FAB   *.....................*
032FE0   00000008 00032F83 40000014 00032F83   C00000C0 00032FC7 40000C00 47709A0A   *..............G......*
```

Figure 8-6. Example of Compare Logical Long instruction (370 only).

where b indicates blank. The padding character for the CLCL is blank, so the strings compare as equal.

VARIABLE-LENGTH STRINGS

The length field of a CLC or MVC instruction is specified at assembly time; it is not a quantity that is calculated at execution time, as is the index in an RX instruction. However, sometimes we need the length to be a variable that is calculated at execution time.

Suppose that we have an arbitrary 80-byte string beginning at ABC, for example,

ABC
b b b b . . . b G E O R G E b b C A M E b b . . .

Suppose that we wish to move the first word in this string to another location, FOUND, where a "word" is a group of contiguous nonblank characters delimited at each end by a blank or the end of the string. However, the location of the first word in ABC is a variable; it depends on the data. Scanning from the left, we set R6 to contain the address of the first character of the first word, and we set R7 to contain the address of the blank following the first word. (The details are left to the reader.) Then the situation would be as follows:

ABC
b b b b . . . b G E O R G E b b C A M E b b . . .
                    ↑   ↑
                    R6   R7

There are several ways to move the first word to FOUND. A first (poor) method is to move one byte at a time, thus:


```
        LA    8,FOUND       initialize destination address
LOOP    MVC   0(1,8),0(6)   move one byte
        LA    6,1(0,6)      increment source pointer
        LA    8,1(0,8)      increment destination pointer
        CR    6,7           end
        BL    LOOP            test
```


This method works, but it requires several statements to write and it is slow in execution.

A more sophisticated method is to use the Execute instruction to insert a calculated length into a MVC instruction prior to execution of the MVC instruction. (This is to be distinguished from a length that is fixed at assembly time.) Before resuming this example, we describe the Execute instruction in general.

Execute

Machine format [RX]:

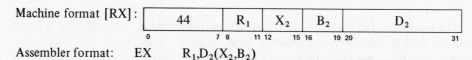

44	R_1	X_2	B_2	D_2
0 7 8	11 12	15 16	19 20	31

Assembler format: EX $R_1,D_2(X_2,B_2)$

Meaning: The effective address is calculated as usual for RX instructions. The effective address points to the *subject instruction,* which must be on a half-word boundary. The meaning is (1) temporarily modify the second byte of the subject instruction, bits 8 to 15, by ORing with bits 24 to 31 of the general register indicated by R_1. If $R_1 = 0$, then do not modify. (2) Then execute the subject instruction once, and resume flow at the instruction following the Execute instruction, except that if the subject instruction is a successful branch the flow of control will not return.

The modification does not permanently affect either $C(R_1)$ or the subject instruction. The subject instruction may not be another Execute instruction. The subject instruction may be any legitimate length, that is, 16, 32, or 48 bits long.

The OR operation mentioned is the ordinary inclusive OR, which may be defined on a bit basis by the following truth table:

a	b	a OR b
0	0	0
0	1	1
1	0	1
1	1	1

The purpose of the Execute instruction is to allow the insertion of calculated second bytes (lengths, masks, immediate data, and so on) into the subject instruction before executing it. It may be helpful to think of the subject instruction as a subroutine that is one instruction long, and the Execute instruction as the call to that subroutine. Some examples for subject instructions in various formats are shown next.

Example 1:

.
.
.

B   L   4,X
       EX   0,XYZ   XYZ   SR   4,5
       ST   4,Y

The subject instruction for the Execute instruction is SR 4,5 = 1B45$_H$. The first operand of the Execute instruction is 0, so instruction modification will not take place. The effect of executing the instructions beginning at B will be as if the sequence

```
        .
        .
        .
   L      4,X
   SR     4,5
   ST     4,Y
        .
        .
        .
```

had been executed.

Example 2:

```
        .
        .
        .
9265_____      QQ    MVI    ZZ,X'65'
        .
        .
41400099       AB    LA     4,X'99'
4440_____            EX     4,QQ
        .
        .
        .
```

The right byte of R4 is	99$_H$ = 1001 1001
The second byte of the subject instruction is	65$_H$ = 0110 0101
The bitwise OR of these two strings is	1111 1101

So the effect of executing the Execute instruction is as if the instruction

```
   MVI      ZZ,X'FD'
```

had been executed. However, after the flow of control has passed by, the MVI instruction and the Execute instruction remain unchanged in memory.

Example 3: Returning to the problem of moving a variable-length string, let us assume the situation indicated schematically in Figure 8-7 in which we want to move all the bytes beginning at i and ending at j $-$ 1 to FOUND. In assembler language the length of the move is

$$l = j - i$$

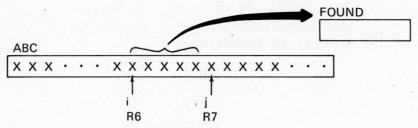

Figure 8-7. Moving a variable length string.

but in machine language the length of the move is

$$L = j - i - 1 = C(R7) - C(R6) - 1$$

Before using the Execute instruction we must calculate this machine language length. The code is

```
                .
                .
                .
            LR      3,7             j
            SR      3,6             j - i
            S       3,ONE           j - i - 1
            EX      3,QRS
            B       NEXT
ONE         DC      F'1'
QRS         MVC     FOUND(0),0(6)
NEXT        .
                .
                .
```

The subject instruction for the Execute is the MVC. The second byte of the MVC is assembled as 00_H. At the time of execution of the Execute instruction, the contents of R3 are $j - i - 1$, which is a small positive integer in the right end of the register. Bits 24 to 31 of R3 are then ORed with the second byte of the subject instruction to form a temporary second byte of the subject instruction. In this case, this is equivalent to inserting $L = j - i - 1$ into the temporary instruction. Thus the execution of the temporarily modified MVC has the effect of moving

$$L + 1 = j - i$$

bytes from 0(6) to FOUND.

EXERCISES

1. Generate object code for the following program.

```
PROB        CSECT
            BALR        10,0
            USING       *,10
            MVC         XYZ+4(2),PER
            MVI         PER,C'$'
            BCR         15,14
PER         DC          3C'T'
XYZ         DC          C'ABCABCABC'
            END
```

   Assume this program is loaded at 06A2B0 and executed. Show the contents of bytes 06A2BC through 06A2C9 after execution.

2. Write a program to read a card and print the card image on the printer. Then replace all occurrences of the digits 0, 1, 2, . . ., 9 by underscore, $=$ X'6D', and print the modified card image.

3. Write a program to read a card, print the card image on the printer, and then print on the next line the first word on that card. A "word" is a string of contiguous nonblank characters delimited by blanks or card boundaries. An example of printer output is

```
b b b G E O R G E b C A M E b T O b b b . . .
G E O R G E b b b . . .
```

4. Write a program to read a card, print the card image on the printer and then print all the words on the card, one word per line. An example of printer output is

```
b b G E O R G E b C A M E b T O b b D I N N E R .
G E O R G E b b b . . .
C A M E b b . . .
T O b b . . .
D I N N E R . b b b . . .
```

   Note that the period is a part of the last word.

5. Repeat Exercise 4, but alphabetize the list of words before printing.

6. Print a heading. Read and print a data card. Then print a list of all the words on the card that begin with the letter G. The first word of the list should be printed on the same line as the card image, and subsequent words should be printed on subsequent single-spaced lines. The card image field of the subsequent lines should be blank. Print three asterisks at the right of all printed lines. Repeat for the next data card for a total

of five data cards; then print a terminating message and quit. An example of correct output is as follows:

DATA AS READ IN	WORD BEGINNING WITH G	***
GEORGE GROWS GORGEOUS GERANIUMS.	GEORGE	***
	GROWS	***
	GORGEOUS	***
	GERANIUMS.	***
NEXT CARD IS BLANK.		***
		***
THE GOOSE IS COOKED.	GOOSE	***
GRACE AND GLADYS LEFT.	GRACE	***
	GLADYS	***

END OF DATA

7. Write a program to read cards and print card images. At the right of each printed card image print a message to indicate whether or not the parentheses on the card, if any, are legally paired as in Fortran statements. Continue until the data deck is exhausted. The program should handle nesting of parentheses to considerable depth.

8. Write a program to read and list a deck. Continue until you encounter a "trip card" containing some special pattern of punches, for example, dollar signs in columns 2 and 3. Then print a message and terminate execution.

9

Decimal conversions

In a binary computer such as the 360, there are substantial differences between the ways numbers are represented externally (at the printer or card reader) and internally (in the memory and CPU). The conversion from one to the other is a significant problem, which is the subject of this chapter.

NUMBER REPRESENTATIONS

In the 360 the four ways in which integers can be represented are as follows[1]:

1. *Character string form.* In this form each decimal digit is represented by one byte, using the regular character code, thus:

Graphic	Hex Byte
0	F0
1	F1
2	F2
.	.
.	.
.	.
9	F9

---

[1] This discussion is restricted to integers. Numbers may also be represented in floating-point form.

This form also permits characters such as minus signs, commas, and decimal points to appear. For example,

$$C'\text{-}1252' = 60 \quad F1 \quad F2 \quad F5 \quad F2_H$$

2. *Zoned decimal form.* In this form each decimal digit occupies one byte. The general form is

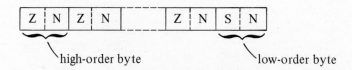

where Z represents the *zone* or left half-byte, and the zone is $1111_2 = F_H$ for EBCDIC coding. N is the *numeric* or right half-byte and represents a decimal digit between 0 and 9, or between 0000 and 1001_2. Numerics in the range 1010 to 1111_2 are illegal. S is the *sign* and lies in the left half of the low-order byte. The encoding of the sign in EBCDIC[2] is

$$1111 = \text{unsigned}$$
$$1101 = \text{minus}$$
$$1100 = \text{plus}$$

A zoned decimal field may be 1 to 16 bytes long, and may begin at any byte address; that is, there is no alignment requirement. For example, the minimum-length zoned decimal representation of $^-1252$ is

$$F1 \quad F2 \quad F5 \quad D2_H$$

If more space is available, the string is extended to the left with (zoned) zeros. Thus an eight-byte zoned decimal representation of $^-1252$ is

$$F0 \quad F0 \quad F0 \quad F0 \quad F1 \quad F2 \quad F5 \quad D2_H$$

3. *Packed decimal form.* In this form, the decimal digits are packed two to a byte except at the right end. The general form is

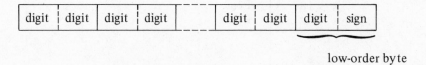

[2]When using USASCII-8 code, plus is 1010, minus is 1011, and the zone is 0101.

A packed decimal number may begin at any byte address and may be 1 to 16 bytes long. For example, the minimum-length packed decimal representation of −1252 is

$$01 \quad 25 \quad 2D_H$$

In this case the number was padded with one zero on the left, because the representation must contain an integral number of bytes. If more space is available, the string will be padded on the left with (packed) zeros. Thus an eight-byte packed decimal version of −1252 is

$$00 \quad 00 \quad 00 \quad 00 \quad 00 \quad 01 \quad 25 \quad 2D_H$$

4. *Binary form.* This is the form already discussed at length in Chapter 3. The 32-bit two's complement form of −1252 is

$$FF \quad FF \quad FB \quad 1C_H$$

COMPARISON OF NUMBER REPRESENTATIONS

Each number representation described is useful in some circumstances. None is superior to all the others for all purposes. The character string representation is used for input and output. (This representation is also used directly for manipulation of characters as described in Chapter 8.) The zoned decimal representation is closely related to the character string representation except for punctuation and signs. The packed decimal representation and the binary representation are used for arithmetic.

Some comparisons between the various number representations are indicated in Figure 9-1. Packed decimal is a more compact representation than zoned decimal, and binary is the most compact representation. The 360/370 contains instructions for performing arithmetic directly on packed decimal numbers; this is called "decimal" arith-

Representation	Number of bits needed to represent one decimal digit	Number of conversion steps from external form	Arithmetic speed
Character string	8	0	Not implemented in 360
Zoned decimal	8	1	Not implemented in 360
Packed decimal	4	2	slower
Binary	$\log_2 10 = 3.32$	3	faster

Figure 9-1.   Comparison of four number representations.

metic.[3] Binary arithmetic operations are somewhat faster than decimal arithmetic operations, but this varies somewhat from model to model within the 360/370 line.[4] The advantages of binary arithmetic with respect to speed and compactness mean that binary arithmetic is usually used in programs in which many arithmetic operations are performed for each number that is input or output. If only a very few arithmetic operations are to be performed for each number that is input or output, it may be faster overall to use packed decimal arithmetic to save on conversions.

CONVERSIONS

To convert from one representation to another, several instructions are provided.

Instruction		Form of Source	Form of Destination
Pack	PACK	Zoned decimal	Packed decimal
Convert to binary	CVB	Packed decimal	Binary
Convert to decimal	CVD	Binary	Packed decimal
Unpack	UNPK	Packed decimal	Zoned decimal

The details are given next.

Pack

Machine format [SS]:

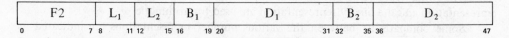

Assembler format: PACK $D_1(l_1,B_1),D_2(l_2,B_2)$

Meaning: The second operand is assumed to be in zoned decimal form. It is converted to packed decimal form, extended with high-order zeros if necessary, and stored in the first operand location.

The length of the first and second operands is indicated by l_1 and l_2 in assembler language and by L_1 and L_2 in machine language, where $l_i = L_i + 1$.

For example, let C(Y) = F3 F6 F7 F1 D9 40 40. Then execute the instruction   PACK   X(8),Y(5). The object code for this instruction will be F274_____ where the assembler will provide base and displacement digits to correspond to the symbols X and Y. Note that the assembler length of the first operand is 8 and the corresponding machine length is 7. The effect of executing this instruction is indicated next.

---

[3]For details of decimal arithmetic, see *Principles of Operation*, Form GA22-6821 or GA22-7000.

[4]For details of speeds, see the "functional characteristics" manual for the model in question.

Before: Y =   F3 F6 F7 F1 D9 40 40

After: X = 00 00 00 00 00 36 71 9D

Here X and Y are presumed to be disjoint strings of bytes in arbitrary memory locations; they are shown with the least significant bytes lined up only for convenience.

The effect of executing a PACK instruction is as if the bytes of the first operand were processed one at a time from right to left (from least significant digit to most significant digit). Because of this, the first and second operands may be overlapped. For example, the result of executing the instruction   PACK   W(5),W(5)   is

Before: W = F3 F6 F7 F1 C9

After: W = 00 00 36 71 9C

The PACK instruction is subject to errors which are sometimes troublesome to diagnose. If the length of the first operand (the destination) is too short to contain all the significant digits of the result, then the high-order digits will be lost, the answer will be incorrect, and there will be no message. Thus execution will proceed until something else goes wrong, or the program may run to completion with incorrect results. Another possible source of difficulty is that in the PACK instruction the sign and digits are moved unchanged from the source string to the destination string without inspection for valid codes. For example, a PACK instruction with an erroneous length is

Before: A = F2 F3 F4 40 40 40

Execute: PACK   B(4),A(4)

After: B = 00 02 34 04
                                         └─────── supplied

Here the length of the first operand was one byte too long, so a spurious low-order byte was picked up. This resulted in an illegal sign digit (= 4_H) in the packed result, plus other problems, but it did not cause an interruption. (However, usually the next instruction following a PACK will be a CVB instruction and trouble will occur there if a sign or digit code is illegal.)

The PACK and EXecute instructions may be used together to allow packing from a calculated position with a calculated length. For example, let ABC be a string of bytes, thus:

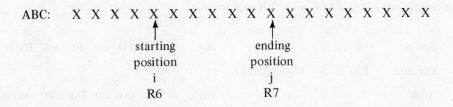

ABC: X X X X X X X X X X X X X X X X X X X X

                      starting   ending
                      position   position
                         i   j
                         R6   R7

To pack the string beginning at i = C(R6) and ending just before j = C(R7) and put the result in DEST, we must first calculate the length, and then EXecute a PACK with the appropriate source and length:

```
                .
                .
                .
          SR      7,6           j - i
          BCTR    7,0           j - i - 1
          EX      7,IJK
          B       NEXT
IJK       PACK    DEST(8),0(0,6)
NEXT      .
                .
                .
                .
```

Here the length of the first operand (the destination) was fixed at 8 at assembly time, but the length of the second operand (the source) was calculated in R7 and inserted with the EX instruction.

Convert to binary

Machine format [RX]:

4F	R_1	X_2	B_2	D_2
0	7 8	11 12	15 16	19 20 31

Assembler format: CVB $R_1,D_2(X_2,B_2)$

Meaning: The second operand is assumed to be an eight-byte packed decimal number aligned on a double-word boundary. It is converted to 32-bit two's complement binary form and stored in R_1.

The second operand *is* checked for valid sign and digit codes. If any of them are illegal, the 360 will produce a data interruption; the 370 will suppress the operation.

The second operand is eight bytes long and contains a sign plus up to 15 decimal digits. However, the range of numbers that can be correctly represented in a 32-bit two's complement form is only

$$\text{from } -2^{31} = -2,147,483,648 \text{ to } +2^{31} - 1 = +2,147,483,647$$

If the number to be converted is too big to fit in R_1, then a fixed-point divide interruption will occur.

An example using both PACK and CVB is as follows:

```
Before:                        AA   = F0 F0 F0 F0 F4 F3 F0

Execute:  PACK    BB(8),AA(7)

After:                         BB   = 00 00 00 00 00 00 43 0F
```

Then

Execute: CVB   8,BB

After: C(R8) = 00 00 01 AE

Note that CVB treats both F and C as plus signs.

As a second example, a program to read a card containing a positive four-decimal-digit integer in columns 12 to 15, with leading zeros punched, and to convert the number to binary and store it in R4 is as follows:

```
        .
        .
        .
        GET     XX,CARD
        PACK    DW(8),CARD+11(4)
        CVB     4,DW
        .
        .
        .
DW      DS      1D
CARD    DS      80C
XX      DCB     DSORG=PS,RECFM=FB,MACRF=GM,DDNAME=SYSIN
        .
        .
        .
```

Convert to decimal

Machine format [RX] :

4E	R$_1$	X$_2$	B$_2$	D$_2$
0 7	8 11	12 15	16 19	20 31

Assembler format: CVD   R$_1$,D$_2$(X$_2$,B$_2$)

Meaning: The first operand is a 32-bit two's complement integer in R$_1$. It is converted to packed decimal format and stored in the double word at the second operand address. The second operand must lie on a double-word boundary. Since the range of the result, 15 decimal digits, is larger than the range of the source, 2^{31}, the result will never be too big to fit.

Unpack

Machine format [SS] :

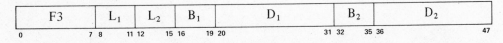

F3	L$_1$	L$_2$	B$_1$	D$_1$	B$_2$	D$_2$
0 7	8 11	12 15	16 19	20 31	32 35	36 47

Assembler format: UNPK   D$_1$(l_1,B$_1$),D$_2$(l_2,B$_2$)

Meaning: The second operand is assumed to be in packed decimal form. It is converted to zoned decimal form and stored in the first operand location, extended with high-order zeros if necessary. The lengths of the two operands are indicated by l_1 and l_2 in assembler language and by L_1 and L_2 in the machine format. If the first operand length is not long enough to hold all the digits of the result, high-order digits will be lost, the result will be incorrect, and there will be no message.

The sign and digits that are moved are not inspected for valid codes. When using EBCDIC encoding, zones of 1111_2 are supplied.

The bytes of the first operand are processed from right to left, with two result bytes stored for each byte fetched except for the first byte. If an attempt is made to overlap the two fields caution must be exercised to avoid destruction of bytes that have not yet been processed.

An example using CVD and UNPK is as follows:

Before:			C(R3) = FF FF FF AB = -85
Execute:	CVD	3,IJK	
After:			C(IJK) = 00 00 00 00 00 00 08 5D
Then			
Execute:	UNPK	X(5),IJK+5(3)	
After:			C(X) = F0 F0 F0 F8 D5

CONVERSION OF ZONED DECIMAL NUMBERS TO PRINTABLE FORM

In the UNPK example, the result at X was F0 F0 F0 F8 D5$_H$ which is almost printable, but not quite. The first four bytes can be printed as they stand to produce the graphics

0008

but the last byte will print as the graphic N because of the sign information contained in it. To fix this, we write a program segment to examine the last byte of the string X. If the last byte is greater than or equal to D0, the number is negative; if the last byte is less than D0, the number is positive. Then we insert the appropriate leading sign character in front of the string, change the sign in the last byte from D or C to F to make the last byte printable, and print the line. The program segment is

```
        MVC    LINE+4(5),X                        move string
        CLI    LINE+8,X'D0'                       examine last byte
        BL     POS
        MVI    LINE+3,C'-'                         insert leading minus sign
        B      J
POS     MVI    LINE+3,C'+'                         insert leading plus sign
J       OI     LINE+8,X'F0'                        remove sign from last byte
        PUT    YY,LINE
                   .
                   .
                   .
LINE    DC     133C'b'
YY      DCB    DSORG=PS,RECFM=FBA,MACRF=PM,BLKSIZE=1064,        X
               LRECL=133,DDNAME=SYSPRINT
```

(Math.Trip/1939)

The sign was deleted from the last byte with the Or Immediate instruction, which has the form   OI $D_1(B_1),I_2$. This OR's the immediate operand with the first operand, and leaves the result in the first operand location. In this case   OI   LINE+8,X'F0' has the effect of forcing the left half of the byte at LINE+8 to F, thus rendering the last byte printable as a 5. The result is that the printed line is

    bb-00085bbbb. . .

An alternative to using Or Immediate is to use the instruction Move Zones, which has the form   MVZ $D_1(l,B_1),D_2(B_2)$. This is the same form as the Move Characters instruction, MVC, and it has the same meaning, except that only the zones, the left half-bytes, are copied from the source to the destination, and the right half-bytes in the destination string remain undisturbed. Thus one could insert a zone of F_H at LINE+8 with the instruction

        MVZ   LINE+8(1),CON

where CON is defined by the statement

    CON   DC   X'F0'

The instruction Move Numerics, MVN, is similar to MVZ, except that it copies only the numerics, the right half-bytes, and leaves the left half-bytes undisturbed.

   A complete program using the PACK, CVB, CVD, and UNPK instructions is shown in Figures 9-2 and 9-3. The program reads a card containing in columns 12 to 15 and 20 to 23 two positive four-digit decimal integers with leading zeros punched. It prints the entire card image. Then it converts the two numbers to binary, subtracts the second from the first using binary arithmetic, converts the result back to character form with a leading sign inserted, and prints the first 29 characters of the card image and the result. Figure 9-2 shows the assembler listing and the execution output. For practice the reader should verify that the assembly of some of the conversion instructions is correct. In this case the input data cards also contained some alphabetic information that was unrelated to the

```
LOC    OBJECT CODE     ADDR1 ADDR2 STMT   SOURCE STATEMENT                                F15OCT70  6/14/72

C00000                              1 MAIN      CSECT
C00000 9CEC C00C            0000C   2          STM    14,12,12(13)
C00004 05C0                         3          BALR   12,0
C00006                              4          USING  *,12
                                    5          PRINT  NOGEN
                                    6 BEGIN     OPEN   (XX,INPUT,YY,OUTPUT)
C00016 4130 0003            0C003  14          LA     3,3
                                   15 LP        GET    XX,CARD
                                   20           PUT    YY,L1
C00036 F273 C1CA C15E C01E0 00164  25           PACK   DW(8),CARD+11(4)
C0003C 4F40 C1DA            001E0  26           CVB    4,DW
C00040 F273 C1E2 C166 C01E8 0C16C  27           PACK   DW2(8),CARD+19(4)
C00046 4F50 C1E2            001E8  28           CVB    5,DW2
C0004A 1B45                        29           SR     4,5
C0004C 4E40 C1E2            001E8  30           CVD    4,DW2
C00050 F337 C209 C1E2 C020F 001E8  31           UNPK   LINE+31(4),DW2(8)
C00056 95DC C20C      C0212        32           CLI    LINE+34,X'D0'
C0005A 4740 C060            0C066  33           BL     POS
C0005E 926C C208      C020E        34           MVI    LINE+30,C'-'
C00062 47F0 C064            0C06A  35           B      J
C00066 924E C2C8      C020E        36 POS       MVI    LINE+30,C'+'
C0006A 96F0 C20C      C0212        37 J         OI     LINE+34,X'F0'
C0006E D21C C1EB C153 001F1 0C159  38           MVC    LINE+1(29),CARD
                                   39           PUT    YY,LINE
C00082 4630 C014            0001A  44           BCT    3,LP
                                   45 ENDDATA   CLOSE  (YY)
C00092 98EC C00C      0C0CC        51           LM     14,12,12(13)
C00096 07FE                        52 YY        BCR    15,14
                                   53 YY        DCB    DSORG=PS,RECFM=FBA,MACRF=PM,BLKSIZE=1064,     X
                                                       LRECL=133,DDNAME=SYSPRINT
                                  107 XX        JCB    DSORG=PS,RECFM=FB,MACRF=GM,DDNAME=SYSIN,EODAD=ENDDATA
000158 40                        161 L1        DC     C' '
000159                           162 CARD      DS     80C
0001A9 5C5C5C5C5C5C5C5C5C        163           DC     52C'*'
0001EC                           164 DW        DS     1D
0001E8                           165 DW2       DS     1D
0001F0 404C404040404040          166 LINE      DC     60C' '
00022C 7B7B7B7B7B7B7B7B7B        167           DC     73C'#'
                                 168           END
```

```
0033    0033 ABC  ABC        ABC       ABC          ***************************************************
0033    0033 ABC  +0000      ABC       ABC          ###################################################
0237    3468 DEF  DEF        DEF       DEF          ***************************************************
0237    3468 DEF  -3231      DEF       DEF          ###################################################
0018    0012 GHI  GHI        GHI       GHI          ***************************************************
0018    0012 GHI  +0006      GHI       GHI          ###################################################
```

Figure 9-2. Assembler F listing of a decimal conversion program and (below the line) the execution output.

problem at hand; the portion that lay in columns 1 to 29 was also reproduced as output. Figure 9-3 shows a listing of the deck for this program to show the ordering of the control cards, the data deck, etc. The ESP version is similar except that the OPEN, CLOSE, and DCB statements are not needed.

EXERCISES

1. Show the contents of D and F at the conclusion of execution of this program segment.

```
        L      5,A
        CVD    5,D
        UNPK   F(8),D(8)
        .
        .
        .
D       DS     1D
F       DS     12C
A       DC     X'FFFFFFE7'
```

****

```
//D227    JOB    'U9329,TIME=3,SIZE=96K',BREARLEY,MSGLEVEL=(1,1)
//STEP2   EXEC   ASMFCLG
//ASM.SYSIN DD   *
MAIN      CSECT
          STM    14,12,12(13)
          BALR   12,0
          USING  *,12
          PRINT  NOGEN
BEGIN     OPEN   (XX,INPUT,YY,OUTPUT)
          LA     3,3
LP        GET    XX,CARD
          PUT    YY,L1
          PACK   DW(8),CARD+11(4)
          CVB    4,DW
          PACK   DW2(8),CARD+19(4)
          CVB    5,DW2
          SR     4,5
          CVD    4,DW2
          UNPK   LINE+31(4),DW2(8)
          CLI    LINE+34,X'D0'
          BL     POS
          MVI    LINE+30,C'-'
          B      J
POS       MVI    LINE+30,C'+'
J         OI     LINE+34,X'F0'
          MVC    LINE+1(29),CARD
          PUT    YY,LINE
          BCT    3,LP
ENDDATA   CLOSE  (YY)
          LM     14,12,12(13)
          BCR    15,14
YY        DCB    DSORG=PS,RECFM=FBA,MACRF=PM,BLKSIZE=1064,          X
                 LRECL=133,DDNAME=SYSPRINT
XX        DCB    DSORG=PS,RECFM=FB,MACRF=GM,DDNAME=SYSIN,EODAD=ENDDATA
L1        DC     C' '
CARD      DS     80C
          DC     52C'*'
DW        DS     1D
DW2       DS     1D
LINE      DC     60C' '
          DC     73C'#'
          END
/*
//GO.SYSPRINT DD SYSCUT=A
//GO.SYSUDUMP DD SYSCUT=A
//GO.SYSIN DD   *
          0033   0033 ABC  ABC       ABC       ABC
          0237   3468 DEF  DEF       DEF       DEF
          0018   0012 GHI  GHI       GHI       GHI
CARD 4    XXXXXXXXXXXXXXXXXXXXXXXXXX
CARD5 YYYYYY        YYYYYYYY      YYYYYYYYY
CARD 6  ZZZZZZ      ZZZZZZZ    ZZZZZZZZZZZZZZZZZZZZZZZZZZZZZZZZZZZZZZZZZZZZ
/*
```

Figure 9-3.   Complete deck for Assembler F decimal conversion program of Figure 9-2.

2. At the conclusion of execution of this program segment, show the contents of R3, R7, and B.

```
          LA      2,2
          LA      3,2
          LA      4,2
          LA      5,A
          MR      2,4
          EX      3,C
          CVB     7,B
          ST      7,D
            .
            .
            .
A    DC     C'000456789'
B    DS     1D
C    PACK   B(8),2(0,5)
D    DS     1F
```

3. Translate the following program into object code by hand; show the results in the form of an assembler listing. Also translate it on an assembler and compare the results. If this program is executed, what will be stored in I?

```
ABC        CSECT
           STM        14,12,12(13)
           BALR       12,0
           USING      *,12
           PACK       DW(8),CARD+10(6)
           CVB        7,DW
           ST         7,I
           LM         2,12,28(13)
           BCR        15,14
DW         DS         1D
I          DS         1F
CARD       DC         C'123123123'
           DC         C'456456456'
           DC         C'789'
           DC         20C' '
X          DS         1F
           END
```

4. Write a program like the example of Figure 9-2, except print the result with a floating minus sign with leading zeros suppressed and plus signs suppressed.

5. Write a program like the example program of Figure 9-2, except allow input of signed integers with the sign in a fixed position and leading zeros punched.

6. Write a program like the example program of Figure 9-2, except allow a variable input format in which the first integer can be anywhere in columns 1 to 20 and the second integer can be anywhere in columns 22 to 42. The input numbers may have up to 12 decimal digits, the leading zeros are suppressed, and there is a floating sign. If the sign is absent, assume that the number is positive.

7. Write a program to read all the numbers on a card, convert them to binary, add them, and print the sum. The number of numbers on the card is variable; the numbers are separated by at least one blank. If the card is all blank, set the sum to zero. If the card contains anything other than legal signed and unsigned integers, print an error message.

8. A deck of cards contains words, where a word is defined to be a string of contiguous nonblank characters delimited by blanks or card boundaries. The deck is terminated by a card with # in column 1. Write a program to read and list the cards in the deck and count the cards and words in the deck. Then print suitable messages and the card count and word count in decimal with leading zeros suppressed. Then terminate execution. The program should work for any reasonable length of deck and number of words, including zero. Assume that words will not be broken across card boundaries.

9. Same as Exercise 8, except allow words to be broken across card boundaries if properly hyphenated. A hyphenated word should count as one word, not two.

10. Same as Exercise 8, except allow data decks that are terminated with a # in column 1 to be concatenated. Each time the program encounters a # it should print a message and the number of cards and words in the previous deck, reset the counters to zero, and begin reading the next deck. Eventually terminate by attempting to read beyond the end of the last #.

11. Write a program to count the number of letters A through Z in a deck of cards and print the result.

12. Write a program to print in hexadecimal the contents of a 20-byte string. For example, if the first byte of the string is $D7_H$, then the program should construct two bytes C4 F7, which when transmitted to the printer will produce the graphics D7. Test the program by using it to print in hex a 20-byte portion of the program itself.

Subprograms

A *subprogram* is a program segment that is used by another program.[1] For example, program BBC might need to scan card images to find a number, and this need might occur at three places in program BBC. One way to handle this problem is to write a program to do the scanning (name it SCAN), and invoke it three times. This is indicated schematically in Figure 10-1.

There are several reasons for using subprograms:

1. To avoid writing the same thing more than once.

2. To avoid writing anything at all by using a subprogram that somebody else wrote.

3. To break a long program into shorter pieces to facilitate assembly, debugging, and possible future modification.

FLOW OF CONTROL

With subprograms there are two problems related to flow of control:

1. How to enter the subprogram.

2. How to exit from the subprogram.

---

[1] Subprograms are also sometimes called subroutines, but in Fortran a subroutine is a particular kind of subprogram. To avoid confusion, we use the more general term subprogram.

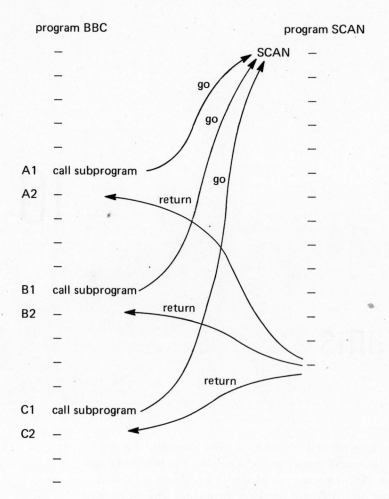

Figure 10-1. Flow of control between a calling program, BBC, and a called program, SCAN.

Consider first the case in which the calling program and the called program are assembled together in one assembly. Then the calling program can refer to the called program symbolically. In Figure 10-1 the flow of control from A1 or B1 or C1 to the beginning of SCAN could be accomplished with an ordinary branch instruction   BC   15,SCAN, but it is not usually done this way because of the problem of exiting. Exiting from the called program and returning control to the calling program involve (in this case) a three-way branch. The flow of control should return to a *return address* which is a variable; that is, it depends on where the subprogram was called from. When SCAN is called from A1, then the return address should be A2; when SCAN is called from B1, the return address should be B2; etc. This can be accomplished with the following instructions:

Branch and link

Machine format [RX] :

45	R_1	X_2	B_2	D_2

0   7 8   11 12   15 16   19 20   31

Assembler format [RX] :   BAL $R_1, D_2(X_2, B_2)$

Machine format [RR] :

05	R_1	R_2

0   7 8   11 12   15

Assembler format [RR] :   BALR R_1, R_2

Meaning: Store the updated instruction address, that is, the address of the next instruction, in R_1; then branch to the branch address where

$$\text{branch address} = C(X_2) + C(B_2) + D_2 \quad \text{in RX format}$$

$$= C(R_2) \quad \text{in RR format}$$

In RR format, when $R_2 = 0$, store the updated instruction address in R_1 but do not branch.

Figure 10-2 shows an example of a calling program and a called program assembled in one assembly. The called program is invoked twice, once at A1 and once at B1, with the instruction

        BAL   11,XXX

This stores the updated instruction address (the return address) in R11 and then branches to XXX, which is at the beginning of the called program. At the end of execution of the called program, the instruction

        BCR   15,11

branches to the address in R11, that is, to 108_H after calling from 104_H and to $3AA_H$ after calling from $3A6_H$, provided that C(R11) has not been destroyed by the subprogram.[2]

TRANSMISSION OF ARGUMENTS

A subprogram may have zero or more *arguments,* which represent information to be transmitted between the calling program and the subprogram. In general, some of the arguments are input arguments representing data that is to be used by the subprogram, and some of them are output arguments or answers. There are several ways to transmit

---

[2]Here we describe the addresses as if the program were loaded and executed at location 000. Actually, it will be relocated before execution and the absolute addresses will be bigger than the values shown by the amount of this relocation.

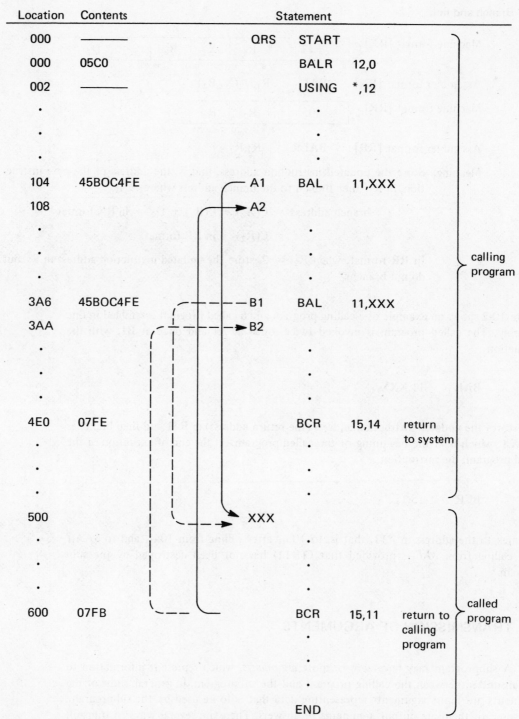

Location	Contents		Statement	
000	——	QRS	START	
000	05C0		BALR	12,0
002	——		USING	*,12
.			.	
.			.	
.			.	
104	45B0C4FE	A1	BAL	11,XXX
108		A2		
.			.	
.			.	
3A6	45B0C4FE	B1	BAL	11,XXX
3AA		B2		
.			.	
.			.	
4E0	07FE		BCR	15,14 return to system
.			.	
.			.	
.			.	
500		XXX		
.			.	
.			.	
600	07FB		BCR	15,11 return to calling program
.			.	
.			.	
			END	

calling program

called program

Figure 10-2. Flow of control for a calling program and a called program assembled in one assembly. Flow at first use of subprogram is indicated by solid lines, flow at second use is indicated by dashed lines.

arguments to and from subprograms. Three ways, in order of increasing sophistication, are as follows:

1. Use common names.

2. Transmit arguments via registers.

3. Use an argument address list.

Method 1 uses common names. This method applies only when the calling and the called programs are assembled together. Then a symbol such as ABC in the calling program and the symbol ABC in the called program both refer to the same location in memory.

As an example of method 1, we write a subprogram named SIGN with one input argument I and one output argument J, where I and J are full words. This is indicated schematically as

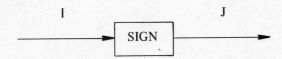

or in function notation as

$$J = SIGN(I)$$

The definition of SIGN is

if I $>$ 0, then J $=$ +1

if I $=$ 0, then J $=$ 0

if I $<$ 0, then J $=$ -1

In the main program we invoke this subprogram twice to calculate

$$CS = SIGN(C)$$

and

$$DS = SIGN(D)$$

We assume that at the time the flow of control passes from the calling to the called program that the input argument is in I and when control passes back that the output argument is in J. Then the calling and the called programs are as shown in Figure 10-3. Note that symbols I and J are known to both programs. The value of the symbol I is 000034 throughout both programs, and I is referred to in statements 9, 16, and 31 as $02E_H$ bytes beyond the address in R12, where C(R12) $=$ 006 relative.

```
LOC    OBJECT CODE    ADDR1 ADDR2  STMT    SOURCE STATEMENT

000000                                1 ABC        START
000000 90EC D00C            0000C     2            STM    14,12,12(13)
000004 05C0                            3            BALR   12,0
000006                                 4            USING  *,12
                                       5 * CALLING PROGRAM
                                       6 *
                                       7 * FIRST CALLING SEQUENCE
000006 5820 C03E            00044      8            L      2,C
00000A 5020 C02E            00034      9            ST     2,I
00000E 45B0 C046            0004C     10            BAL    11,SIGN
000012 5820 C032            00038     11            L      2,J
000016 5020 C036            0003C     12            ST     2,CS
                                      13 *
                                      14 * SECOND CALLING SEQUENCE
00001A 5820 C042            00048     15            L      2,D
00001E 5020 C02E            00034     16            ST     2,I
000022 45B0 C046            0004C     17            BAL    11,SIGN
000026 5820 C032            00038     18            L      2,J
00002A 5020 C03A            00040     19            ST     2,DS
                                      20 *
00002E 98EC D00C            0000C     21            LM     14,12,12(13)
000032 07FE                           22            BCR    15,14
000034                                23 I          DS     1F
000038                                24 J          DS     1F
00003C                                25 CS         DS     1F
000040                                26 DS         DS     1F
000044 FFFFFFFD                       27 C          DC     F'-3'
000048 00000000                       28 D          DC     F'0'
                                      29 *
                                      30 * CALLED PROGRAM
00004C 5840 C02E            00034     31 SIGN       L      4,I
000050 1244                           32            LTR    4,4
000052 4720 C064            0006A     33            BP     PLUS
000056 4740 C05A            00060     34            BM     MIN
00005A 5040 C032            00038     35            ST     4,J         J=0
00005E 07FB                           36            BCR    15,11
000060 1B44                           37 MIN        SR     4,4
000062 0640                           38            BCTR   4,0
000064 5040 C032            00038     39            ST     4,J         J=-1
000068 07FB                           40            BCR    15,11
00006A 4140 0001            00001     41 PLUS       LA     4,1
00006E 5040 C032            00038     42            ST     4,J         J=+1
000072 07FB                           43            BCR    15,11
                                      44 *
                                      45            END
```

Figure 10-3.   Argument transmission via common names. Input argument is always at I, output argument is always at J.

Method 2 involves the transmission of arguments via registers. When using this method, the author of the calling program and the author of the called program must agree on register use. As an example we rewrite the SIGN example using the conventions that the input argument is in R2 upon entry, the output argument is in R2 upon exit, and R11 contains the return address. The calling and the called programs are shown in Figure 10-4. This shows both programs in one assembly, but the method is also applicable to separate assemblies. This method is useful only when the arguments are small enough to fit in registers and there are enough registers available.

Before describing method 3 for argument transmission, we discuss address constants.

ADDRESS CONSTANTS

A DC statement containing an address constant is of the following form:

Name	Operation	Operand
Symbol or blank	DC	A(one or more relocatable or absolute expressions separated by commas)

```
   LOC    OBJECT CODE    ADDR1 ADDR2   STMT      SOURCE STATEMENT

000000                                  1 ABC        START
000000  90EC D00C               0000C    2           STM    14,12,12(13)
000004  05C0                             3           BALR   12,0
000006                                   4           USING  *,12
                                         5 *
                                         6 * CALLING PROGRAM
                                         7 *
                                         8 * FIRST CALLING SEQUENCE
000006  5820 C026               0002C    9           L      2,C
00000A  45B0 C02E               00034   10           BAL    11,SIGN2
00000E  5020 C01E               00024   11           ST     2,CS
                                        12 *
                                        13 * SECOND CALLING SEQUENCE
000012  5820 C02A               00030   14           L      2,D
000016  45B0 C02E               00034   15           BAL    11,SIGN2
00001A  5020 C022               00028   16           ST     2,DS
                                        17 *
00001E  98EC D00C               0000C   18           LM     14,12,12(13)
000022  07FE                            19           BCR    15,14
000024                                  20 CS         DS     1F
000028                                  21 DS         DS     1F
00002C  FFFFFFFD                        22 C          DC     F'-3'
000030  00000006                        23 D          DC     F'6'
                                        24 *
                                        25 * CALLED PROGRAM
000034  1222                            26 SIGN2      LTR    2,2
000036  4720 C040               00046   27           BP     PLUS
00003A  4740 C03A               00040   28           BM     MIN
00003E  07FB                            29           BCR    15,11     ANS=0
000040  1B22                            30 MIN        SR     2,2
000042  0620                            31           BCTR   2,0
000044  07FB                            32           BCR    15,11     ANS=-1
000046  4120 0001               00001   33 PLUS       LA     2,1
00004A  07FB                            34           BCR    15,11     ANS=+1
                                        35 *
                                        36           END
```

Figure 10-4.   Argument transmission via registers.

Address constants are enclosed in parentheses instead of in single quotes as for other types of constants. The object code corresponding to this statement consists of one four-byte address for each expression, aligned on a full-word boundary. For example, the object code for

        AD   DC   A(PAT)

is a four-byte constant containing the address of the symbol PAT. If PAT is a relocatable symbol, then the address constant is relocatable. This means that upon relocation the loader must adjust the value of the address constant by adding the relocation amount. If the relative address of PAT is 02C and the program is relocated by 04C020, then the absolute value of the address constant at execution time is

$$
\begin{array}{r}
02C \\
+\ 04C020 \\
\hline
04C04C
\end{array}
$$

If the constant is an absolute expression as in

        DEF   DC   A(21)

then a four-byte constant, 00000015, is created. However, this is an absolute address and it will *not* be adjusted upon relocation.[3]

Address constants as described have an implied length of four bytes and automatic alignment on full-word boundaries. If an explicit length is specified by the insertion of a length modifier of the form L*n* following the A, then a constant *n* bytes long will be generated and there will be no automatic boundary alignment. For example,

JOE   DC   AL3(JACK)

will cause the creation of a three-byte address constant at the next available byte. Figure 10-5 shows some absolute and relocatable address constants as assembled and as loaded.

ARGUMENT ADDRESS LISTS

A more general method of argument transmission is by means of an *argument address list,* also called an argument list. This method is applicable to programs that are assembled together or separately, and it can handle any number of arguments of any length. To use this method one creates in the calling program a list of addresses of arguments and then sets R1 to point to the first word in this list. The list of addresses lies in consecutive full words in memory, but the arguments referred to can be of any length and can lie anywhere in memory.

```
LOC   OBJECT CODE      ADDR1 ADDR2   STMT    SOURCE STATEMENT

000000                            1 ABC     START
000000 00000018                   2 A       DC    A(JOHN)          RELOCATABLE
000004 00000015                   3 B       DC    A(21)            ABSOLUTE
000008 0000000E                   4 C       DC    A(PAT-JOHN+2)    ABSOLUTE EXPRESSION
00000C 0000001700000006           5 D       DC    A(23,6,JOE-4)    MULTIPLE OPERANDS
                                  6 *                              RELOCATABLE EXPRESSION
000018 0006                       7 JOHN    DC    AL2(6)    ABSOLUTE, LENGTH MODIFIER
00001A 000018                     8 JOE     DC    AL3(JACK)  RELOCATABLE, LENGTH MODIFIER
00001D 00000018                   9 K       DC    AL4(JACK)        UNALIGNED
000021 000000
000024 00000018                  10 PAT     DC    A(JACK)          ALIGNED
000028 00000007                  11 JILL    DC    A(CON)           ABSOLUTE
000018                           12 JACK    EQU   JOHN
000007                           13 CON     EQU   7
                                 14         END
```

```
LOAD MODULE    GO

06EFC0
06EFE0     00000006 0006EFE6 0J0606EF E80006EF      0006EFE8 00000015 0000000E 00000017
                                                    E8000000 0006EFE8 00000007 807C419B
```

Figure 10-5. Relocatable and absolute address constants. Above the line is the assembler listing. Below the line is the object code after relocation to 06EFD0. Note which constants were increased by 06EFD0.

---

[3]The information about which constants need to be adjusted upon relocation and which do not need to be adjusted is kept in a table called the relocation dictionary. This table is created by the assembler and used by the loader. For further details, see *Assembler [F] Programmer's Guide,* Form GC26-3756.

When using this method we follow the standard conventions for register usage to avoid confusion. The conventions are as follows:

Register	Contents
15	Address of the program being called, also called the entry-point address
14	Return address
13	Address of an 18-word area in which the called program can store the register contents (see section on register saving)
1	Address of the argument address list
0	Optional result register, which may be used to return a single four-byte fixed-point result

Registers 2 through 12 should be used for all other purposes, including base registers.

Using these conventions, the calling sequence for method 3 is as follows:

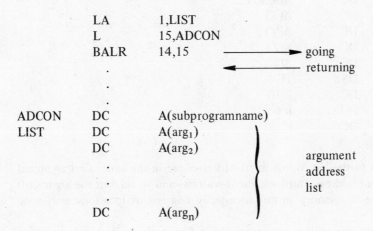

```
         LA      1,LIST
         L       15,ADCON
         BALR    14,15    ──────────▶ going
            .             ◀────────── returning
            .
            .
ADCON    DC      A(subprogramname)
LIST     DC      A(arg₁)          ⎫
         DC      A(arg₂)          ⎬  argument
            .                     ⎪  address
            .                     ⎪  list
         DC      A(argₙ)          ⎭
```

The instruction

```
     L          15,ADCON
```

puts the address of the called program into R15 and then

```
     BALR    14,15
```

branches to that address. In the called program the addresses of the arguments can be retrieved by fetching the address from 0, 4, 8, 12, and so on, bytes beyond the address in R1. Then that number can be used as an address to fetch or store the argument itself.

To exit from the called program, one writes   BCR   15,14   to return control to the instruction following   BALR   14,15.

As an example, we show a subprogram named MSQ with three input arguments X, Y, and Z and one output argument W, where $W = X^2 + Y^2 + Z^2$. This is indicated schematically as follows:

$$X, Y, Z \qquad\qquad W = MSQ(X,Y,Z) = X^2 + Y^2 + Z^2$$

To invoke this subprogram to calculate MSQ(10,−3,6), the calling sequence is

```
        LA      1,LST
        L       15,ADCON
        BALR    14,15
          .
          .
          .
ADCON   DC      A(MSQ)
LST     DC      A(X)
        DC      A(Y)
        DC      A(Z)
        DC      A(W)
W       DS      1F
X       DC      F'10'
Z       DC      F'6'
Y       DC      F'-3'
```

Note that the addresses in the list of argument addresses are in the order first argument address, second argument address, third argument address, and so on, but the arguments themselves lie elsewhere in memory in not necessarily contiguous locations and in no particular order.

Figure 10-6 shows the calling sequence, the subprogram, and a postexecution dump. Note the address constants. In the assembler listing the address constant A(X) lies at 00001C and has contents 00000030. After relocation, it lies at

$$\begin{array}{r} 00001C \\ + 06A2B0 \\ \hline 06A2CC \end{array}$$

and has contents

$$\begin{array}{r} 000030 \\ + 06A2B0 \\ \hline 06A2E0 \end{array}$$

The relation between the argument address list and the arguments is indicated schematically in Figure 10-7.

```
      LOC    OBJECT          ADDR1 ADDR2 STMT SOURCE STATEMENT

      000000                             1 MAIN      CSECT
      000000 90EC D00C                   2           STM     14,12,12(13)
      000004 05C0                        3           BALR    12,0
      000006                             4           USING   *,12
                                         5 * CALLING SEQUENCE
      000006 4110 C016       0001C       6           LA      1,LST
      00000A 58F0 C012       00018       7           L       15,ADCON
      00000E 05EF                        8           BALR    14,15
                                         9 * CONTINUATION OF MAIN PROGRAM
      000010 98EC D00C                  10           LM      14,12,12(13)
      000014 07FE                       11           BCR     15,14
      000018 0000003C                   12 ADCON     DC      A(MSQ)
      00001C 00000030                   13 LST       DC      A(X)
      000020 00000038                   14           DC      A(Y)
      000024 0C000034                   15           DC      A(Z)
      000028 0000002C                   16           DC      A(W)
      00002C                            17 W         DS      1F
      000030 0000000A                   18 X         CC      F'10'
      000034 00000006                   19 Z         DC      F'6'
      000038 FFFFFFFD                   20 Y         DC      F'-3'
                                        21 *
                                        22 *  SUBPROGRAM BEGINS HERE
      00003C 9825 1000                  23 MSQ       LM      2,5,0(1)    FETCH FOUR ARGUMENT ADDRESSES
      000040 5870 2000                  24           L       7,0(0,2)    FETCH FIRST ARGUMENT
      000044 1C67                       25           MR      6,7         SQUARE FIRST ARGUMENT
      000046 5890 3000                  26           L       9,0(0,3)    FETCH SECOND ARGUMENT
      00004A 1C89                       27           MR      8,9         SQUARE SECOND ARGUMENT
      00004C 1A79                       28           AR      7,9
      00004E 5890 4000                  29           L       9,0(0,4)    FETCH THIRD ARGUMENT
      000052 1C89                       30           MR      8,9         SQUARE  THIRD ARGUMENT
      000054 1A79                       31           AR      7,9
      000056 5070 5000                  32           ST      7,0(0,5)
      00005A 07FE                       33           BCR     15,14       RETURN
      000000                            34           END

      NC  ERRORS/WARNINGS FOUND IN THIS ASSEMBLY
```

```
PROGRAM WAS ENTERED AT 06A2B0

06A2A0                                                    90ECD00C  05C04110  C01658F0  C01205EF
06A2C0   98ECD00C  07FEC1D4  0006A2EC  0006A2E0  0006A2E8  0006A2E4  0006A2DC  00000091
06A2E0   0000000A  00000006  FFFFFFFD  98251000  58702000  1C675890  30001C89  1A795890
C6A300   40001C89  1A795070  500007FE  D6E6C140  C9D6E6C1  40E2E3C1  E3C540E4  D5C9E5C5
06A320   D9E2C9E3  E840C1D4  C5E26BC9  D6E6C140  C9D6E6C1  40E2E3C1  E3C540E4  D5C9E5C5
```

Figure 10-6.   Argument transmission via a fixed length argument address list.

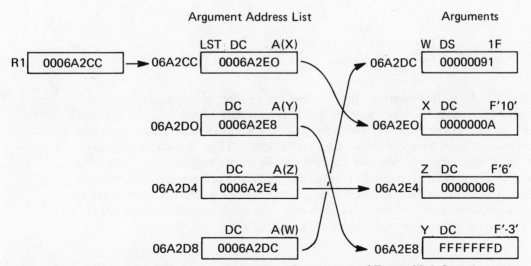

Figure 10-7.   Argument address list and arguments for program of Figure 10-6. Locations and contents are shown symbolically and in hexadecimal as read from the dump.

In the subprogram the first instruction is

    LM   2,5,0(1)

This fetches the four argument addresses into registers 2 through 5. If there were not enough registers available, the arguments could be fetched one at a time. Then the arguments themselves are fetched and manipulated, and finally the result is stored with

    ST   7,0(0,5)

VARIABLE-LENGTH ARGUMENT LISTS

The subprogram MSQ was written with a fixed number of arguments. It was known when the calling program was written and when the called program was written that there were to be exactly three input arguments and one output argument. It is also possible to write a subprogram to handle a variable number of arguments; that is, the number of arguments is not known at assembly time. For example, consider a subprogram named SUM with n arguments. The subprogram is to add the first $n - 1$ arguments and store the sum into the nth argument. This can be accomplished by fetching the argument addresses and arguments one at a time and adding the arguments to a running sum, with the process continuing until the end of the argument address list. The end of the argument address list may be indicated by inserting a flag, thus:

    LIST   DC   A(arg$_1$)
            DC   A(arg$_2$)
            DC   A(arg$_3$)
             .
             .
             .
            DC   A(arg$_{n-1}$)
            DC   X'80'
            DC   AL3(arg$_n$)

The first $n - 1$ DC statements in this list cause the creation of four-byte address constants. However, since the largest possible 360 address is only 24 bits long, the left-hand byte of each address constant will always be 00_H. The next-to-last DC statement causes the creation of a one-byte constant, $80_H = 10000000_2$. There is no automatic alignment for X-type constants, but this constant will lie at the beginning of a full word because of the previous statement. The last DC statement contains an explicit-length modifier, L3, which overrides the implied length and causes the creation of a three-byte address constant without any automatic alignment. The combined effect of the last two DC statements is to create one full word in the argument address list, thus:

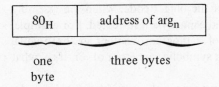

80$_H$	address of arg$_n$

one
byte

three bytes

The subprogram can sense this full word by noting that it is negative when interpreted arithmetically, while all the other full words in the list are positive. The insertion of the negative sign does not interfere with the use of this word as an address, because the addition that occurs in the calculation of the effective address of an operand is only 24 bits wide and the left-hand 8 bits are ignored.

The subprogram and a calling program are shown in Figure 10-8. The subprogram contains a loop. One argument is fetched and examined for sign on each trip through the loop. If it is positive, the program continues; if it is negative, the sum is stored and control returns to the calling program.

```
LOC     OBJECT CODE     ADDR1 ADDR2  STMT   SOURCE STATEMENT

000000                                  1 MAIN    CSECT
000300  90EC D00C             0000C      2         STM    14,12,12(13)
000004  05C0                             3         BALR   12,0
000006                                   4         USING  *,12
                                         5 * CALLING SEQUENCE
000006  4110 C00E             00014      6         LA     1,LST
00000A  45E0 C036             0003C      7         BAL    14,SUM
                                         8 * CONTINUATION OF MAIN PROGRAM
00000E  98EC D00C             0000C      9         LM     14,12,12(13)
000012  07FE                            10         BCR    15,14
000014  00000028                        11 LST     DC     A(X)
000018  0000002C                        12         DC     A(Y)
00001C  00000030                        13         DC     A(Z)
000020  00000034                        14         DC     A(W)
000024  80                              15         DC     X'80'
000025  000038                          16         DC     AL3(Q)
000028  0000000A                        17 X       DC     F'10'
00002C  FFFFFFFD                        18 Y       DC     F'-3'
000030  00000006                        19 Z       DC     F'6'
000034  0000000E                        20 W       DC     F'14'
000038                                  21 Q       DS     1F
                                        22 *
                                        23 * SUBPROGRAM
00003C  1B44                            24 SUM     SR     4,4          SUM=0
00003E  1B22                            25         SR     2,2          INDEX = 0
000040  5852 1000             00000     26 LOOP    L      5,0(2,1)     FETCH (FIRST) ADDRESS
000044  1255                            27         LTR    5,5          TEST SIGN
000046  4740 C050             00056     28         BM     NEG          OF ADDRESS
00004A  5A40 5000             00000     29         A      4,0(0,5)     ADD (FIRST) ARGUMENT
00004E  4120 2004             00004     30         LA     2,4(0,2)     STEP INDEX
000052  47F0 C03A             00040     31         B      LOOP
000056  5040 5000             00000     32 NEG     ST     4,0(0,5)     STORE SUM
00005A  07FE                            33         BCR    15,14        RETURN
                                        34         END
```

Figure 10-8. A subprogram that uses a variable length argument address list.

SEPARATELY ASSEMBLED PROGRAMS[4]

So far the example subprograms have been assembled in the same assembly with the calling program. If the calling and the called programs are assembled separately and then linked together before execution, some new problems arise.

First, we distinguish between *ordinary* or local symbols and *external* or global symbols. An ordinary symbol is the kind we have used almost exclusively so far. An ordinary symbol has meaning only throughout one assembly. During assembly it is used

---

[4]This section applies only to the IBM assemblers; ESP does not handle separate assemblies.

to create the symbol table and thence to construct the object code. When the assembly process is complete, the ordinary symbols vanish and cannot be resurrected. For example, one cannot tell by looking at the object code of a program whether in the original assembler language version a particular word had a symbolic name or not, or, if so, what that name was.

External symbols are used for linkages between separately assembled programs. An external symbol does not vanish forever at the end of assembly; rather, its character string form is preserved in a table called the external symbol dictionary, which is used by the linkage editor to establish the linkages between programs.[5] One can declare a symbol to be external in several ways:

1. The name of a CSECT statement is automatically an external symbol; it does not need to be declared further.

2. A symbol can be declared to be external by writing

Name	Operation	Operand
Blank	EXTRN	One or more relocatable symbols separated by commas

3. By using a V-type operand in a DC statement. The effect of a V-type operand is the same as the effect of an A-type operand plus an EXTRN statement.

For example, to branch to a separately assembled subprogram named DEF, one can write

```
          L        15,ADCON
          BALR     14,15
            .
            .
            .
ADCON     DC       A(DEF)
          EXTRN    DEF
```

This has the effect of declaring ADCON to be the symbolic name of an address constant of an external symbol DEF. The same thing can be done by writing

```
          L        15,ADCON
          BALR     14,15
            .
            .
            .
ADCON     DC       V(DEF)
```

---

[5]For further details see *Assembler [F] Programmer's Guide*, GC26-3756, and J. J. Donovan, *Systems Programming* (New York: McGraw-Hill, 1972).

Both sequences have the effect of allowing a branch out of this program to external symbol DEF. In both cases the value of the address of DEF is unknown to the assembler at assembly time, so the assembler will create an address constant of 00000000_H. Later the linkage editor will have to fill in the value of the address of DEF after all the program segments that will run together have been prepared for loading into the memory for execution.

DEF must be defined as an entry point in one of the programs that is loaded into the machine with this program. This will be true if it appears in the name field of a CSECT statement in one of the other programs or if it is the name of a statement in one of the other programs which is also defined in that program to be an entry point. This can be done by an ENTRY statement of the form

Name	Operation	Operand
Blank	ENTRY	One or more symbols separated by commas

If DEF is not defined as an entry point in any of the programs loaded with the calling program, it is an error.

Figure 10-9 shows part of the output from a job in which two programs were assembled separately, then linkedited together, relocated, loaded, and executed.[6,7] The programs are similar to those in Figure 10-8, and the main program contains a deliberate illegal instruction to force a dump. To illustrate the use of the ENTRY statement, the called program is entered at SUM, which is not the beginning of the control section.

The two programs are assembled separately, with addresses in each beginning at 000, as indicated in column 1 of Figure 10-10. Next the linkage editor takes the object code from these two assemblies and constructs a single load module with addresses running from 000 to 071, as shown in column 2 of Figure 10-10 and in the linkage editor cross-reference table in Figure 10-9. Finally, the loader relocates the object module by (in this case) 70788 bytes and loads it into the memory for execution. The corresponding addresses are shown in column 3 of Figure 10-10. One can verify these addresses from the dump. Note that in MAIN the address constant   DC   A(SUM)   was assembled as 00000000; in the load module as constructed its value was 00000050, as indicated by the linkage editor cross-reference table; and in the load module as executed its value was 000707D8.

SAVING REGISTER CONTENTS

When writing two or more programs to run together, one must avoid conflicts in register usage. In Figure 10-9 one potential conflict concerns return addresses. MAIN uses C(R14) to branch back to the system at the end of execution. AAA uses C(R14) to branch back to MAIN. Conflict is avoided in MAIN by saving C(R14) before calling the subprogram and restoring it just before returning to the system, using the scheme de-

---

[6]This example is simplified in that it does not follow the standard conventions for saving registers. The next three sections discuss these conventions and the reasons for them.

[7]The control cards and other details of separate assembly are not shown here. For details, see *Assembler [F] Programmer's Guide.*

```
       LOC   OBJECT CODE    ADDR1 ADDR2  STMT    SOURCE STATEMENT                           F150CT70   7/21/72

      000000                                        1 MAIN     CSECT
                                                    2 *
                                                    3 * CALLING PROGRAM
      000000 90EC D00C            0000C              4          STM   14,12,12(13)
      000004 05C0                                    5          BALR  12,0
      000006                                         6          USING *,12
                                                    7 * CALLING SEQUENCE
      000006 4110 C01A            00020              8          LA    1,LST
      00000A 58F0 C016            0001C              9          L     15,ADCON
      00000E 05EF                                   10          BALR  14,15
                                                   11 * END OF CALLING SEQUENCE
      000010 00000000                              12          DC    F'0'
      000014 98EC D00C            0000C             13          LM    14,12,12(13)
      000018 07FE                                   14          BCR   15,14
      00001A 0000
      00001C 00000000                              15 ADCON    DC    A(SUM)
                                                   16          EXTRN SUM
      000020 00000034                              17 LST      DC    A(X)
      000024 00000038                              18          DC    A(Y)
      000028 0000003C                              19          DC    A(Z)
      00002C 00000040                              20          DC    A(W)
      000030 80                                    21          DC    X'80'
      000031 000044                                22          DC    AL3(Q)
      000034 0000000A                              23 X        DC    F'10'
      000038 FFFFFFFD                              24 Y        DC    F'-3'
      00003C 00000006                              25 Z        DC    F'6'
      000040 0000000E                              26 W        DC    F'14'
      000044 00000042                              27 Q        DC    F'66'
                                                   28          END
```

```
       LOC   OBJECT CODE    ADDR1 ADDR2  STMT    SOURCE STATEMENT                           F150CT70   7/21/72

      000000                                        1 AAA      CSECT
                                                    2 *        SUBPROGRAM
      000000                                         3 SUM      DS    2F
      000008 05B0                                    4 SUM      BALR  11,0
      00000A                                         5          USING *,11
      00000A 1B44                                    6          SR    4,4          SUM=0
      00000C 1B22                                    7          SR    2,2          INDEX = 0
      00000E 5852 1000            00000              8 LOOP     L     5,0(2,1)     FETCH (FIRST) ADDRESS
      000012 1255                                    9          LTR   5,5          TEST SIGN
      000014 4740 B01A            0C024             10          BM    NEG          OF ADDRESS
      000018 5A40 5000            00000             11          A     4,0(0,5)     ADD (FIRST) ARGUMENT
      00001C 4120 2004            00004             12          LA    2,4(0,2)     STEP INDEX
      000020 47F0 B004            0000E             13          B     LOOP
      000024 5040 5000            00000             14 NEG      ST    4,0(0,5)     STORE SUM
      000028 07FE                                  15          BCR   15,14         RETURN
                                                   16          ENTRY SUM
                                                   17          END
```

```
F44-LEVEL LINKAGE EDITOR OPTIONS SPECIFIED LIST,XREF
         DEFAULT OPTION(S) USED -  SIZE=(90112,12288)


                                    CROSS REFERENCE TABLE


    CONTROL SECTION                        ENTRY

      NAME    ORIGIN  LENGTH         NAME    LOCATION   NAME   LOCATION   NAME   LOCATION   NAME   LOCATION

      MAIN      00      48
      AAA       48      2A
                                     SUM       50


    LOCATION  REFERS TO SYMBOL  IN CONTROL SECTION          LOCATION  REFERS TO SYMBOL  IN CONTROL SECTION

        1C          SUM         AAA
    ENTRY ADDRESS   00
    TOTAL LENGTH    78

    ****GO       DOES NOT EXIST BUT HAS BEEN ADDED TO DATA SET
```

*Figure 10-9. A calling and a called program assembled separately and executed together.
An illegal instruction, DC F'0', was inserted in the calling program to force a dump.*

```
REGS AT ENTRY TC ABEND

    FLTR 0-6     0001762800000088    02CA0600D000C197         C4F2F2F7C6404040    0000000000000000

    REGS 0-7     FD000008  000707A8  00000010  5C018CA8       0000001B  800707CC  000195DC  00023150
    REGS 8-15    00018C80  00017630  00018CA8  400707DA       4007078E  0007F768  40070798  000707D8

LOAD MODULE    GO

070780                     90ECD00C  05C04110    C01A58F0 C01605EF 00000000 98ECD00C   *................o............*
0707A0   07FE0000 000707D8 000707BC  000707C0    000707C4 000707C8 800707CC 0000000A   *...........Q............D...H........*
0707C0   FFFFFFFD 00000006 0000000E  0000001B    40114710 812C48C0 05B01B44 1B225852   *.........................*
0707E0   10001255 4740B01A 5A405000  41202004    47F0B004 50405000 07FE58B0 401812BB   *.... ..... .........o... ....... ...*
```

Figure 10-9. (Continued)

scribed on page 99. Another potential conflict concerns base registers. MAIN uses R12 as a base register. If AAA also used R12 as a base register, that would destroy the base address for MAIN—then upon returning control to MAIN all the effective addresses would be incorrect. We avoided conflict in this case by using a different base register in AAA, but this simple strategy is not adequate for more complicated cases.

In general, one should presume that the calling program and the called program each use most of the registers, so conflict must be avoided by saving and restoring all of

	Symbol	Col. 1 Address as assembled	Col. 2 Address in load module	Col. 3 Address after relocation by 70788 bytes
First program	MAIN	000	000	70788
		047	047	707CF
Second program	AAA	000	048	707DO
	SUM	008	050	707D8
		029	071	707F9

Figure 10-10. Addresses in two separately assembled programs that are loaded and executed together.

them. The standard scheme for saving register contents is as follows. Each calling program defines an 18-word *save area* in which the called program can save the register contents. The standard save area format is shown in Figure 10-11. The calling program also sets R13, the *save area pointer,* to contain the address of that save area. Then the called program saves the registers with

STM   14,12,12(13)

soon after entering the called program, and it restores the registers with

LM   14,12,12(13)

before returning control to its caller.[8]

	Location	Contents
word 1	AREA + 0	Used by operating system, but not ordinarily used by application programs.
word 2	AREA + 4	Backward pointer, to next higher level save area.
word 3	AREA + 8	Forward pointer, to next lower level save area.
word 4	AREA + 12	C(R14), the return address. The first byte is set to FF_H when the called program has returned control.
word 5	AREA + 16	C(R15), the entry point address.
word 6	AREA + 20	C(R0). This may contain a result.
word 7	AREA + 24	C(R1), the address of the argument address list.
word 8	AREA + 28	C(R2)
.	.	.
.	.	.
.	.	.
word 18	AREA + 68	C(R12)

Figure 10-11.   Standard save area layout. (From Basic Fortran IV (E) Programmer's Guide, Form GC28-6603, © 1966 by International Business Machines Corporation, reproduced by permission.)

Figure 10-12 shows three programs MAIN, SUB1, and SUB2. MAIN and SUB1 call other programs, so each of them must define a save area within itself in which its called program can save the register contents. Details of setting up save areas are given in a later section. An important feature of the scheme is that the main program is considered to be a subprogram of the system, and it is treated like any other subprogram. Lowest-level programs, for example, SUB2, use the save area in the program that called them, but they do not define a new save area. (So far in this book we have written all programs as lowest-level subprograms; hence we did not define a new save area.)

---

[8]Except that if R0 contains a result, it should not be restored.

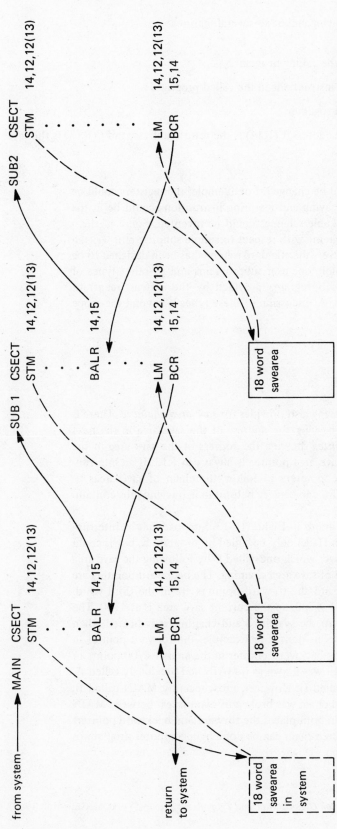

Figure 10-12. *Save areas for nested subprograms. MAIN is treated as a subprogram of the system. Solid lines indicate flow of control. Dashed lines indicate storing and loading of registers.*

The standard scheme for register saving embodies several features:

1. The registers are saved in the calling program.

2. The registers are saved by instructions in the called program.

3. The save areas are chained together.

4. C(R15) is the entry point address, C(R14) is the return address, and C(R13) is the save area pointer.

Each of these features of the design could be changed. For example, the registers could be saved in the called program. Also, the saving and restoring instructions could be in the calling program. And so on. Many workable schemes could be invented. Some of them might be just as good as the standard scheme with respect to simple subprograms written by one user and used only by him. However, the standard scheme has been designed to be applicable to, or extensible to, both simple one-user subprograms and to other types of subprograms. Among these types are subprograms provided by the system, reentrant subprograms, and recursive subprograms. A discussion of these types is beyond the scope of this text.[9]

SAVE AREA CHAINING

The standard scheme for register saving also provides for *save area chaining*. There is in each save area a *backward pointer* showing the address of the save area in the next higher-level program, and a *forward pointer* showing the address of the save area in the next lower-level program. The current save area pointer is always in R13. If an interruption occurs, it is possible to use these pointers to follow the chain of save areas to discover which program called which. This can be very helpful in debugging jobs containing many subprograms.

For example, consider the calling graph in Figure 10-13. Suppose that an interruption occurs while in program H. Program H can only be called by program E, but E could have been called by D or B. We can discover which one called E by following the save area pointers. Figure 10-14 shows an example of save area chaining. The backward pointers are in the second word of each save area, and the forward pointers are in the third word. When the interruption occurs, C(R13) = 4700, so the current save area is at 4700. The chain can be followed all the way back to the system. Valid chaining is indicated when the forward and backward pointers are consistent. For example, the forward pointer in the area at 4100 points to 4700, and the backward pointer in the area at 4700 points to 4100, so they are consistent. Figure 10-14 was drawn as if MAIN had previously called A, which called D which called E which called H. However, most recently MAIN called B, which called E which called H, so the old chain was broken in two places: between MAIN and A and between D and E. Note that in both places the forward and backward pointers no longer agree. The tracing of the save area chain can be done by a computer program or by a human reading a postexecution dump.

---

[9]See C. W. Gear, *Computer Organization and Programming* (New York: McGraw-Hill, 1969), and Donovan, *op. cit.*

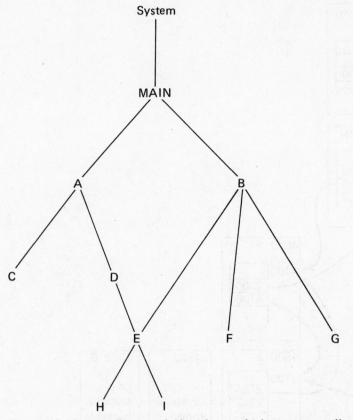

Figure 10-13.   A calling graph that shows which programs call which programs.

FULL CONVENTIONS FOR SUBPROGRAMS

The full conventions for a lowest-level subprogram, one that does not call another subprogram, are shown in Figure 10-15. It begins with a character string name in a standard position and a branch around it. The presence of a name in character string form makes it easier to find this subprogram in a dump containing many subprograms.[10] This subprogram does not define a new save area, but it does save registers 14 through R in the current save area.

At the end, registers 2 through R are restored. R14 containing the return address is presumed to have been undisturbed. R0 is not restored because it may contain a new result. A flag of X'FF' is inserted in the otherwise unused left byte of the fourth word of the current save area to indicate completion.

The full conventions for a program that is not a lowest-level program are shown in Figure 10-16. This is similar to Figure 10-15 except for the statements that

1. Define a new save area.

2. Branch around it.

_____

[10]The control section name, "deckname," and the character string name do not necessarily have to be the same.

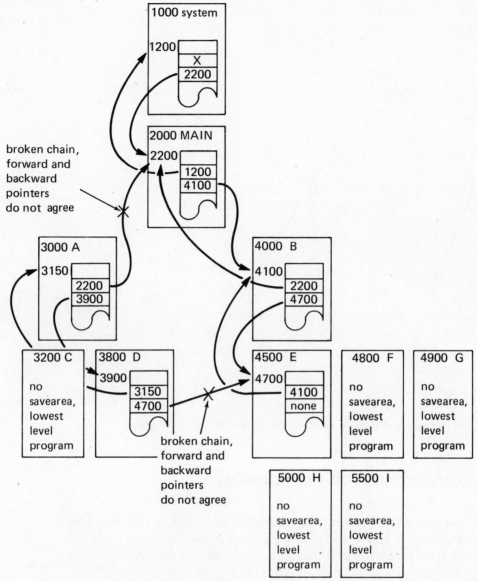

Figure 10-14.   Example of save area chaining.

3. Switch current save area pointers.

4. Store backward and forward pointers.

5. Branch to lower-level program.

Two separately assembled programs that follow all the conventions for character string names, save area definition, and save area chaining are shown in Figure 10-17. The assembler listings are first, followed by the linkage editor cross-reference table. Then comes part of the dump. Note that in the first assembly

$$C(000090_{rel}) = A(SUM) = 00000000$$

Name	Operation	Operand	
deckname	START		
	BC	15,m+1+4(15)	Branch around constants
	DC	X'm'	m must be an odd integer to insure that the STM instruction starts on a half-word boundary. The name may be padded with blanks.
	DC	CLm'name'	
	STM	14,R,12(13)	Save contents of registers 14 through R in the save area in the calling program. $2 \leqslant R \leqslant 12$
	BALR	B,0	Establish base register, $2 \leqslant B \leqslant 12$
	USING	*,B	
	.		
	.	}	body of subprogram
	.		
	LM	2,R,28(13)	Restore registers
	MVI	12(13),X'FF'	Set flag to indicate completion
	BCR	15,14	Return to calling program

Figure 10-15. Conventions for a lowest level subprogram. (From Basic Fortran IV (E) Programmer's Guide, Form GC28-6603, © 1966 by International Business Machines Corporation, reproduced by permission.)

but in the postexecution dump

$$C(030798_{abs}) = A(SUM) = 000307C8$$

The dump also contains two save area traces. One trace begins at the system save area and follows the forward pointers to the current save area. The other trace begins at the current save area and follows the chain backward.[11] The reader should verify that the save area traces are correct, that the forward and backward pointers agree where expected, etc. Note that in the lowest-level save area at 03072C the forward pointer is spurious—there is no lower-level save area.

In this example the chain is only two save areas long. It might be much longer in a job involving many subprograms. If one makes a programming error that damages the save area pointers and then gets a dump, the diagnostic program will print the save area traces up to the place where the forward and backward pointers disagree, and then it will print a message saying that the chain was broken.

---

[11] The abbreviations used in the trace are HSA = higher save area, LSA = lower save area, RET = return address, and EPA = entry point address (C(R15)).

Name	Operation	Operand	
deckname	START		
	BC	15,m+1+4(15)	
	DC	X'm'	
	DC	CLm'name$_1$'	
	STM	14,R,12(13)	
	BALR	B,O	
	USING	*,B	
	LR	Q,13	Save old save area pointer
	LA	13,AREA	Set new save area pointer
	ST	13,8(O,Q)	Store forward pointer in old save area.
	ST	Q,4(0,13)	Store backward pointer in this save area.
	BC	15,prob$_1$	Branch around save area.
AREA	DS	18F	Reserve 18 words for save area
prob$_1$	·		
	·		
	·		
	LA	1,ARGLIST	Example of
	L	15,ADCON	a calling
	BALR	14,15	sequence
	·		
	·		
	·		
	L	13,AREA+4	Load the address of the previous save area into R13
	LM	2,R,28(13)	Restore registers
	L	14,12(0,13)	Restore return address
	MVI	12(13),X'FF'	Set flag to indicate completion
	BCR	15,14	Return to calling program
ADCON	DC	A(name$_2$)	Name of subprogram called by this subprogram
	EXTRN	name$_2$	
ARGLIST	DC	A(arg$_1$)	Address of first argument
	·		
	·		
	·		
	DC	X'80'	Flag to indicate last argument
	DC	AL3(arg$_n$)	Address of last argument
	·		
	·		
	·		
	END		

The body of the subprogram comment bracket (spanning the LA/L/BALR calling sequence rows) reads: body of subprogram.

Figure 10-16. Conventions for a subprogram which is not a lowest level subprogram. (From Basic Fortran IV (E) Programmer's Guide, Form GC28-6603, © 1966 by International Business Machines Corporation, reproduced by permission.)

```
LOC    OBJECT CODE    ADDR1 ADDR2  STMT   SOURCE STATEMENT                                F150CT70   7/24/72
                                    1 * CALLING PROGRAM
000000                              2 MAIN    CSECT
000000 47FF 000A            0000A   3          BC    15,10(15)           BRANCH AROUND CHARACTER STRING NAME
000004 05                           4          DC    X'5'
000005 D4C1C9D540                   5          DC    CL5'MAIN'
                                    6 * SAVE ROUTINE
00000A 90EC D00C            0000C   7          STM   14,12,12(13)
00000E 05C0                         8          BALR  12,0
000010                              9          USING *,12
000010 184D                        10          LR    4,13                SAVE R13
000012 41D0 C014            00024  11          LA    13,AREA             SET NEW CURRENT SAVE AREA POINTER
000016 50D0 4008            00008  12          ST    13,8(0,4)           STORE FORWARD POINTER
00001A 5040 D004            00004  13          ST    4,4(0,13)           STORE BACKWARDS POINTER
00001E 47F0 C05C            0006C  14          BC    15,BEGIN
000024                             15 AREA     DS    18F                 RESERVE 18 WORDS FOR SAVE AREA
                                   16 *
                                   17 * CALLING SEQUENCE
00006C 4110 C084            00094  18 BEGIN    LA    1,LST
000070 58F0 C080            00090  19          L     15,ADCON
000074 05EF                        20          BALR  14,15
000076 0000
000078 00000000                    21          DC    F'0'
                                   22 * RETURN ROUTINE
00007C 58D0 C018            00028  23          L     13,AREA+4
000080 982C D01C            0001C  24          LM    2,12,28(13)
000084 58ED D00C            0000C  25          L     14,12(13)           RESTORE RETURN ADDRESS
000088 92FF D00C      0000C        26          MVI   12(13),X'FF'        SET FLAG TO INDICATE COMPLETION
00008C 07FE                        27          BCR   15,14
00008E 0000
000090 00000000                    28 ADCON    DC    A(SUM)
                                   29          EXTRN SUM
000094 000000A8                    30 LST      DC    A(X)
000098 000000AC                    31          DC    A(Y)
00009C 000000B0                    32          DC    A(Z)
0000A0 000000B4                    33          DC    A(W)
0000A4 80                          34          DC    X'80'
0000A5 0000B8                      35          DC    AL3(Q)
0000A8 0000000A                    36 X        DC    F'10'
0000AC FFFFFFFD                    37 Y        DC    F'-3'
0000B0 00000006                    38 Z        DC    F'6'
0000B4 0000000E                    39 W        DC    F'14'
0000B8 00000042                    40 Q        DC    F'66'
                                   41          END
```

```
LOC    OBJECT CODE    ADDR1 ADDR2  STMT   SOURCE STATEMENT                                F150CT70   7/24/72
                                    1 * CALLED PROGRAM
000000                              2 SUM     CSECT
000000 47FF 0008            00008   3          BC    15,8(15)            BRANCH AROUND CHARACTER STRING NAME
000004 03                           4          DC    X'3'
000005 E2E4D4                       5          DC    CL3'SUM'
000008 90EC D00C            0000C   6          STM   14,12,12(13)        SAVE REGISTERS
00000C 05C0                         7          BALR  12,0
00000E                              8          USING *,12
00000E 1B44                         9          SR    4,4                 SUM=0
000010 1B22                        10          SR    2,2                 INDEX = 0
000012 5852 1000            00000  11 LOOP     L     5,0(2,1)            FETCH (FIRST) ADDRESS
000016 1255                        12          LTR   5,5                 TEST SIGN
000018 4740 C01A            00028  13          BM    NEG                 OF ADDRESS
00001C 5A40 5000            00000  14          A     4,0(0,5)            ADD (FIRST) ARGUMENT
000020 4120 2004            00004  15          LA    2,4(0,2)            STEP INDEX
000024 47F0 C004            00012  16          B     LOOP
000028 5040 5000            00000  17 NEG      ST    4,0(0,5)            STORE SUM
00002C 982C D01C            0001C  18          LM    2,12,28(13)         RESTORE REGISTERS
000030 92FF D00C      0000C        19          MVI   12(13),X'FF'        SET FLAG TO INDICATE COMPLETION
000034 07FE                        20          BCR   15,14               RETURN
                                   21          END
```

Figure 10-17. Part of the output from the separate assembly, linkediting and execution of a main program and a subprogram. These programs follow the full conventions for register saving and linking of save areas. The dump includes two save area traces.

```
F44-LEVEL LINKAGE EDITOR OPTIONS SPECIFIED LIST,XREF
        DEFAULT OPTION(S) USED -  SIZE=(90112,12288)


                                      CROSS REFERENCE TABLE

     CONTROL SECTION                    ENTRY

       NAME    ORIGIN  LENGTH           NAME  LOCATION   NAME  LOCATION   NAME  LOCATION   NAME  LOCATION

      MAIN      00     BC
      SUM       CO     36


     LOCATION  REFERS TO SYMBOL  IN CONTROL SECTION       LOCATION  REFERS TO SYMBOL  IN CONTROL SECTION

         90           SUM                SUM
     ENTRY ADDRESS    00
     TOTAL LENGTH     F8

     ****GO       DOES NOT EXIST BUT HAS BEEN ADDED TO DATA SET
```

```
     SAVE AREA TRACE

     GO        WAS ENTERED VIA LINK
```

PAGE 0003

```
     SA   03F768   WD1 00000000   HSA 00000000   LSA 0003072C   RET 000068A0   EPA 01030708   R0  FD000008
                   R1  0003F7F8   R2  00019358   R3  5C0186B0   R4  000203F0   R5  00020598   R6  00018EDC
                   R7  00022278   R8  00018688   R9  00019528   R10 000186B0   R11 00000000   R12 400AAC82

     GO        WAS ENTERED VIA CALL

     SA   03072C   WD1 1BAA1DA9   HSA 0003F768   LSA 807C41BB   RET FF03077E   EPA 000307C8   R0  FD000008
                   R1  0003079C   R2  00019358   R3  5C0186B0   R4  0003F768   R5  00020598   R6  00018EDC
                   R7  00022278   R8  00018688   R9  00019528   R10 000186B0   R11 00000000   R12 40030718


     INTERRUPT AT 030780


     PROCEEDING BACK VIA REG 13

     GO        WAS ENTERED VIA CALL

     SA   03072C   WD1 1BAA1DA9   HSA 0003F768   LSA 807C41BB   RET FF03077E   EPA 000307C8   R0  FD000008
                   R1  0003079C   R2  00019358   R3  5C0186B0   R4  0003F768   R5  00020598   R6  00018EDC
                   R7  00022278   R8  00018688   R9  00019528   R10 000186B0   R11 00000000   R12 40030718

     GO        WAS ENTERED VIA LINK

     SA   03F768   WD1 00000000   HSA 00000000   LSA 0003072C   RET 000068A0   EPA 01030708   R0  FD000008
                   R1  0003F7F8   R2  00019358   R3  5C0186B0   R4  000203F0   R5  00020598   R6  00018EDC
                   R7  00022278   R8  00018688   R9  00019528   R10 000186B0   R11 00000000   R12 400AAC82


     REGS AT ENTRY TO ABEND

         FLTR 0-6     0000000000000000      0000000000000000        0000000000000000     0000000005050505

         REGS 0-7     FD000008  0003079C  00019358  5C0186B0      0003F768  00020598  00018EDC  00022278
         REGS 8-15    00018688  00019528  000186B0  00000000      40030718  0003072C  4003077E  000307C8

     LOAD MODULE    GO

     030700                    47FF000A 05D4C1C9   D54090EC D00C05C0 184D41D0 C01450D0   *.............MAIN ...........*
     030720   40085040 D00447F0 C05C1BBC 1BAA1DA9   0003F768 807C41BB FF03077E 000307C8   *. ...0........7........H*
     030740   FD000008 0003079C 00019358 5C0186B0   0003F768 00020598 00018EDC 00022278   *.. ....0............7.......*
     030760   00018688 00019528 000186B0 00000000   40030718 4110C084 58F0C080 05EF0000   *..............O.......*
     030780   00000000 58D0C018 982CD01C 58ED000C   92FFD00C 07FE0000 000307C8 000307B0   *......................*
     0307A0   000307B4 000307B8 000307BC 800307C0   0000000A FFFFFFFD 00000006 0000000E   *..................H....*
     0307C0   0000001B C0004180 47FF0008 03E2E4D4   90ED000C 05C01844 18225852 10001255   *.............SUM..........*
     0307E0   4740C01A 5A405000 41202004 47F0C004   50405000 982CD01C 92FFD00C 07FE84EE   *. ... .......0... ........*
```

Figure 10-17. (Continued)

EXERCISES

1. Write a subprogram named MOD to calculate

$$\text{arg}_3 = \text{arg}_1 \text{ modulo arg}_2$$

that is, the remainder after dividing arg_1 by arg_2. Write a driving program to test it.

2. Write a subprogram named DIGIT. The first argument is an 80-byte string. If the string contains any decimal digits 0 through 9, then the subprogram should return 1 as the second argument; otherwise, it should return 0. The second argument is a full word. Write a program to invoke DIGIT.

3. Write a subprogram to find the next group of contiguous nonblank characters in a string. The arguments are as follows:

Inputs: first argument   = starting address of string (full word)
            second argument = number of bytes in string (full word)
            third argument   = address at which to begin searching
Outputs: fourth argument = address of first byte in next group of contiguous non-
                               blank bytes
            fifth argument   = address of last byte in next group of contiguous non-
                               blank bytes

For example, let the string be as follows:

    F I N D b b T H E b b W O R D . b

where b = blank. Then the arguments might be as follows:

    first argument   = 0007070C
    second argument = 00000011
    third argument   = 00070710
    fourth argument = 00070712
    fifth argument   = 00070714

When there are no more nonblank characters in the string, return the address of the last byte in the string as the fourth and fifth arguments.

4. Write a subprogram to evaluate a polynomial

$$f = a_n x^n + a_{n-1} x^{n-1} + \ldots + a_1 x^1 + a_0$$

where the argument list is of the form

    LIST   DC   A(x)
             DC   A(a_n)
             DC   A(a_{n-1})
              .
              .
              .
             DC   A(a_0)
             DC   X'80'
             DC   AL3(f)

Write a driving program to test this subprogram for several cases. What is the smallest n the subprogram will handle?

5. Variable numbers of arguments can be handled by a flag in the argument address list as described earlier, or by a count showing the number of arguments. Write a subprogram to add the elements of a one-dimensional array. The elements of the array are in consecutive full words.

first argument   = first word of the array
second argument = n, a four-byte integer showing the number of elements to be added
third argument   = output, the sum of the first n elements of the array

6. Write a subprogram, HEX, to print in hexadecimal the contents of the memory from X to Y, where X and Y are symbols in the calling program. The calling sequence should be of the form

```
        LA      1,LIST
        L       15,XXX
        BALR    14,15
          .
          .
          .

LIST    DC      A(X)
        DC      A(Y)
XXX     DC      A(HEX)
```

If $X \geqslant Y$, then print an error message. After execution of the subprogram, return control to the calling program. Write a driver program to debug HEX.

Note that GET and PUT (both the O.S. and ESP versions) use and do not restore registers 14, 15, 0, and 1. Also the O.S. GET and PUT instructions invoke subprograms that use the current save area, so a program containing a GET or PUT should follow the conventions for a subprogram that is not a lowest level subprogram.

7. Write a subprogram to print a backward save area trace.

8. Invent a scheme for saving register contents that is similar to the standard scheme, except that the return address and the address of the save area are always related by a fixed amount, for example, eight bytes, so that the contents of one register is sufficient to determine both addresses. Discuss the good and bad features of this scheme.

9. Invent a different scheme for register saving in which both the save area and the instructions that do the saving and restoring are in the called program. Discuss the good and bad features of this scheme. Does it allow save area chaining?

Appendix A

The ESP assembler-interpreter

The ESP Assembler-Interpreter[1] allows the translation and execution of an assembler language program to occur almost as if it were done by one of the IBM-supplied assemblers. First, the ESP Assembler program translates the source statements into object code. Then the ESP Interpreter program executes the object code interpretively, with control returning to the ESP Interpreter after the execution of each object instruction. This allows the Interpreter to provide features that are not normally available to a program running freely in the hardware computer. In this case the features provided are

1. Simplified input-output.

2. Check against excessive number of instructions executed.

3. Memory protection to prevent the user from referring to addresses outside the 4096-byte region assigned to him.

4. A trace to print the contents of pertinent registers and memory after the execution of each instruction.

---

[1]ESP is a mnemonic for "easy symbolic programming." The assembler was written by D. E. Elliott, the interpreter by Lawrence Schutte, both at Iowa State University. It can operate in a 128K-byte region under O.S.

In execution an ESP program is slower than an Assembler F program. To execute one addition in an Assembler F program takes just the time for one add instruction, whereas in an ESP program one addition takes the time for many instructions, including the time needed to construct and print the trace. However, ESP has a speed advantage because it allows batching and Assembler F does not. Batching means that when processing several ESP jobs in succession the ESP Assembler-Interpreter can remain constantly in the main memory instead of having to be reloaded from backup memory for each job. The overall result is that when processing in one batch several short programs, such as those typically written by students learning assembler language, ESP is faster.

An ESP program should be punched on cards according to the rules for 360 assembler language, except that continuation cards are not permitted. The arrangement of an ESP deck is as follows:

/ESP   accounting information
       }   assembler language statements
  END
       }   data deck, if any

The first card is the /ESP card, whose layout is shown in Figure A-2. The end of the assembler language deck is denoted only by the assembler language END; no additional delimiter is needed. Also, the data deck has no delimiters, either preceding or following. Decks arranged as shown may be concatenated for batch processing. A sample deck is shown in Figure A-1.

```
/ESP    CCCO    US329.SC01.P01.BREARLEY,E=500,T=50,A=1,P=10
* ESP SAMPLE PROGRAM
        CSECT
        STM    14,12,12(13)   SAVE REGISTER CONTENTS
        EALR   12,0
        LSING  *,12
        L      2,A
        A      2,B
        ST     2,C
        GET    CARD
        MVC    CARD+4(1),DCLLAR
        PUT    LINE
        LM     14,12,12(13)   RESTORE REGISTER CONTENTS
        ECR    15,14
A       CC     F'-23'
B       DC     F'4'
C       CS     1F
LINE    CC     C' '                   CARRIAGE CONTROL CHARACTER
CARD    CC     8CC' '
        CC     52C'*'
COLLAR  CC     C'$'
        END
ABCDEFGHI
```

Figure A-1. Listing of an ESP deck. In this sample the data deck consists of only one card containing ABCDEFGHI.

ESP PSEUDOINSTRUCTIONS

ESP provides two pseudoinstructions for simplified input-output. The input instruction is

Assembler language: GET $D_1(B_1)$

Machine language format:

51		B_1	D_1
0 7 8	15 16	19 20	31

The meaning is to read 80 characters from the next card in the card reader, and put the corresponding EBCDIC bytes into the 80-byte region of memory indicated by the operand $D_1(B_1)$ or by a symbol. The output instruction is

Assembler language: PUT $D_1(B_1)$

Machine language format:

52		B_1	D_1
0 7 8	15 16	19 20	31

The meaning is to transmit to the printer the contents of the 133-byte region of memory indicated by the operand $D_1(B_1)$ or a symbol. The printer uses the first character as a carriage control character and prints the following 132 characters. A carriage control character of blank means single space, 0 means double space, and 1 means advance to the top of the next page.

During execution, the ESP Interpreter can print a trace showing after the execution of each instruction the following:

1. Location of the instruction.

2. Instruction.

3. Condition code.

4. Contents of pertinent registers and memory locations.

The instruction location and the instruction are printed in hexadecimal; the contents of the pertinent locations are printed in hexadecimal or as characters. Normally, the object code is assembled starting at location 000000. At execution time the program is relocated, and the relocated values are the ones shown in the trace.

The number of instructions to be traced may be controlled by the T parameter on the /ESP card, as shown in Figure A-2. The number of instructions to be traced may also be controlled by a pseudoinstruction of the form

Name	Operation	Operand	Comments
	TRACE	n	

where n is a decimal integer between 0 and 255. The assembler translates this into $03XX_H$, where XX is the hexadecimal equivalent of n. This tells the interpreter to print the trace of the next n instructions including itself, then stop printing the trace, print the message END OF TRACE, but continue execution and execution printing, if any, until a

Column	Contents
1-4	/ESP
5-8	blank
9-11	File number
12-15	blank
16-20	account number
21-22	.S
23-25	Student number
26-27	.P
28-29	Problem number
30	,
31-38	student name
39	,
40-70	input parameters of the form:

$$E = 100, T = 50, A = 0, P = 10$$

where E is the maximum number of instructions to be executed

T is the number of instructions to be traced, minimum 1.

A dump option: 1 always give full dump
                  0 full dump only in trouble
           -1 indicative dump if trouble

P is the maximum number of pages of output (including trace)

defaults are as indicated in the above example

Column	Contents
71-72	blank
73-80	sequence number

Figure A-2. Format of ESP job card.

subsequent TRACE instruction is encountered. The trace may be turned off by the instruction   TRACE   0. Note that 03 is not a legal 360 operation code; this is a pseudoinstruction for the ESP Interpreter.

At the conclusion of execution, the interpreter prints a postmortem dump showing the contents of the registers and of the 4096-byte region allocated to this program. In the dump the byte addresses are shown in hexadecimal; the byte contents are shown in both hexadecimal and character form. In the character portion of the dump, bytes that contain blanks, the letters A through Z, and the digits 0 through 9 are printed correctly; all other bytes are printed as periods.

REGISTER USAGE CONVENTIONS

The register usage conventions under ESP are the same as the register usage conventions under O.S., which were described in Chapter 6. At the beginning of execution, register 15 contains the entry point address, register 14 contains the address to which control should be returned at the end of execution of the problem program, and register 13 contains the address of an 18-word area in which the register contents can be saved. In ESP, R13 points to 4024_{10} bytes beyond the beginning of the region allocated to this program. In the example program we save the register contents at the beginning with

        STM   14,12,12(13)

and restore them just before branching back to the system with

        LM   14,12,12(13)

SAMPLE PROGRAM

The complete output from a program that runs correctly is shown in Figure A-3. The first part of the program calculates $A + B \rightarrow C$ or $-23 + 4 \rightarrow C$. The answer can be found in the trace and in the dump to be $FFFFFFED_H = -19_{10}$. The second part of the program reads 80 characters from a card, replaces the fifth character with a dollar sign, and prints the result. The condition of the character string after the insertion of the dollar sign can be seen in four places:

1. In the trace of the MVC instruction.

2. In the line printed by the PUT instruction.

3. In the trace of the PUT instruction.

4. In the dump.

Figure A-4 shows the output from the same program except that the trace is turned off with the instruction   TRACE   0   at statement 6. Note that execution continues even though the trace is off and the same execution output is printed, but this time the output is easier to find since it is not buried in the trace. At the end of execution, a dump is printed as before.

The complete output from a program that contains a source language error is shown in Figure A-5. The error was in statement 16

        C   DC   1F

as indicated by the message

        ERROR   35

The list in Figure A-6 shows that message 35 means "no required constant for a DC statement." Statement 16 could be corrected by providing a constant or by changing DC

```
/ESP    0000    U9329.SC01.P01.BREARLEY,E=500,T=50,A=1,P=10                                      PAGE      1
LOC   CBJECT        ADDR1 ADDR2 STMT SOURCE STATEMENT                VERSION 2 1/1/69           DATE 06-29-72
                                    1 * ESP SAMPLE PROGRAM
C00000                              2       CSECT
C0000C 9CEC D00C                    3       STM    14,12,12(13)   SAVE REGISTER CONTENTS
000004 05C0                         4       BALR   12,0
C00006                              5       USING  *,12
C00006 5820 C022          00028     6       L      2,A
00000A 5A20 C026          C0C2C     7       A      2,B
C0000E 5020 C02A          00030     8       ST     2,C
000012 5100 C02F    00035           9       GET    CARD
000016 D200 C033 C0B3  C0039 000B9 10       MVC    CARD+4(1),DCLLAR
00001C 5200 C02E    00034          11       PUT    LINE
00002C 98EC D00C                   12       LM     14,12,12(13)   RESTORE REGISTER CONTENTS
000024 07FE                        13       BCR    15,14
000028 FFFFFFE9                    14 A     DC     F'-23'
00002C CCC00C04                    15 B     DC     F'4'
000030                             16 C     DS     1F
000034 40                          17 LINE  DC     C' '          CARRIAGE CCNTROL CHARACTER
000035 40                          18 CARD  DC     80C' '
0000E5 5C                          19       DC     52C'*'
0000B9 5B                          20 DOLLAR DC    C'$'
C00000                             21       END

       NC  ERRORS/WARNINGS FOUNC IN THIS ASSEMBLY
```

```
C00000  C332          CC=0   GR 0-7   827C59E0  00000000  47C0700A  D203827C  B904588C  0000D203  D0E8827C  58E0B900
                             GR 8-F   80800088  7C70588C  00005870  82744177  B2315850  0003B268  0003CFB8  0003A2B0
                             FR 0-6   D9E2C9E340404040    C033C0B35200C02E    4040404040404040    98ECD00C07FEE3C1

03A2B0  90ECD00C      CC=0   GR E-5   0003CFB8  0003A2B0  827C59E0  00000000  47C0700A  D203827C  B904588C  0000D203
                             GR 6-C   D0E8827C  58E0B900  80800088  7070588C  00005870  82744177  B2315850                 TO  03B274

03A2B4  05C0          CC=0   GR 0-7   827C59E0  00000000  47C0700A  D203827C  B904588C  0000D203  D0E8827C  58E0B900
NEXT INSTRUCTICN AT 03A2B6   GR 8-F   80800088  7070588C  00005870  82744177  4003A2B6  0003B268  0003CFB8  0003A2B0

03A2B6  5820C022      CC=0   GR 2    FFFFFFE9                    OP 2    FFFFFFE9        AT  03A2D8

03A2BA  5A20C026      CC=1   GR 2    FFFFFFED                    OP 2    00000004        AT  03A2DC

03A2BE  5020C02A      CC=1   GR 2   (FFFFFFED)   C = -19         OP 2    FFFFFFED        AT  03A2E0

03A2C2  5100C02F      CC=1           ABCDEFGHI                                                                      *     AT  03A2E5

03A2C6  D200C033C0B3  CC=1   CP 1  5BC6C7C8C9404040404040404040 AT 03A2E9  OP 2  5B                                       AT  03A369
 ABCD$FGHI                                                                   *********************************************************
03A2CC  5200C02E      CC=1   CCNTROL=40  ABCD$FGHI       PRINTED  BY  PUT  STATEMENT                                AT  03A2E5

03A2D0  98ECD00C      CC=1   GR E-5   0003CFB8  0003A2B0  827C59E0  00000000  47C0700A  D203827C  B904588C  0000D203
                             GR 6-C   D0E8827C  58E0B900  80800088  7070588C  00005870  82744177  B2315850                FROM 03B274

C00000  07FE          CC=1   GR 0-7   827C59E0  00000000  47C0700A  D203827C  B904588C  0000D203  D0E8827C  58E0B900
NEXT INSTRUCTION AT 03CFB8    GR 8-F   80800088  7070588C  00005870  82744177  B231585C  0003B268  0003CFB8  0003A2B0
```

```
NORMAL CCMPLETICN DUMP REQUESTEC

REGISTERS AT TERMINATICN
GR 0-7    827C59E0  CCC00000  47C0700A  D203827C  B904588C  0000D203  D0E8827C  58E0B900
GR 8-F    8C8000B8  7C7C588C  C0005870  82744177  B2315850  0003B268  0003CFB8  0003A2B0
FR 0-6    C9E2C9E340404040    C033C0B35200C02E    4040404040404040    98ECD00C07FEE3C1

PROGRAM WAS ENTERED AT 03A2B0

03A2A0   C = -19              CARD                                                                   CARD
03A2C0                                                   90ECD00C  05C05820  C0225A20  C0265020  *.......................................*
03A2CC   C02A5100  C02FD200  C033C0B3  5200C02E  98ECD00C  07FEE3C1  FFFFFFE9  00000000  *....K.............TA...Z......*
03A2E0   FFFFFFED  40C1C2C3  C45BC6C7  C8C94040  40404040  40404040  40404040  40404040  *....ABCD.FGHI                  *
03A300   40404040  404C4040  40404040  40404040  40404040  40404040  40404040  40404040  *                              *
03A320   40404040  404C4040  40404040  40404040  40404040  405C5C5C  5C5C5C5C  5C5C5C5C  *............................*
03A340   5C5C5C5C  5C5C5C5C  5C5C5C5C  5C5C5C5C  5C5C5C5C  5C5C5C5C  5C5C5C5C  5C5C5C5C  *............................*
03A360   5C5C5C5C  5C5C5C5C  5C5B68C9  D6E6C140  C9D6E6C1  40E2E3C1  E3C540E4  D5C9E5C5  *............IOWA IOWA STATE UNIVE*
03A380   CSE2C9E3  E840C1D4  C5E268C9  D6E6C140  C9D6E6C1  40E2E3C1  E3C540E4  D5C9E5C5  *RSITY AMES.IOWA IOWA STATE UNIVE*
         LINES 03A3A0-C3B240 SAME AS ABOVE
03B260   D5E2C9E3  E84CC1D4  CCC00000  00000000  00000000  0003CFB8  0003A2B0  827C59E0  *RSITY AM....................*
03B280   CCC00000  47CC700A  D203827C  B904588C  0000D203  D0E8827C  58E0B900  80800088  *.......K..........K..Y..........*
03B2A0   7070588C  000C5870  82744177  B2315850                                          *..............*

END CF DUMP

0000010 INSTRUCTICNS EXECUTED
```

Figure A-3.   Output from an ESP job.

```
/ESP    0000    L9329.S001.P01.BREARLEY,E=500,T=50,A=1,P=10                              PAGE    1
  LOC   OBJECT            ADDR1 ADDR2 STMT SOURCE STATEMENT              VERSION 2 1/1/69      DATE 06-29-72

                                  1  *     ESP SAMPLE PROGRAM  USING TRACE INSTRUCTICN
C0C000                            2        CSECT
000000  90EC D00C                 3        STM   14,12,12(13)   SAVE REGISTER CONTENTS
C00004  05C0                      4        BALR  12,0
000006                            5        USING *,12
C00006  0300                      6        TRACE 0
000008  5820 C022        C0C028   7        L     2,A
0J000C  5A20 C026        00C2C    8        A     2,B
00001C  5020 CC2A        00030    9        ST    2,C
000014  5100 C02F        00035   10        GET   CARD
000018  D200 C033 C0B3  00039 00CB9  11    MVC   CARD+4(1),DCLLAR
00001E  5200 C02E        00034   12        PUT   LINE
000022  98EC C00C                13        LM    14,12,12(13)   RESTORE REGISTER CONTENTS
000026  C7FE                      14        BCR   15,14
000028  FFFFFFE9                  15 A      DC    F'-23'
00002C  CCC00004                  16 B      DC    F'4'
000030                            17 C      DS    1F
000034  40                        18 LINE   DC    C' '            CARRIAGE CONTROL CHARACTER
000035  40                        19 CARD   DC    80C' '
000085  5C                        20        DC    52C'*'
0000B9  5B                        21 DOLLAR DC    C'$'
C00000                            22        END

      NO  ERRORS/WARNINGS FOUND IN THIS ASSEMBLY
```

```
C00000  0332          CC=0    GR 0-7   827C59E0  00000000  47C0700A  D203827C  B904588C  0000D203  D0E8827C  58E0B900
                               GR 8-F   80800088  7070588C  00005870  82744177  82315850  0003B268  0003CF88  0003A2B0
                               FR 0-6   D9E2C9E340404040  D200C033C0B35200  4040404040404040  C02E98ECD00C07FE

03A2BC  90ECD00C      CC=0    GR E-5   0003CF88  0003A2B0  827C59E0  00000000  47C0700A  D203827C  B904588C  0000D203
                               GR 6-C   D0E8827C  58E0B900  80800088  7070588C  00005870  82744177  82315850              TO  03B274

03A2B4  05C0          CC=0    GR 0-7   827C59E0  00000000  47C0700A  D203827C  B904588C  0000D203  D0E8827C  58E0B900
NEXT INSTRUCTION AT 03A2B6      GR 8-F   80800088  7070588C  00005870  82744177  4003A2B6  0003B268  0003CF88  0003A2B0

END OF FULL TRACE
ABCD$FGHI                                      ***************************************************
```

```
NORMAL CCMPLETICN DUMP REQUESTED

REGISTERS AT TERMINATICN
GR 0-7   827C59E0  CCC00000  47C0700A  D203827C  B904588C  0000D203  D0E8827C  58E0B900
GR 8-F   8C8C00B8  7070588C  C0005870  82744177  82315850  0003B268  0003CF88  0003A2B0
FR 0-6   C9E2C9E340404C40  D200C033C0B35200  4040404040404040  C02E98ECD00C07FE

PROGRAM WAS ENTERED AT C3A2B0

03A2A0                                          90ECD00C  05C00300  5820C022  5A20CC26  *....................*...............*
03A2C0   5020C02A  510CC02F  D200C033  C0B35200  C02E98EC  D00C07FE  FFFFFFE9  00000004  *................Z.....*
03A2E0   FFFFFFED  40C1C2C3  C45BC6C7  C8C94040  40404040  40404040  40404040  40404040  *.... ABCD.FGHI      *
C3A300   404C4040  40404040  40404040  40404040  40404040  40404040  40404040  40404040  *                    *
03A320   4C404040  40404040  40404040  405C5C5C  5C5C5C5C  5C5C5C5C  5C5C5C5C  5C5C5C5C   *..........***********
03A340   5C5C5C5C  5C5C5C5C  5C5C5C5C  5C5C5C5C  5C5C5C5C  5C5C5C5C  5C5C5C5C  5C5C5C5C   *********************
03A360   5C5C5C5C  5C5C5C5C  5C5B6BC9  D6E6C140  C9D6E6C1  40E2E3C1  E3C540E4  D5C9E5C5   *.......IOWA IOWA STATE UNIVE*
03A380   C9E2C9E3  E840C1D4  C5E26BC9  D6E6C140  C9D6E6C1  40E2E3C1  E3C540E4  D5C9E5C5   *RSITY AMES.IOWA IOWA STATE UNIVE*
         LINES 03A3A0-C3B240 SAME AS ABOVE
03B260   D9E2C9E3  E840C1D4  C0C00000  00000000  00000000  0003CF88  0003A2B0  827C59E0  *RSITY AM.............*
C3B280   CCC00000  47C0700A  D203827C  B904588C  0000D203  D0E8827C  58E0B900  80800088  *.........K..........K..Y.........*
03B2A0   7070588C  C0005870  82744177  82315850                                          *.................... *

END OF DUMP

0000011 INSTRUCTIONS EXECUTED
```

Figure A-4. Output from an ESP job containing instruction TRACE 0.

```
/ESP    0000    US329.SCC1.P01.BREARLEY,E=500,T=50,A=1,P=10                                    PAGE     1
        LOC  CBJECT      ADDR1 ADDR2 STMT SOURCE STATEMENT              VERSION 2 1/1/69        DATE 06-29-72

                                        1 * SAMPLE PROGRAM WITH SOURCE LANGUAGE ERROR
        C00000                          2         CSECT
        C000CC 90EC 000C                3         STM    14,12,12(13)   SAVE REGISTER CONTENTS
        000004 05C0                     4         BALR   12,0
        C00006                          5         USING  *,12
        C00006 5820 C022       C0028    6         L      2,A
        C0000A 5A2C C026       0002C    7         A      2,B
        00000E 5020 C02A       C0C30    8         ST     2,C
        000012 5100 C02B       00031    9         GET    CARD
        000016 D200 C02F C0AF  00035 C0CB5  10    MVC    CARD+4(1),DCLLAR
        00001C 5200 C02A       C0030   11         PUT    LINE
        00002C 98EC 000C                12         LM     14,12,12(13)   RESTORE REGISTER CONTENTS
        000024 07FE                     13         BCR    15,14
        000028 FFFFFFE9                 14 A       DC     F'-23'
        C0002C CCC00004                 15 B       DC     F'4'
        000030                          16 C       DC     1F
                    **ERROR** 35                                        $
        000030 40                       17 LINE    DC     C' '
        000031 40                       18 CARD    DC     80C' '         CARRIAGE CONTROL CHARACTER
        000081 5C                       19         DC     52C'*'
        0000B5 5B                       20 DOLLAR  DC     C'$'
        000000                          21         END

            1  ERRORS/WARNINGS FOUND IN THIS ASSEMBLY
```

```
000000  0332         CC=0    GR 0-7   827C59E0  00000000  47C0700A  D203827C  B904588C  0000D203  D0E8827C  58E0B900
                              GR 8-F   80800088  7070588C  00005870  82744177  B2315850  0003B268  0003CF88  0003A2B0
                              FR 0-6   4040404040404040    C02FC0AF5200C02A    4040404040404040    98ECD00C07FEE3C1

03A2B0  90ECD00C     CC=0    GR E-5   0003CF88  0003A2B0  827C59E0  00000000  47C0700A  D203827C  B904588C  00000203
                              GR 6-C   D0E8827C  58E0B900  80800088  7070588C  00005870  82744177  B2315850            TO  03B274

03A2B4  05C0         CC=0    GR 0-7   827C59E0  00000000  47C0700A  D203827C  B904588C  0000D203  D0E8827C  58E0B900
NEXT INSTRUCTION AT 03A2B6   GR 8-F   80800088  7070588C  00005870  82744177  4003A2B6  0003B268  0003CF88  0003A2B0

03A2B6  5820C022     CC=0    GR 2    FFFFFFE9           OP 2    FFFFFFE9      AT  03A2D8

03A2BA  5A20C026     CC=1    GR 2    FFFFFFED           OP 2    00000004      AT  03A2DC

03A2BE  5020C02A     CC=1    GR 2    FFFFFFED           OP 2    FFFFFFED      AT  03A2E0

03A2C2  5100C02B     CC=1            ABCDEFGHI                                          AT  03A2E1

03A2C6  D200C02FC0AF CC=1    OP 1   5BC6C7C8C94040404040404040404040 AT 03A2E5  OP 2  5B          AT  03A365
```

```
SYSTEM COMPLETION CODE  0C6

INTERRUPT AT LOCATION C3A2D0

SAVE AREA BACKWARDS CHAIN

        GR D - CONTENTS AT ABEND 0003B268

REGISTERS AT TERMINATION
GR 0-7   827C59E0  CCCC0000  FFFFFFED  D203827C  B904588C  0000D203  D0E8827C  58E0B900
GR 8-F   8C800088  707C588C  C0005870  82744177  4003A286  0003B268  0003A2C6  0003DBBE
FR 0-6   404040404040C40     C02FC0AF5200C02A    4040404040404040    98ECD00C07FEE3C1

PROGRAM WAS ENTERED AT 03A2B0

03A2A0
03A2C0  C02A5100  C02ED200  C02FC0AF  5200C02A    90ECD00C  05C05820  C0225A20  C0265020 *.........K.......................*
03A2E0  FFC1C2C3  C45EC6C7  C8C94040  40404040    40404040  40404040  40404040  40404040 *.ABCD.FGHI.......................*
C3A300  40404040  40404040  40404040  40404040    40404040  40404040  40404040  40404040 *................................*
03A320  404C404C  40404040  40404040  40404040    405C5C5C  5C5C5C5C  5C5C5C5C  5C5C5C5C *................................*
03A340  5C5C5C5C  5C5C5C5C  5C5C5C5C  5C5C5C5C    5C5C5C5C  5C5C5C5C  5C5C5C5C  5C5C5C5C *................................*
03A360  5C5C5C5C  5C5E5C1D4  C5E268C9  D6E6C140    C9D6E6C1  40E2E3C1  E3C540E4  D5C9E5C5 *......AMES.IOWA IOWA STATE UNIVE*
03A380  C9E2C9E3  E840C1D4  C5E268C9  D6E6C140    C9D6E6C1  40E2E3C1  E3C540E4  D5C9E5C5 *RSITY AMES.IOWA IOWA STATE UNIVE*
        LINES 03A3A0-C3B240 SAME AS ABOVE
03B260  D9E2C9E3  E84C C1D4  C0000000  00000000    00000000  0003CF88  0003A2B0  827C59E0 *RSITY AM.........................*
03B280  CCC00000  47CC700A  D203827C  B904588C    0000D203  D0E8827C  58E0B900  80800088 *.........K...........K..Y........*
C3B2A0  707C588C  C0C05870  82744177  82315850                                          *................................*
                                                                                        *.....................     .......*

END OF DUMP

C000008 INSTRUCTIONS EXECUTED
```

Figure A-5. Output from an ESP job with an error.

0 - Not supported
1 - No continuation cards allowed
2 - Missing operation code
3 - Missing/redundant operand
4 - Missing/redundant label
5 - Missing END statement
6 - Invalid operation code
7 - Too many control sections
8 - Duplicate label
9 - Program too long

20 - Invalid operand
21 - Negative displacement required
22 - No active base register (missing USING statement)
23 - No closing right parenthesis
24 - No blank following operand
25 - Too many operands for operation code
26 - Not enough operands for operation code

30 - Duplication factor less than zero
31 - Invalid type for DC/DS statement
32 - Invalid length modifier for type of DC/DS
33 - Length modifier too large for type of DC statement
34 - Invalid separator for multiple constants in DC/DS
35 - No required constant for DC statement
36 - Length not 3 or 4 for relocatable A type constant
37 - No closing parenthesis or quote for constant in DC/DS statement
38 - Invalid constant for DC/DS statement
39 - Too many constants for DC/DS statement

50 - Invalid symbol or label
51 - Undefined symbol in operand
52 - Label too long (truncated)

60 - Invalid expression in EQU statement
61 - Invalid expression in ORG statement (not relocatable)
62 - Invalid expression value in ORG statement (negative)
63 - Invalid CNOP statement
64 - Invalid USING statement
65 - Invalid DROP statement

Figure A-6. ESP assembly time error messages.

to DS. Note that no object code was generated corresponding to the offending statement. Thus symbols C and LINE both have relative address 30_H.

Even though the assembler found an error, the interpreter attempted to execute the defective object code. In this program the only instruction that uses symbol C is ST   2,C, so one might expect execution to hang there, but it did not. The instruction ST   2,C   stored FFFFFFED into the four bytes beginning at relative address 30, or 03A2E0 absolute, overwriting the carriage control character at LINE and the first three bytes of CARD. Execution finally stopped during the attempted execution of the PUT instruction because FF_H is not a legal carriage control character.

Upon abnormal termination, ESP also prints one of several *system completion codes*. Some of the ESP codes are as follows:

222	Exceeded limit on number of pages printed.
322	Exceeded limit on number of instructions executed.
337	Attempted to read beyond the end of the data deck.
0CX	X is a hexadecimal digit, 1 to F, which indicates what kind of program interruption occurred. For a list of interruption codes, see *Principles of Operation*, page 16.

In the sample program the completion code is 0C6, which means a specification interruption. This is not particularly helpful information in this case since the details of the PUT operation are not visible to the user—the real problem is as indicated previously.

The amount by which the object code is relocated before execution varies from run to run. The sample programs were relocated to 03A2B0.

LIMITATIONS OF ESP

For completeness we list here the limitations of ESP. The ESP Assembler will accept all problem state machine instructions except SVC. It will not accept any of the supervisor state instructions, including the input-output instructions. It will accept the following assembler language pseudoinstructions: CSECT, DSECT, USING, DROP, EQU, ORG, DC, DS, EJECT, SPACE, TITLE, and END. It will not accept the START instruction, so CSECT should be used instead. It will also accept GET, PUT, and TRACE, as described previously.

The space allowed for the object code is 4096 bytes. Multiple control sections are allowed within this space limitation. The number of control sections plus the number of dummy sections must be less than or equal to 16. The number of operands in a DC statement must be less than 17.

The assembler does not allow

1. Literals.

2. Macros, either user or system.

3. Continuation cards.

4. Linkages to programs outside the 4096-byte region.

5. V constants.

Appendix B

IBM system/360
reference data

IBM System/360 Reference Data

MACHINE INSTRUCTIONS

NAME	MNEMONIC	OP CODE	FORMAT	OPERANDS
Add (c)	AR	1A	RR	R1,R2
Add (c)	A	5A	RX	R1,D2(X2,B2)
Add Decimal (c,d)	AP	FA	SS	D1(L1,B1),D2(L2,B2)
Add Halfword (c)	AH	4A	RX	R1,D2(X2,B2)
Add Logical (c)	ALR	1E	RR	R1,R2
Add Logical (c)	AL	5E	RX	R1,D2(X2,B2)
AND (c)	NR	14	RR	R1,R2
AND (c)	N	54	RX	R1,D2(X2,B2)
AND (c)	NI	94	SI	D1(B1),I2
AND (c)	NC	D4	SS	D1(L,B1),D2(B2)
Branch and Link	BALR	05	RR	R1,R2
Branch and Link	BAL	45	RX	R1,D2(X2,B2)
Branch and Store (e)	BASR	0D	RR	R1,R2
Branch and Store (e)	BAS	4D	RX	R1,D2(X2,B2)
Branch on Condition	BCR	07	RR	M1,R2
Branch on Condition	BC	47	RX	M1,D2(X2,B2)
Branch on Count	BCTR	06	RR	R1,R2
Branch on Count	BCT	46	RX	R1,D2(X2,B2)
Branch on Index High	BXH	86	RS	R1,R3,D2(B2)
Branch on Index Low or Equal	BXLE	87	RS	R1,R3,D2(B2)
Compare (c)	CR	19	RR	R1,R2
Compare (c)	C	59	RX	R1,D2(X2,B2)
Compare Decimal (c,d)	CP	F9	SS	D1(L1,B1),D2(L2,B2)
Compare Halfword (c)	CH	49	RX	R1,D2(X2,B2)
Compare Logical (c)	CLR	15	RR	R1,R2
Compare Logical (c)	CL	55	RX	R1,D2(X2,B2)
Compare Logical (c)	CLC	D5	SS	D1(L,B1),D2(B2)
Compare Logical (c)	CLI	95	SI	D1(B1),I2
Convert to Binary	CVB	4F	RX	R1,D2(X2,B2)
Convert to Decimal	CVD	4E	RX	R1,D2(X2,B2)
Diagnose (p)		83	SI	
Divide	DR	1D	RR	R1,R2
Divide	D	5D	RX	R1,D2(X2,B2)
Divide Decimal (d)	DP	FD	SS	D1(L1,B1),D2(L2,B2)
Edit (c,d)	ED	DE	SS	D1(L,B1),D2(B2)
Edit and Mark (c,d)	EDMK	DF	SS	D1(L,B1),D2(B2)
Exclusive OR (c)	XR	17	RR	R1,R2
Exclusive OR (c)	X	57	RX	R1,D2(X2,B2)
Exclusive OR (c)	XI	97	SI	D1(B1),I2
Exclusive OR (c)	XC	D7	SS	D1(L,B1),D2(B2)
Execute	EX	44	RX	R1,D2(X2,B2)
Halt I/O (c,p)	HIO	9E	SI	D1(B1)
Insert Character	IC	43	RX	R1,D2(X2,B2)
Insert Storage Key (a,p)	ISK	09	RR	R1,R2
Load	LR	18	RR	R1,R2
Load	L	58	RX	R1,D2(X2,B2)
Load Address	LA	41	RX	R1,D2(X2,B2)
Load and Test (c)	LTR	12	RR	R1,R2
Load Complement (c)	LCR	13	RR	R1,R2
Load Halfword	LH	48	RX	R1,D2(X2,B2)
Load Multiple	LM	98	RS	R1,R3,D2(B2)
Load Multiple Control (e,p)	LMC	B8	RS	R1,R3,D2(B2)
Load Negative (c)	LNR	11	RR	R1,R2
Load Positive (c)	LPR	10	RR	R1,R2
Load PSW (n,p)	LPSW	82	SI	D1(B1)
Load Real Address (c,e,p)	LRA	B1	RX	R1,D2(X2,B2)
Move	MVI	92	SI	D1(B1),I2
Move	MVC	D2	SS	D1(L,B1),D2(B2)
Move Numerics	MVN	D1	SS	D1(L,B1),D2(B2)
Move with Offset	MVO	F1	SS	D1(L1,B1),D2(L2,B2)
Move Zones	MVZ	D3	SS	D1(L,B1),D2(B2)
Multiply	MR	1C	RR	R1,R2
Multiply	M	5C	RX	R1,D2(X2,B2)
Multiply Decimal (d)	MP	FC	SS	D1(L1,B1),D2(L2,B2)
Multiply Halfword	MH	4C	RX	R1,D2(X2,B2)
OR (c)	OR	16	RR	R1,R2
OR (c)	O	56	RX	R1,D2(X2,B2)
OR (c)	OI	96	SI	D1(B1),I2
OR (c)	OC	D6	SS	D1(L,B1),D2(B2)
Pack	PACK	F2	SS	D1(L1,B1),D2(L2,B2)
Read Direct (b,p)	RDD	85	SI	D1(B1),I2
Set Program Mask (n)	SPM	04	RR	R1
Set Storage Key (a,p)	SSK	08	RR	R1,R2
Set System Mask (p)	SSM	80	SI	D1(B1)
Shift Left Double (c)	SLDA	8F	RS	R1,D2(B2)
Shift Left Double Logical	SLDL	8D	RS	R1,D2(B2)
Shift Left Single (c)	SLA	8B	RS	R1,D2(B2)
Shift Left Single Logical	SLL	89	RS	R1,D2(B2)
Shift Right Double (c)	SRDA	8E	RS	R1,D2(B2)
Shift Right Double Logical	SRDL	8C	RS	R1,D2(B2)
Shift Right Single (c)	SRA	8A	RS	R1,D2(B2)
Shift Right Single Logical	SRL	88	RS	R1,D2(B2)
Start I/O (c,p)	SIO	9C	SI	D1(B1)
Store	ST	50	RX	R1,D2(X2,B2)
Store Character	STC	42	RX	R1,D2(X2,B2)
Store Halfword	STH	40	RX	R1,D2(X2,B2)
Store Multiple	STM	90	RS	R1,R3,D2(B2)
Store Multiple Control (e,p)	STMC	B0	RS	R1,R3,D2(B2)
Subtract (c)	SR	1B	RR	R1,R2
Subtract (c)	S	5B	RX	R1,D2(X2,B2)
Subtract Decimal (c,d)	SP	FB	SS	D1(L1,B1),D2(L2,B2)
Subtract Halfword (c)	SH	4B	RX	R1,D2(X2,B2)
Subtract Logical (c)	SLR	1F	RR	R1,R2
Subtract Logical (c)	SL	5F	RX	R1,D2(X2,B2)
Supervisor Call	SVC	0A	RR	I
Test and Set (c)	TS	93	SI	D1(B1)
Test Channel (c,p)	TCH	9F	SI	D1(B1)
Test I/O (c,p)	TIO	9D	SI	D1(B1)
Test under Mask (c)	TM	91	SI	D1(B1),I2
Translate	TR	DC	SS	D1(L,B1),D2(B2)
Translate and Test (c)	TRT	DD	SS	D1(L,B1),D2(B2)
Unpack	UNPK	F3	SS	D1(L1,B1),D2(L2,B2)
Write Direct (b,p)	WRD	84	SI	D1(B1),I2
Zero and Add (c,d)	ZAP	F8	SS	D1(L1,B1),D2(L2,B2)

NOTES FOR PANELS 1-3

a. Protection feature
b. Direct control feature
c. Condition code is set
d. Decimal feature
e. Model 67
n. New condition
code is loaded
p. Privileged instruction
x. Extended precision
floating point feature

MACHINE FORMATS

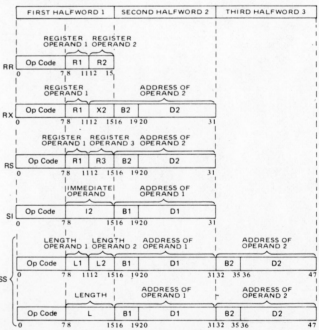

208

FLOATING-POINT FEATURE INSTRUCTIONS

Add Normalized, Extended (c,x)	AXR	36	RR	R1,R2
Add Normalized, Long (c)	ADR	2A	RR	R1,R2
Add Normalized, Long (c)	AD	6A	RX	R1,D2(X2,B2)
Add Normalized, Short (c)	AER	3A	RR	R1,R2
Add Normalized, Short (c)	AE	7A	RX	R1,D2(X2,B2)
Add Unnormalized, Long (c)	AWR	2E	RR	R1,R2
Add Unnormalized, Long (c)	AW	6E	RX	R1,D2(X2,B2)
Add Unnormalized, Short (c)	AUR	3E	RR	R1,R2
Add Unnormalized, Short (c)	AU	7E	RX	R1,D2(X2,B2)
Compare, Long (c)	CDR	29	RR	R1,R2
Compare, Long (c)	CD	69	RX	R1,D2(X2,B2)
Compare, Short (c)	CER	39	RR	R1,R2
Compare, Short (c)	CE	79	RX	R1,D2(X2,B2)
Divide, Long	DDR	2D	RR	R1,R2
Divide, Long	DD	6D	RX	R1,D2(X2,B2)
Divide, Short	DER	3D	RR	R1,R2
Divide, Short	DE	7D	RX	R1,D2(X2,B2)
Halve, Long	HDR	24	RR	R1,R2
Halve, Short	HER	34	RR	R1,R2
Load and Test, Long (c)	LTDR	22	RR	R1,R2
Load and Test, Short (c)	LTER	32	RR	R1,R2
Load Complement, Long (c)	LCDR	23	RR	R1,R2
Load Complement, Short (c)	LCER	33	RR	R1,R2
Load, Long	LDR	28	RR	R1,R2
Load, Long	LD	68	RX	R1,D2(X2,B2)
Load Negative, Long (c)	LNDR	21	RR	R1,R2
Load Negative, Short (c)	LNER	31	RR	R1,R2
Load Positive, Long (c)	LPDR	20	RR	R1,R2
Load Positive, Short (c)	LPER	30	RR	R1,R2
Load Rounded, Extended to Long (x)	LRDR	25	RR	R1,R2
Load Rounded, Long to Short (x)	LRER	35	RR	R1,R2
Load, Short	LER	38	RR	R1,R2
Load, Short	LE	78	RX	R1,D2(X2,B2)
Multiply, Extended (x)	MXR	26	RR	R1,R2
Multiply, Long	MDR	2C	RR	R1,R2
Multiply, Long	MD	6C	RX	R1,D2(X2,B2)
Multiply, Long/Extended (x)	MXDR	27	RR	R1,R2
Multiply, Long/Extended (x)	MXD	67	RX	R1,D2(X2,B2)
Multiply, Short	MER	3C	RR	R1,R2
Multiply, Short	ME	7C	RX	R1,D2(X2,B2)
Store, Long	STD	60	RX	R1,D2(X2,B2)
Store, Short	STE	70	RX	R1,D2(X2,B2)
Subtract Normalized, Extended (c,x)	SXR	37	RR	R1,R2
Subtract Normalized, Long (c)	SDR	2B	RR	R1,R2
Subtract Normalized, Long (c)	SD	6B	RX	R1,D2(X2,B2)
Subtract Normalized, Short (c)	SER	3B	RR	R1,R2
Subtract Normalized, Short (c)	SE	7B	RX	R1,D2(X2,B2)
Subtract Unnormalized, Long (c)	SWR	2F	RR	R1,R2
Subtract Unnormalized, Long (c)	SW	6F	RX	R1,D2(X2,B2)
Subtract Unnormalized, Short (c)	SUR	3F	RR	R1,R2
Subtract Unnormalized, Short (c)	SU	7F	RX	R1,D2(X2,B2)

NOTES

EXTENDED MNEMONIC INSTRUCTION CODES

GENERAL

Extended Code		Machine Instruction		Meaning
B	D2(X2,B2)	BC 15,	D2(X2,B2)	Branch Unconditionally
BR	R2	BCR 15,	R2	Branch Unconditionally
NOP	D2(X2,B2)	BC 0,	D2(X2,B2)	No Operation
NOPR	R2	BCR 0,	R2	No Operation (RR)

AFTER COMPARE INSTRUCTIONS (A:B)

BH	D2(X2,B2)	BC 2,	D2(X2,B2)	Branch on A High
BL	D2(X2,B2)	BC 4,	D2(X2,B2)	Branch on A Low
BE	D2(X2,B2)	BC 8,	D2(X2,B2)	Branch on A Equal B
BNH	D2(X2,B2)	BC 13,	D2(X2,B2)	Branch on A Not High
BNL	D2(X2,B2)	BC 11,	D2(X2,B2)	Branch on A Not Low
BNE	D2(X2,B2)	BC 7,	D2(X2,B2)	Branch on A Not Equal B

AFTER ARITHMETIC INSTRUCTIONS

BO	D2(X2,B2)	BC 1,	D2(X2,B2)	Branch on Overflow
BP	D2(X2,B2)	BC 2,	D2(X2,B2)	Branch on Plus
BM	D2(X2,B2)	BC 4,	D2(X2,B2)	Branch on Minus
BZ	D2(X2,B2)	BC 8,	D2(X2,B2)	Branch on Zero
BNP	D2(X2,B2)	BC 13,	D2(X2,B2)	Branch on Not Plus
BNM	D2(X2,B2)	BC 11,	D2(X2,B2)	Branch on Not Minus
BNZ	D2(X2,B2)	BC 7,	D2(X2,B2)	Branch on Not Zero

AFTER TEST UNDER MASK INSTRUCTIONS

BO	D2(X2,B2)	BC 1,	D2(X2,B2)	Branch if Ones
BM	D2(X2,B2)	BC 4,	D2(X2,B2)	Branch if Mixed
BZ	D2(X2,B2)	BC 8,	D2(X2,B2)	Branch if Zeros
BNO	D2(X2,B2)	BC 14,	D2(X2,B2)	Branch if Not Ones

CNOP ALIGNMENT

Double Word							
Word				Word			
Half Word		Half Word		Half Word		Half Word	
Byte	Byte	Byte	Byte	Byte	Byte	Byte	Byte
0,4		2,4		0,4		2,4	
0,8		2,8		4,8		6,8	

EDIT AND EDMK PATTERN CHARACTERS (in hex)

20–digit selector	40–blank	5C--asterisk
21–start of significance	4B--period	6B--comma
22–field separator	5B--dollar sign	C3D9--CR

SUMMARY OF CONSTANTS (OS and DOS Assemblers)

TYPE	IMPLIED LENGTH, BYTES	ALIGNMENT	FORMAT	TRUNCA-TION/ PADDING
C	–	byte	characters	right
X	–	byte	hexadecimal digits	left
B	–	byte	binary digits	left
F	4	word	fixed-point binary	left
H	2	halfword	fixed-point binary	left
E	4	word	short floating-point	right
D	8	doubleword	long floating-point	right
L	16	doubleword	extended floating-point	right
P	–	byte	packed decimal	left
Z	–	byte	zoned decimal	left
A	4	word	value of address	left
Y	2	halfword	value of address	left
S	2	halfword	address in base-displacement form	–
V	4	word	externally defined address value	left
Q*	4	word	symbol naming a DXD or DSECT	left

*OS only

ASSEMBLER INSTRUCTIONS ⑤

Source: GC24-3414 for DOS
GC28-6514 for OS

Function	Mnemonic	Meaning
Data definition	DC	Define constant
	DS	Define storage
	CCW	Define channel command word
Program	START	Start assembly
sectioning	CSECT	Identify control section
and linking	DSECT	Identify dummy section
	DXD*	Define external dummy section
	CXD*	Cumulative length of external dummy section
	COM	Identify blank common control section
	ENTRY	Identify entry-point symbol
	EXTRN	Identify external symbol
	WXTRN	Identify weak external symbol
Base register	USING	Use base address register
assignment	DROP	Drop base address register
Control of listings	TITLE	Identify assembly output
	EJECT	Start new page
	SPACE	Space listing
	PRINT	Print optional data
Program control	ICTL	Input format control
	ISEQ	Input sequence checking
	PUNCH	Punch a card
	REPRO	Reproduce following card
	ORG	Set location counter
	EQU	Equate symbol
	OPSYN*	Equate operation code
	LTORG	Begin literal pool
	CNOP	Conditional no operation
	COPY	Copy predefined source coding
	END	End assembly
Macro definition	MACRO	Macro definition header
	MNOTE	Request for error message
	MEXIT	Macro definition exit
	MEND	Macro definition trailer
Conditional	ACTR	Conditional assembly loop counter
assembly	AGO	Unconditional branch
	AIF	Conditional branch
	ANOP	Assembly no operation
	GBLA	Define global SETA symbol
	GBLB	Define global SETB symbol
	GBLC	Define global SETC symbol
	LCLA	Define local SETA symbol
	LCLB	Define local SETB symbol
	LCLC	Define local SETC symbol
	SETA	Set arithmetic variable symbol
	SETB	Set binary variable symbol
	SETC	Set character variable symbol

*OS only

CONDITION CODES ⑥

	0	1	2	3
Condition Code Setting	0	1	2	3
Mask Bit Position	8	4	2	1

Floating-Point Arithmetic

	0	1	2	3
Add Normalized S/L/E	zero	<zero	>zero	--
Add Unnormalized S/L	zero	<zero	>zero	--
Compare S/L (A:B)	equal	A low	A high	--
Load and Test S/L	zero	<zero	>zero	--
Load Complement S/L	zero	<zero	>zero	--
Load Negative S/L	zero	<zero	--	--
Load Positive S/L	zero	-	>zero	--
Subtract Normalized S/L/E	zero	<zero	>zero	--
Subtract Unnormalized S/L	zero	<zero	>zero	--

Fixed-Point and Decimal Arithmetic

	0	1	2	3
Add H/F/Dec.	zero	<zero	>zero	overflow
Add Logical	zero, no carry	not zero, no carry	zero, carry	not zero, carry
Compare H/F/Dec. (A:B)	equal	A low	A high	-
Load and Test	zero	<zero	>zero	
Load Complement	zero	<zero	>zero	overflow
Load Negative	zero	<zero	--	--
Load Positive	zero	-	>zero	overflow
Shift Left Single/Double	zero	<zero	>zero	overflow
Shift Right Single/Double	zero	<zero	>zero	-
Subtract H/F/Dec.	zero	<zero	>zero	overflow
Subtract Logical	-	not zero, no carry	zero, carry	not zero, carry
Zero and Add	zero	<zero	>zero	overflow

Logical Operations

	0	1	2	3
AND	zero	not zero	--	--
Compare Logical (A:B)	equal	A low	A high	-
Edit	zero	<zero	>zero	--
Edit and Mark	zero	<zero	>zero	--
Exclusive OR	zero	not zero	--	--
OR	zero	not zero	-	--
Test under Mask	zero	mixed	-	one
Translate and Test	zero	incomplete	complete	-

Input/Output Operations

	0	1	2	3
Halt I/O	interruption pending	CSW stored	halted	not oper
Start I/O	started	CSW stored	busy	not oper
Test I/O	available	CSW stored	busy	not oper
Test Channel	available	interruption pending	burst mode	not oper

Miscellaneous Operations

	0	1	2	3
Test and Set	zero	one	--	--
Load Real Address (Mod. 67)	successful	segment unavailable	page unavailable	--

NOTES

CODES FOR PROGRAM INTERRUPTION

Interruption Code Dec	Hex	Program Interruption Cause	Interruption Code Dec	Hex	Program Interruption Cause
1	0001	Operation	10	000A	Decimal overflow
2	0002	Privileged operation	11	000B	Decimal divide
3	0003	Execute	12	000C	Exponent overflow
4	0004	Protection	13	000D	Exponent underflow
5	0005	Addressing	14	000E	Significance
6	0006	Specification	15	000F	Floating-point divide
7	0007	Data	16 *	0010	Segment translation
8	0008	Fixed-point overflow	17 *	0011	Page translation
9	0009	Fixed-point divide			

*Model 67

HEXADECIMAL AND DECIMAL CONVERSION

From hex: locate each hex digit in its corresponding column position and note the decimal equivalents. Add these to obtain the decimal value.

From decimal: (1) locate the largest decimal value in the table that will fit into the decimal number to be converted, and (2) note its hex equivalent and hex column position. (3) Find the decimal remainder. Repeat the process on this and subsequent remainders.

Note: Decimal, hexadecimal, (and binary) equivalents of all numbers from 0 to 255 are listed on panels 11-14.

HEXADECIMAL COLUMNS

6 HEX	= DEC	5 HEX	= DEC	4 HEX	= DEC	3 HEX	= DEC	2 HEX	= DEC	1 HEX	= DEC
0	0	0	0	0	0	0	0	0	0	0	0
1	1,048,576	1	65,536	1	4,096	1	256	1	16	1	1
2	2,097,152	2	131,072	2	8,192	2	512	2	32	2	2
3	3,145,728	3	196,608	3	12,288	3	768	3	48	3	3
4	4,194,304	4	262,144	4	16,384	4	1,024	4	64	4	4
5	5,242,880	5	327,680	5	20,480	5	1,280	5	80	5	5
6	6,291,456	6	393,216	6	24,576	6	1,536	6	96	6	6
7	7,340,032	7	458,752	7	28,672	7	1,792	7	112	7	7
8	8,388,608	8	524,288	8	32,768	8	2,048	8	128	8	8
9	9,437,184	9	589,824	9	36,864	9	2,304	9	144	9	9
A	10,485,760	A	655,360	A	40,960	A	2,560	A	160	A	10
B	11,534,336	B	720,896	B	45,056	B	2,816	B	176	B	11
C	12,582,912	C	786,432	C	49,152	C	3,072	C	192	C	12
D	13,631,488	D	851,968	D	53,248	D	3,328	D	208	D	13
E	14,680,064	E	917,504	E	57,344	E	3,584	E	224	E	14
F	15,728,640	F	983,040	F	61,440	F	3,840	F	240	F	15
0 1 2 3		4 5 6 7		0 1 2 3		4 5 6 7		0 1 2 3		4 5 6 7	
BYTE				BYTE				BYTE			

POWERS OF 2

2^n	n
256	8
512	9
1 024	10
2 048	11
4 096	12
8 192	13
16 384	14
32 768	15
65 536	16
131 072	17
262 144	18
524 288	19
1 048 576	20
2 097 152	21
4 194 304	22
8 388 608	23
16 777 216	24

POWERS OF 16

	16^n	n
$2^0 = 16^0$	1	0
$2^4 = 16^1$	16	1
$2^8 = 16^2$	256	2
$2^{12} = 16^3$	4 096	3
$2^{16} = 16^4$	65 536	4
$2^{20} = 16^5$	1 048 576	5
$2^{24} = 16^6$	16 777 216	6
$2^{28} = 16^7$	268 435 456	7
$2^{32} = 16^8$	4 294 967 296	8
$2^{36} = 16^9$	68 719 476 736	9
$2^{40} = 16^{10}$	1 099 511 627 776	10
$2^{44} = 16^{11}$	17 592 186 044 416	11
$2^{48} = 16^{12}$	281 474 976 710 656	12
$2^{52} = 16^{13}$	4 503 599 627 370 496	13
$2^{56} = 16^{14}$	72 057 594 037 927 936	14
$2^{60} = 16^{15}$	1 152 921 504 606 846 976	15

PROGRAM STATUS WORD

System Mask*	Key	AMWP*	Interruption Code
0 7	8 11	12 15	16 23 24 31

ILC	CC	Program Mask*	Instruction Address
32 34 36 39		40	47 48 55 56 63
33 35			

0 Channel 0 mask	13 Machine check mask (M)
1 Channel 1 mask	14 Wait state (W)
2 Channel 2 mask	15 Problem state (P)
3 Channel 3 mask	32-33 Instruction length code (ILC)
4 Channel 4 mask	34-35 Condition code (CC)
5 Channel 5 mask	36 Fixed-point overflow mask
6 Mask for channel 6 and up	37 Decimal overflow mask
7 External mask	38 Exponent underflow mask
12 ASCII-8 mode (A)	39 Significance mask

*A one-bit equals on, and permits an interrupt.

CHANNEL ADDRESS WORD

Key	0000	Command Address
0 3	4 7	8 15 16 23 24 31

CHANNEL COMMAND WORD

Command Code	Data Address
0 7	8 15 16 23 24 31

Flags	000	///////	Byte Count
32 36	37 39	40 47	48 55 56 63

CD—bit 32 (80) causes use of address portion of next CCW.
CC—bit 33 (40) causes use of command code and data address of next CCW.
SLI—bit 34 (20) causes suppression of possible incorrect length indication.
Skip—bit 35 (10) suppresses transfer of information to main storage.
PCI—bit 36 (08) causes a channel Program Controlled Interruption.

CHANNEL STATUS WORD

Key	0000	Command Address
0 3	4 7	8 15 16 23 24 31

Status	Byte Count
32 39	40 47 48 55 56 63

32 (8000) Attention	40 (0080) Program-controlled interruption
33 (4000) Status modifier	41 (0040) Incorrect length
34 (2000) Control unit end	42 (0020) Program check
35 (1000) Busy	43 (0010) Protection check
36 (0800) Channel end	44 (0008) Channel data check
37 (0400) Device end	45 (0004) Channel control check
38 (0200) Unit check	46 (0002) Interface control check
39 (0100) Unit exception	47 (0001) Chaining check

Byte Count: bits 48-63 form the residual count for the last CCW used.

Comments about this card may be sent to the Technical Publications Department at the White Plains address below. All comments and suggestions become the property of IBM.

IBM ®

International Business Machines Corporation
Data Processing Division
1133 Westchester Ave., White Plains, N.Y. 10604
(U.S.A. only)

IBM World Trade Corporation
821 United Nations Plaza, New York, New York 10017
(International)

Printed in U.S.A. GX20-1703-9

PERMANENT STORAGE ASSIGNMENTS

Dec	Hex	Length	Purpose
0	0	double word	Initial program loading PSW
8	8	double word	Initial program loading CCW1
16	10	double word	Initial program loading CCW2
24	18	double word	External old PSW
32	20	double word	Supervisor Call old PSW
40	28	double word	Program old PSW
48	30	double word	Machine-check old PSW
56	38	double word	Input/output old PSW
64	40	double word	Channel status word
72	48	word	Channel address word
76	4C	word	Unused
80	50	word	Timer (uses bytes 50, 51 & 52)
84	54	word	Unused
88	58	double word	External new PSW
96	60	double word	Supervisor Call new PSW
104	68	double word	Program new PSW
112	70	double word	Machine-check new PSW
120	78	double word	Input/output new PSW
128	80	(1)	Diagnostic scan-out area

(1) The size of the diagnostic scan-out area depends on the particular model and I/O channels; for models 30 through 75, maximum size is 256 bytes.

CHANNEL COMMANDS

2314, 2311/2321 DASD   Source: GA26-3599, GA26-5988

Command for CCW‡		Count	MT Off	MT On†
Control	Seek	6	07	
	Seek Cylinder	6	0B	
	Seek Head	6	1B	
	Set File Mask	1	1F	
	Space Count	3	0F	
	Recalibrate (Note 1)	Not zero	13	
	Restore (2321 only)	Not zero	17	
Sense	Sense I/O	6	04	
	Release Device } (Note 2)	6	94	
	Reserve Device	6	B4	
Search	Home Address EQ	4 (usually)	39	B9
	Identifier EQ	5 (usually)	31	B1
	Identifier HI	5 (usually)	51	D1
	Identifier EQ or HI	5 (usually)	71	F1
	Key EQ	1 to 255	29	A9
	Key HI	1 to 255	49	C9
	Key EQ or HI	1 to 255	69	E9
	Key & Data EQ		2D	AD
	Key & Data HI	Number	4D	CD
	Key & Data EQ or HI	of bytes	6D	ED
Continue	Search EQ	in search	25	A5
Scan	Search HI	argument,	45	C5
	Search HI or EQ	including	65	E5
	Set Status Modifier*	mask bytes.	35	B5
	Set Status Modifier*	(Special	75	F5
	No Status Modifier	feature.)	55	D5
Read	Home Address	5	1A	9A
	Count	8	12	92
	Record 0		16	96
	Data	Number	06	86
	Key & Data	of bytes	0E	8E
	Count, Key & Data	transferred	1E	9E
	IPL		02	
Write	Home Address	5 (usually)	19	
	Record 0	8+KL+DL of R0	15	
	Count, Key & Data	8+KL+DL	1D	
	Special Count, Key & Data	8+KL+DL	01	
	Data	DL	05	
	Key & Data	KL+DL	0D	
	Erase	8+KL+DL	11	

1. For 2311 or 2314 only.
2. Two-channel switch required except for a 2314/2844 combination.

*Sense byte determines command used.
†Code same as MT Off except as listed.
‡See also standard commands, panel 10.

CHANNEL COMMANDS (Contd)

Standard Command Code Assignments (CCW bits 0-7) for I/O Operations

xxxx 0000	Invalid	†††† ††01	Write	
†††† 0100	Sense	†††† ††10	Read	
xxxx 1000	Transfer in Channel	†††† ††11	Control	
†††† 1100	Read Backward	0000 0011	Control No Operation	

x—Bit ignored.   †Modifier bit for specific type of I/O device

1052 CONSOLE   Source: GA22-6877

Read Inquiry BCD	0A	Sense	04
Write BCD, Auto Carrier Return	09	Alarm	0B
Write BCD, No Carrier Return	01		

2540 CARD READ PUNCH   Source: GA24-3312

Command	Type	Code	Bit Meanings	
Read, Feed, Select Stacker	AA	SSD0 0010	SS	Stacker
Read	AB	11D0 0010	00	R1 or P1
Read, Feed (1400 Compatibility*)	—	11D1 0010	01	R2 or P2
Feed, Select Stacker	BA	SS10 0011	10	RP3
PFR* Write, Feed, Select Stacker	BA	SSD0 1001	D	Data Mode
Write, Feed, Select Stacker	BB	SSD0 0001	0	1-EBCDIC
Sense	—	0000 0100	1	2-Col. binary*

1442-N1 CARD READ PUNCH   Source: GA21-9025

Write	01	Read	02
Write, Select Stacker 2	41	Read, Select Stacker 2	42
Write, Feed	81	Read Card Image	22
Write, Feed, Select Stacker 2	C1	Read Card Image, Sel Stkr 2	62
Write Card Image*	21	Read 1442 Compatibility*	12
Write Card Image, Sel Stkr 2	61	Read 1442 Compat, Sel Stkr 2	52
Write Card Image, Feed	A1	Control Feed	83
Write Card Image, Feed, Sel Stkr 2	E1	Control Feed, Select Stkr 2	C3
Sense	04	Control Select Stacker 2	43

1403, 1443 PRINTERS   Source: GA24-3312, GA24-3120

	After Write	Immed			
Skip to Channel 1	89	8B		Diagnostic Data Read	02
Skip to Channel 2	91	93		Diagnostic Check Read	06
Skip to Channel 3	99	9B	1403	UCS Gate*	EB
Skip to Channel 4	A1	A3	only	UCS Load (No Folding)*	F3
Skip to Channel 5	A9	AB		UCS Load (Folding)*	F3
Skip to Channel 6	B1	B3		Block Data Check*	73
Skip to Channel 7	B9	BB		Reset Block Data Check*	7B
Skip to Channel 8	C1	C3		Write without Spacing	01
Skip to Channel 9	C9	CB		Sense	04
Skip to Channel 10	D1	D3			
Skip to Channel 11	D9	DB			After Write	Immed
Skip to Channel 12	E1	E3		Space 1 Line	09	0B
				Space 2 Lines	11	13
				Space 3 Lines	19	1B

2400-SERIES MAGNETIC TAPE

Note: Refer to GA22-6866 for operation of specific models, special features required, mode resets, and precedence of commands.

			Density	Parity	DC	Trans	Cmd
Sense	04						
Read Backward	0C				on	off	13
Write	01			odd	off	off	33
Read	02		200		off	on	3B
Rewind (REW)	07			even	off	off	23
Rewind-Unload (RUN)	0F				off	on	2B
Erase Gap (ERG)	17				on	off	53
Write Tape Mark (WTM)	1F			odd	off	off	73
Backspace Block (BSB)	27		556		off	on	7B
Backspace File (BSF)	2F			even	off	off	63
Forward Space Block (FSB)	37				off	on	6B
Forward Space File (FSF)	3F				on	off	93
Request Track in Error (TIE)	1B			odd	off	off	B3
Diagnostic Mode Set	0B		800		off	on	BB
Set Mode 2 (9-track), 1600 bpi	C3			even	off	off	A3
Set Mode 2 (9-track), 800 bpi	CB				off	on	AB

(Set Mode 1 (7-track))

*Special feature required.

Decimal	Hexadecimal	Instruction Mnemonic (RR Format)	Graphic & Control Symbols (5) BCDIC	EBCDIC	7-Track Tape BCDIC	Punched Card Code	System/360 8-bit Code
0	00			NUL		12-0-1-8-9	0000 0000
1	01			SOH		12-1-9	0000 0001
2	02			STX		12-2-9	0000 0010
3	03			ETX		12-3-9	0000 0011
4	04	SPM		PF		12-4-9	0000 0100
5	05	BALR		HT		12-5-9	0000 0101
6	06	BCTR		LC		12-6-9	0000 0110
7	07	BCR		DEL		12-7-9	0000 0111
8	08	SSK				12-8-9	0000 1000
9	09	ISK				12-1-8-9	0000 1001
10	0A	SVC		SMM		12-2-8-9	0000 1010
11	0B			VT		12-3-8-9	0000 1011
12	0C			FF		12-4-8-9	0000 1100
13	0D	BASR(4)		CR		12-5-8-9	0000 1101
14	0E			SO		12-6-8-9	0000 1110
15	0F			SI		12-7-8-9	0000 1111
16	10	LPR		DLE		12-11-1-8-9	0001 0000
17	11	LNR		DC1		11-1-9	0001 0001
18	12	LTR		DC2		11-2-9	0001 0010
19	13	LCR		TM		11-3-9	0001 0011
20	14	NR		RES		11-4-9	0001 0100
21	15	CLR		NL		11-5-9	0001 0101
22	16	OR		BS		11-6-9	0001 0110
23	17	XR		IL		11-7-9	0001 0111
24	18	LR		CAN		11-8-9	0001 1000
25	19	CR		EM		11-1-8-9	0001 1001
26	1A	AR		CC		11-2-8-9	0001 1010
27	1B	SR		CU1		11-3-8-9	0001 1011
28	1C	MR		IFS		11-4-8-9	0001 1100
29	1D	DR		IGS		11-5-8-9	0001 1101
30	1E	ALR		IRS		11-6-8-9	0001 1110
31	1F	SLR		IUS		11-7-8-9	0001 1111
32	20	LPDR		DS		11-0-1-8-9	0010 0000
33	21	LNDR		SOS		0-1-9	0010 0001
34	22	LTDR		FS		0-2-9	0010 0010
35	23	LCDR				0-3-9	0010 0011
36	24	HDR		BYP		0-4-9	0010 0100
37	25	LRDR		LF		0-5-9	0010 0101
38	26	MXR		ETB		0-6-9	0010 0110
39	27	MXDR		ESC		0-7-9	0010 0111
40	28	LDR				0-8-9	0010 1000
41	29	CDR				0-1-8-9	0010 1001
42	2A	ADR		SM		0-2-8-9	0010 1010
43	2B	SDR		CU2		0-3-8-9	0010 1011
44	2C	MDR				0-4-8-9	0010 1100
45	2D	DDR		ENQ		0-5-8-9	0010 1101
46	2E	AWR		ACK		0-6-8-9	0010 1110
47	2F	SWR		BEL		0-7-8-9	0010 1111
48	30	LPER				12-11-0-1-8-9	0011 0000
49	31	LNER				1-9	0011 0001
50	32	LTER		SYN		2-9	0011 0010
51	33	LCER				3-9	0011 0011
52	34	HER		PN		4-9	0011 0100
53	35	LRER		RS		5-9	0011 0101
54	36	AXR		UC		6-9	0011 0110
55	37	SXR		EOT		7-9	0011 0111
56	38	LER				8-9	0011 1000
57	39	CER				1-8-9	0011 1001
58	3A	AER				2-8-9	0011 1010
59	3B	SER		CU3		3-8-9	0011 1011
60	3C	MER		DC4		4-8-9	0011 1100
61	3D	DER		NAK		5-8-9	0011 1101
62	3E	AUR				6-8-9	0011 1110
63	3F	SUR		SUB		7-8-9	0011 1111

Decimal	Hexadecimal	Instruction Mnemonic (RX Format)	Graphic & Control Symbols (5) BCDIC	EBCDIC	7-Track Tape BCDIC (1)	Punched Card Code	System/360 8-bit Code
64	40	STH		SP	(2)	no punches	0100 0000
65	41	LA				12-0-1-9	0100 0001
66	42	STC				12-0-2-9	0100 0010
67	43	IC				12-0-3-9	0100 0011
68	44	EX				12-0-4-9	0100 0100
69	45	BAL				12-0-5-9	0100 0101
70	46	BCT				12-0-6-9	0100 0110
71	47	BC				12-0-7-9	0100 0111
72	48	LH				12-0-8-9	0100 1000
73	49	CH				12-1-8	0100 1001
74	4A	AH		¢		12-2-8	0100 1010
75	4B	SH	.	.	B A 8 2 1	12-3-8	0100 1011
76	4C	MH	⌷)	<	B A 8 4	12-4-8	0100 1100
77	4D	BAS(4)	[.	(	B A 8 4 1	12-5-8	0100 1101
78	4E	CVD	<	+	B A 8 4 2	12-6-8	0100 1110
79	4F	CVB	‡	¦	B A 8 4 2 1	12-7-8	→ 0100 1111
80	50	ST	& +	&	B A	12	0101 0000
81	51					12-11-1-9	0101 0001
82	52					12-11-2-9	0101 0010
83	53					12-11-3-9	0101 0011
84	54	N				12-11-4-9	0101 0100
85	55	CL				12-11-5-9	0101 0101
86	56	O				12-11-6-9	0101 0110
87	57	X				12-11-7-9	0101 0111
88	58	L				12-11-8-9	0101 1000
89	59	C				11-1-8	0101 1001
90	5A	A		!		11-2-8	0101 1010
91	5B	S	$	$	B 8 2 1	11-3-8	0101 1011
92	5C	M	°	°	B 8 4	11-4-8	0101 1100
93	5D	D	]	)	B 8 4 1	11-5-8	0101 1101
94	5E	AL	;	;	B 8 4 2	11-6-8	0101 1110
95	5F	SL	Δ	¬	B 8 4 2 1	11-7-8	0101 1111
96	60	STD	-	-	B	11	0110 0000
97	61		/	/	A 1	0-1	0110 0001
98	62					11-0-2-9	0110 0010
99	63					11-0-3-9	0110 0011
100	64					11-0-4-9	0110 0100
101	65					11-0-5-9	0110 0101
102	66					11-0-6-9	0110 0110
103	67	MXD				11-0-7-9	0110 0111
104	68	LD				11-0-8-9	0110 1000
105	69	CD				0-1-8	0110 1001
106	6A	AD		¦		12-11	0110 1010
107	6B	SD	,	,	A 8 2 1	0-3-8	0110 1011
108	6C	MD	% (	%	A 8 4	0-4-8	0110 1100
109	6D	DD	Y	_	A 8 4 1	0-5-8	0110 1101
110	6E	AW	\	>	A 8 4 2	0-6-8	0110 1110
111	6F	SW	⧻	?	A 8 4 2 1	0-7-8	0110 1111
112	70	STE				12-11-0	0111 0000
113	71					12-11-0-1-9	0111 0001
114	72					12-11-0-2-9	0111 0010
115	73					12-11-0-3-9	0111 0011
116	74					12-11-0-4-9	0111 0100
117	75					12-11-0-5-9	0111 0101
118	76					12-11-0-6-9	0111 0110
119	77					12-11-0-7-9	0111 0111
120	78	LE				12-11-0-8-9	0111 1000
121	79	CE		`		1-8	0111 1001
122	7A	AE	ƀ	:	A	2-8	0111 1010
123	7B	SE	# =	#	8 2 1	3-8	0111 1011
124	7C	ME	@ '	@	8 4	4-8	0111 1100
125	7D	DE		'	8 4 1	5-8	0111 1101
126	7E	AU	>	=	8 4 2	6-8	0111 1110
127	7F	SU	√	"	8 4 2 1	7-8	0111 1111

NOTES FOR PANELS 11-14

1. Add C (check bit) for odd or even parity as needed, except as noted
2. For even parity use CA
3. Decimal feature
4. Model 67
5. EBCDIC graphics shown are standard bit pattern assignments. For specific print train/chain see printer manual.

RR FORMAT

Op Code	R₁	R₂
0	78 1112	15

RX FORMAT

Op Code	R₁	X₂	B₂	D₂
0	78	1112 1516	1920	31

R1, D2 (X2, B2) or R1, S2 (X2)
R1, D2 (0, B2) or R1, S2

Decimal	Hexadecimal	Instruction Mnemonic (Var.Formats)	Graphic & Control Symbols (5) BCDIC	EBCDIC	7-Track Tape BCDIC	Punched Card Code	System/360 8-bit Code
128	80	SSM				12-0-1-8	1000 0000
129	81			a		12-0-1	1000 0001
130	82	LPSW		b		12-0-2	1000 0010
131	83	(Diagnose)		c		12-0-3	1000 0011
132	84	WRD		d		12-0-4	1000 0100
133	85	RDD		e		12-0-5	1000 0101
134	86	BXH		f		12-0-6	1000 0110
135	87	BXLE		g		12-0-7	1000 0111
136	88	SRL		h		12-0-8	1000 1000
137	89	SLL		i		12-0-9	1000 1001
138	8A	SRA				12-0-2-8	1000 1010
139	8B	SLA				12-0-3-8	1000 1011
140	8C	SRDL				12-0-4-8	1000 1100
141	8D	SLDL				12-0-5-8	1000 1101
142	8E	SRDA				12-0-6-8	1000 1110
143	8F	SLDA				12-0-7-8	1000 1111
144	90	STM				12-11-1-8	1001 0000
145	91	TM		j		12-11-1	1001 0001
146	92	MVI		k		12-11-2	1001 0010
147	93	TS		l		12-11-3	1001 0011
148	94	NI		m		12-11-4	1001 0100
149	95	CLI		n		12-11-5	1001 0101
150	96	OI		o		12-11-6	1001 0110
151	97	XI		p		12-11-7	1001 0111
152	98	LM		q		12-11-8	1001 1000
153	99			r		12-11-9	1001 1001
154	9A					12-11-2-8	1001 1010
155	9B					12-11-3-8	1001 1011
156	9C	SIO				12-11-4-8	1001 1100
157	9D	TIO				12-11-5-8	1001 1101
158	9E	HIO				12-11-6-8	1001 1110
159	9F	TCH				12-11-7-8	1001 1111
160	A0					11-0-1-8	1010 0000
161	A1					11-0-1	1010 0001
162	A2			s		11-0-2	1010 0010
163	A3			t		11-0-3	1010 0011
164	A4			u		11-0-4	1010 0100
165	A5			v		11-0-5	1010 0101
166	A6			w		11-0-6	1010 0110
167	A7			x		11-0-7	1010 0111
168	A8			y		11-0-8	1010 1000
169	A9			z		11-0-9	1010 1001
170	AA					11-0-2-8	1010 1010
171	AB					11-0-3-8	1010 1011
172	AC					11-0-4-8	1010 1100
173	AD					11-0-5-8	1010 1101
174	AE					11-0-6-8	1010 1110
175	AF					11-0-7-8	1010 1111
176	B0	STMC (4)				12-11-0-1-8	1011 0000
177	B1	LRA (4)				12-11-0-1	1011 0001
178	B2					12-11-0-2	1011 0010
179	B3					12-11-0-3	1011 0011
180	B4					12-11-0-4	1011 0100
181	B5					12-11-0-5	1011 0101
182	B6					12-11-0-6	1011 0110
183	B7					12-11-0-7	1011 0111
184	B8	LMC (4)				12-11-0-8	1011 1000
185	B9					12-11-0-9	1011 1001
186	BA					12-11-0-2-8	1011 1010
187	BB					12-11-0-3-8	1011 1011
188	BC					12-11-0-4-8	1011 1100
189	BD					12-11-0-5-8	1011 1101
190	BE					12-11-0-6-8	1011 1110
191	BF					12-11-0-7-8	1011 1111

RS FORMAT

Op Code	R₁	R₃	B₂	D₂

0 78 11 12 15 16 19 20 31

R1, R3, D2 (B2) or R1, R3, S2: BXH, BXLE, LM, LMC, STM, STMC
R1, D2 (B2) or R1, S2: All shift instructions

SI FORMAT

OP Code	I₂	B₁	D₁

0 78 15 16 19 20 31

D1 (B1) or S1: LPSW, SSM, HIO, SIO, TIO, TCH, TS
D1 (B1), I2 or S1, I2: MVI, CLI, NI, OI, XI, TM, WRD, RDD

Decimal	Hexadecimal	Instruction Mnemonic (SS Format)	Graphic & Control Symbols (5) BCDIC	EBCDIC	7-Track Tape BCDIC (1)	Punched Card Code	System/360 8-bit Code
192	C0		?	{	B A 8 2	12-0	1100 0000
193	C1		A	A	B A 1	12-1	1100 0001
194	C2		B	B	B A 2	12-2	1100 0010
195	C3		C	C	B A 2 1	12-3	1100 0011
196	C4		D	D	B A 4	12-4	1100 0100
197	C5		E	E	B A 4 1	12-5	1100 0101
198	C6		F	F	B A 4 2	12-6	1100 0110
199	C7		G	G	B A 4 2 1	12-7	1100 0111
200	C8		H	H	B A 8	12-8	1100 1000
201	C9		I	I	B A 8 1	12-9	1100 1001
202	CA					12-0-2-8-9	1100 1010
203	CB					12-0-3-8-9	1100 1011
204	CC			ſ		12-0-4-8-9	1100 1100
205	CD					12-0-5-8-9	1100 1101
206	CE			Ⴒ		12-0-6-8-9	1100 1110
207	CF					12-0-7-8-9	1100 1111
208	D0		!	}	B 8 2	11-0	1101 0000
209	D1	MVN	J	J	B 1	11-1	1101 0001
210	D2	MVC	K	K	B 2	11-2	1101 0010
211	D3	MVZ	L	L	B 2 1	11-3	1101 0011
212	D4	NC	M	M	B 4	11-4	1101 0100
213	D5	CLC	N	N	B 4 1	11-5	1101 0101
214	D6	OC	O	O	B 4 2	11-6	1101 0110
215	D7	XC	P	P	B 4 2 1	11-7	1101 0111
216	D8		Q	Q	B 8	11-8	1101 1000
217	D9		R	R	B 8 1	11-9	1101 1001
218	DA					12-11-2-8-9	1101 1010
219	DB					12-11-3-8-9	1101 1011
220	DC	TR				12-11-4-8-9	1101 1100
221	DD	TRT				12-11-5-8-9	1101 1101
222	DE	ED (3)				12-11-6-8-9	1101 1110
223	DF	EDMK (3)				12-11-7-8-9	1101 1111
224	E0		*	\	A 8 2	0-2-8	1110 0000
225	E1					11-0-1-9	1110 0001
226	E2		S	S	A 2	0-2	1110 0010
227	E3		T	T	A 2 1	0-3	1110 0011
228	E4		U	U	A 4	0-4	1110 0100
229	E5		V	V	A 4 1	0-5	1110 0101
230	E6		W	W	A 4 2	0-6	1110 0110
231	E7		X	X	A 4 2 1	0-7	1110 0111
232	E8		Y	Y	A 8	0-8	1110 1000
233	E9		Z	Z	A 8 1	0-9	1110 1001
234	EA					11-0-2-8-9	1110 1010
235	EB					11-0-3-8-9	1110 1011
236	EC			Ⴄ		11-0-4-8-9	1110 1100
237	ED					11-0-5-8-9	1110 1101
238	EE					11-0-6-8-9	1110 1110
239	EF					11-0-7-8-9	1110 1111
240	F0		0	0	8 2	0	1111 0000
241	F1	MVO	1	1	1	1	1111 0001
242	F2	PACK	2	2	2	2	1111 0010
243	F3	UNPK	3	3	2 1	3	1111 0011
244	F4		4	4	4	4	1111 0100
245	F5		5	5	4 1	5	1111 0101
246	F6		6	6	4 2	6	1111 0110
247	F7		7	7	4 2 1	7	1111 0111
248	F8	ZAP (3)	8	8	8	8	1111 1000
249	F9	CP (3)	9	9	8 1	9	1111 1001
250	FA	AP (3)				12-11-0-2-8-9	1111 1010
251	FB	SP (3)				12-11-0-3-8-9	1111 1011
252	FC	MP (3)				12-11-0-4-8-9	1111 1100
253	FD	DP (3)				12-11-0-5-8-9	1111 1101
254	FE					12-11-0-6-8-9	1111 1110
255	FF					12-11-0-7-8-9	1111 1111

SS FORMAT

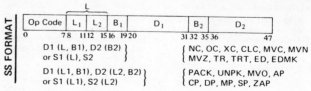

Op Code	L₁	L₂	B₁	D₁	B₂	D₂

0 78 11 12 15 16 19 20 31 32 35 36 47

D1 (L, B1), D2 (B2) or S1 (L), S2 } { NC, OC, XC, CLC, MVC, MVN MVZ, TR, TRT, ED, EDMK

D1 (L1, B1), D2 (L2, B2) or S1 (L1), S2 (L2) } { PACK, UNPK, MVO, AP CP, DP, MP, SP, ZAP

214

Index

A

A-type constant, 175
Abbreviations, mnemonic, 39
ABEND dump, 105
Absolute address, 106
  constants, 175-76
Absolute symbols, 86
Accumulator, 7
Add (A), 58
  (AR), 40
Addition, one's complement, 33
  two's complement, 30
Address
  arithmetic, 56
  base, 56, 75
  byte, 3, 4
  effective, 56, 57
  in separately assembled programs, 185f
  symbolic, 68
Address constants, 174-76
Address lists, argument, 176-80
  variable length, 180-81
Addressability, and base register, 74-78
Alignment, automatic, 69, 74, 134
Argument address lists, 176-80
  variable length, 180-81
Arguments, transmission of, 171-74

Arithmetic
  binary, 19-20
  decimal, 157
  fixed point, 37-63
  hexadecimal, 20-21
Arithmetic comparison, 114, 118
Arithmetic unit, 6-7
Arrays, 122-27
  element of, 122
  index or subscript of, 122, 125-27
  multidimensional, 123, 126
  one-dimensional, 122
  rectangular representation of, 123
  referencing elements of, 124
    by indexing, 125
  storing, by rows and by columns, 123, 124
  subscripts of, 122, 125-27
  two-dimensional, 123
ASMFCLG, 94
Assembler, 39, 65
Assembler coding form, 66
Assembler F, 93-94, 100
Assembler instructions, 69-72
Assembler language, 39, 65-80
  format of, 58-59
  indexing and, 125
  listing, 67, 100
  translation process and, 65-78

Assembly process, 73-74
Assembly step, 95
Assembly time, 70, 74
Assembly time error messages, 107-108, 205f
Asterisk
    as location counter reference, 76
    on comment card, 58

B

Backward pointer, 186f, 188
Base address, 56, 75
Base of a number system, 12
Base register, 56
    conflict in, 185
    establishing, 74-78
Batching, 198
Binary arithmetic, 19-20
Binary number system, 12
Bits, 3, 12
    in character codes, 131, 133
    mask, 115
Blanks, leading zeros and, 145-46
Branch address, 115, 171
Branch and link (BAL, BALR), 76, 171
Branch on condition (BC, BCR), 113-16, 127
Branch on count (BCT, BCTR), 129
Branch on index high (BXH), 128-29
Branch on index low or equal (BXLE), 127-28
Branch on minus (BM), 116
Branch on plus (BP), 116
Branch on zero (BZ), 116
Branching, 113-30
    after logical and byte comparisons, 144, 145
Buffer, 99
Bytes, 3-5
    carriage-control, 136, 199
    in packed and zoned decimal, 155-57
Byte comparisons, 143-49
Byte manipulation, 131-54
Byte strings, variable length, 149-52

C

C-type constant, 134
Called program, 170

Calling graph, 188, 189f
Calling program, 170
Card(s)
    control, 94-96, 198
    for input, 9-10
    job, 94, 200f
    listing a deck of, 136
    punched, and character code, 132f, 133
    reading and printing, 136-38
Card code, 9f, 131-33
Card punch, 10
Card reader, 10
Carriage-control byte, 136, 199
Carry, end-around, 33
Cataloged procedure, 94
Chaining of save areas, 188-90
Character codes, 131-33
Character manipulation, 131-54
Character strings, 134, 155
Characters
    define storage and define constant for, 133-35
    moving, 138-43
CLOSE, 97-99
Codes, character, 131-33
Coding form, 66f
Collating sequence, 144
Columns
    arrays stored by, 123
    on cards, 9-10
Comments card, 58
Comments field, 58
Compare (C,CR), 118
Compare logical (CL,CLR), 143
    (CLC), 146
Compare logical immediate (CLI), 144
Compare logical long (CLCL), 147-48
Comparing strings of bytes, 146-49
Comparisons
    arithmetic, 118, 144
    logical and byte, 143-46
    of number representations, 157-58
Complement
    bitwise, 32
    one's, 32
    two's, 29
Completion code, 105, 206
Computer
    organization of a, 1-10

Computer (Cont.)
  360 and 370, 1
    speeds of, 5
Condition code, 113-15
Contents of byte, 3
Continuation of assembler statement, 98n
Control cards, 94-96
  in ESP, 198
Control, flow of, 87-89, 113
Control sections, 73
Control unit, 7, 9
Conventions for register usage, 99, 177, 200
Conventions for subprograms, 189-94
Conversion(s)
  between bases, 14-19
    fractions, 17-19
    integers, 14-17
  decimal, 155-67
  instructions for, 158-62
  of zoned decimal numbers to printable
    form, 162-64
Convert to binary (CVB), 160-61
Convert to decimal (CVD), 161
Core memory, 5-6
Counter, instruction, 87, 88
Cross reference table
  of assembler, 105
  of linkage editor, 105, 183, 184f
CSECT, 73, 182

D

Data control block, 97, 98
Data set, 97, 98
Decimal, convert to, 161
Decimal arithmetic, 157
Decimal conversions, 155-67
Decimal form
  packed, 156-57
  zoned, 156, 157
Decimal numbers, zoned, conversion of,
  to printable form, 162-64
Deck
  arrangement of, 94-96
    under ESP, 198
  data, reading beyond end of, 137-38
  listing of sample
    under O.S., 100
    under ESP, 198
  program to list, 136-37
Decoding instructions, 88

Define constant (DC), 69-71
  for characters, 133-35
Define storage (DS), 71-72
  for characters, 134-35
Definition of a symbol, 68-72
Digit, 11
Digit position, 11
Dimension of array, 123-24, 126
Diminished radix complement, 32
Displacement, 56
Displacement-index-base form D(X,B),
  59, 116
Divide (D), 58
  (DR), 49
Divide interruption, 50, 51
Dump, 104-106, 191, 200
  forcing, 105, 183, 184
  save area traces in, 191, 194f
  SNAP, 107-11
Duplication factor, 134-35

E

EBCDIC code, 133
Effective address, 56, 57
Elements of array, 122
  referencing, 124-25
END, 72
End-around carry, 33
End test in loop, 117, 118
ENTRY, 183
Entry point, 177, 183
Equate symbol (EQU), 86
Error(s)
  associated with symbols, 72
  deliberate, 105, 183, 184
  finding, with SNAP dumps, 107-11
  flow of control and, 89
  in pack instruction, 159
  in subprograms, 191
Error messages, 105-107
  in ESP, 201, 204f, 205f
ESP Assembler-Interpreter, 93, 197-206
  job card, 200
  job, output from, 202-204
  limitations of, 206
  program to read and print cards, 136, 137
  pseudoinstructions, 199-200
  register usage conventions, 200-201
  sample program, 201-206

Establishing a base register, 74-78
Even-odd register pairs, 44-47, 49-53
Excess three code, 24
Execute (EX), 150-51
    with pack, 159-60
Execute statement in job control language,
    94
Execution of instructions
    in control unit, 7, 9
    flow chart for, 88
    termination of, 90
Execution time, 70, 74
Executive system, 93
Expansion of macro instructions, 96-97
Explicit form, 59, 116
Extended Binary-Coded-Decimal Inter-
    change Code (EBCDIC), 133
Extended mnemonics, 115-16
External symbol dictionary, 105, 182
External symbols, 181-83
EXTRN, 182

F

F-type constant, 69
Fetch of instruction, 7, 9, 88
Fields
    of assembler language statement, 58-59
    of instruction, 38, 56
Fixed-point divide interruption, 50, 51
Fixed-point instructions, 37-63, 118-22
Flow chart, and indexing, 125
Flow of control, 87-89, 113
    with subprograms, 169
Format, assembler language, 58
Format of instructions, 37, 55, 62, 138,
    140
Fortran language, 113
Forward pointer, 186f, 188
Fractions, conversion between bases, 17-19
Full word, 3, 37

G

General registers, 6
GET, 97
    in ESP, 199
Go step, 95, 107
Graph, calling, 188, 189f
Graphic, 132f, 133

H

Half word, 3, 37
Hexadecimal
    arithmetic, 20-21
    constant, 70
    number system, 12-13
    object code, 60-62

I

IBM system/360 reference data, 208-14
Identification-sequence field, 59
Illegal instruction to force a dump, 105,
    183, 184
Illegal sign digit, 159
Immediate operand, 140
Index
    branch on, high, 128-29
    branch on, low or equal, 127-28
    field of instruction, 56
    of array, 122, 125-27
    register, 56, 125
Indexing, 125-27
Infinite loop, 118
Information boundaries, 3
Input-output
    media for, 9-10
    under ESP, 199
    under O.S., 96-99
Instruction counter, 7, 87-89
Instruction fetching, 9, 88
Instruction formats
    RR, 37
    RS, 62
    RX, 55
    SI, 140
    SS, 138
Instruction lengths, 87-89
Instruction register, 88
Instructions, *see entries for individual
    names*
Integer
    conversion between bases, 14-17
    four ways to represent, 155-57
    representation, 11-13
    representation of positive and negative,
        26-27
Interpreter, 197
Interruption, 44n
    address, 105-106

Interruption (Cont.)
  code, 105
  fixed point divide, 50

J

Job card, 94, 104
  in ESP, 200*f*
Job control statements, 94-95

K

Keypunch, 10

L

Leading zeros, suppression of, 145
Length
  field of move instruction, 139
  of instruction, 88, 89
  specification for DC, DS, 133, 134, 176
Limitations of ESP, 206
Linkage editor, 183
Linkage editor cross reference table, 105,
  183, 184*f*
Linkedit step, 95
Linkediting, 193*f*, 194*f*
Listing a deck, 136
Lists, address, 176-81
Load (L), 56
  (LR), 38-39
Load address (LA), 119-20
Load and test (LTR), 118
Load complement (LCR), 118
Load module, 106, 107
Load multiple (LM), 62-63
Load negative (LNR), 119
Load positive (LPR), 119
Loader, 67, 82
Location counter, 73-74, 107
  define storage and, 74, 135
  reference with asterisk, 76
Logical comparison, 143-49
Logical interpretation of 32-bit words,
  144
Loops, 117-18
  infinite, 118
Lowest level subprogram, 189, 191*f*

M

Machine versus assembler instructions,
  69-72
Macro instructions, 96
Magnetic cores, 6
Mask, 115
Mechanics of running a program, 93-112
Memory, 2-6
  speed, 4
Memory address
  calculation of RX, 56
  relocation and, 84
Memory allocation, example of, 8, 82, 87
Memory size, and relocation, 82-83
Messages, error, 105-107
  in ESP, 201, 204*f*, 205*f*
Mnemonic abbreviations, 39
Mnemonics, extended, 115-16
Move character (MVC), 139-40
Move immediate (MVI), 140-41
Move long (MVCL), 141-43
Move numerics (MVN), 163
Move zones (MVZ), 163
Moving variable length strings, 149-52
Multiple definition of symbols, 72
Multiplication, number system for speeding
  up, 24
Multiply (M), 58
  (MR), 44

N

Name field, 58
Negative numbers, representation of, 26-34
Nested subprograms, 187
Nine's complement, 32
Noninteger base, positional number with,
  21-24
No operation, 116
Number representations, comparison of
  360, 155-57
Number systems, 11-35
  arabic, 24
  binary, 12
  excess 3, 24
  hexadecimal, 12-13
  octal, 13
  one's complement, 27, 32-34
  positional, 11-12

Number systems (Cont.)
    roman, 24
    sign-magnitude, 27-29
    two's complement, 27, 29-32
    with noninteger base, 21
Numeric, 156

O

Object code, 60, 65-67
    relocation of, 84-86
Object deck, 67
Object program, 65-67
Octal number system, 13
Offset within array, 126
One-dimensional array, 122
One's complement representation, 27,
    32-34
Op code, 38
OPEN, 96-98
Operand field, 58
Operating System 360, 93-111
Operation code, 38
Operation field, 58
Or, 150
Organization of a computer, 1-10
Or immediate (OI), 163
Output
    SNAP instruction and, 107-11
    under ESP, 199
    under O. S., 96-99
Output devices, 10
Overflow, 41-43
Overlapping operands of move, 141, 142

P

PACK, 158-60
Packed decimal, 156
Padding character, 141, 148
Padding zoned decimal numbers, 157
Paper tape, 10
Pointer
    backward, 186, 188, 191
    forward, 186, 188, 191
Positional number representation, 11
PRINT, 97, 105
Printable characters, 133
Printable form, conversion to, 162-64
Printer, 10

Printer carriage control, 136, 199
Program, 7
Program status word, 108
Pseudoinstructions, 69n
    in ESP, 199
Punched card codes, 9, 133
PUT, 98
    in ESP, 199

Q

Quotient, 49

R

Radix complement representation, 31
Random access memory, 5
Reading beyond the end of data deck, 137
Reading memory, 4
Redundant binary, 23
Reference data, 207-14
Referencing arrays, 124-26
Register, instruction, 88
Register contents, saving, 99, 136, 183,
    185-88, 191, 192
Register and indexed storage (RX) format,
    55-56
Register and storage (RS) format, 62-63
Register pairs, even-odd, 44-47, 49-53
Register saving, 99, 136, 183, 185-88, 191,
    192
Register-to-register (RR) format, 37-39
Register usage conventions, 99, 177
    in ESP, 200, 201
Registers
    argument transmission via, 171-75
    base, conflict in, 185
    even-odd, 44-47, 49-53
    general, 6-7
Relocatable address constants, 175-76
Relocatable symbols, 86
Relocation, 81-86
    need for, 81-83
Relocation amount, 83
Relocation dictionary, 105, 176n
Remainder, 49
Repetitive part of loop, 117
Representation(s)
    of instructions, 39-41
    one's complement, 27, 32-34

Representation(s) (Cont.)
  positive and negative integer, 26-34
  radix complement, 31
  sign-magnitude, 27-29
  two's complement, 27, 29-32
Restoring register contents, 99, 136, 183,
    185-88, 191, 192
Return address, 170-71
  conflict concerning, 183
Returning from a subprogram, 170
Rows, arrays stored by, 123, 124
RR format, 37-39
RS format, 62-63
Running a program, 93-112
RX format, 55-56

S

Save area, 137, 186, 187f
Save area chaining, 188-90
Save area pointers, 186, 188-91
Save area trace, 191, 193f, 194f
Saving register contents, 99, 136, 183,
    185-88, 191, 192
Separately assembled programs, 181
Sequences of instructions, 53-54
Severity codes, 107
SI format, 140
Sign in packed and zoned decimal, 156
Sign-magnitude representation, 27-29
SNAP dumps, 107-11
Source program, 65
Speed of memory, 4-5
SS format, 138
START, 72
Statement field, 58
Stop, 90
Storage, 2-6
Storage and immediate (SI) format,
    140
Storage to storage (SS) format, 138
Store (ST), 57
Store multiple (STM), 63
String, byte, 146-52
Subject instruction, 150-52
Subprograms, 81, 169-96
  full conventions for, 189-94
Subroutines, 81, 169-96
Subscripts of array, 122, 125-27

Subtract (S), 58
  (SR), 40
Subtraction, one's complement, 34
  two's complement, 34-35
Symbol(s)
  absolute, 86
  definition and value of, 68
  errors associated with, 72
  Equate (EQU), 86
  external, 181-84
  multiply defined, 72
  ordinary, 181-84
  relocatable, 86
  undefined, 72
Symbol table, 68, 105
Symbolic addresses, 68
SYSIN data set, 95
SYSPRINT data set, 95
System completion code, 105
  in ESP, 206
SYSUDUM, 95

T

Teletype machines, 10
Ten's complement, 31-32
Termination
  of execution, 90
  reading beyond end of data deck and, 137
TRACE, in ESP, 199-201, 203f
Traces, save area, 191
Translation process, 65-78
Transmission of arguments, 171-75
Two-dimensional array, 123
Two's complement
  addition, 30-31
  representation, 27, 29-32
  subtraction, 34-35

U

Undefined symbol, 72
Unpack (UNPK), 161-62
Users, multiple, and relocation, 83
USING, 75-78

V

V-type constant, 182
Value of a symbol, 68

Variable length argument lists, 180
Variable length strings, 149-52
Vinculum, fractions containing, 18

W

Weight, 11
Word, full, 3
    half, 3
Writing memory, 4

X

X-type constant, 70

Z

Zeros, leading, 145
Zone, 156
Zoned decimal, 156